VOICE: TECHNIQUE

Your Singing Voice

CONTEMPORARY TECHNIQUES, EXPRESSION, AND SPIRIT

To access audio visit:
www.halleonard.com/mylibrary

"Enter Code"
4100-0687-8001-0458

Edited by Jonathan Feist

Jeannie Gagné

BERKLEE PRESS

Vice President: David Kusek
Dean of Continuing Education: Debbie Cavalier
Assistant Vice President of Operations/CFO: Robert F. Green
Managing Editor: Jonathan Feist
Editorial Assistants: Jimmy Haas, David Hume, Shilpa Narayan,
Andrea Penzel, Ben Scudder, Jacqueline Sim, Won (Sara) Hwang
Cover Designer: Kathy Kikkert
Cover Photo: Mark Stallings

Lyrics and music © by Jeannie Gagné. No use except for educational purposes is permitted without the expressed written permission of the author. All Rights Reserved.

ISBN 978-0-87639-126-6

1140 Boylston Street
Boston, MA 02215-3693 USA
(617) 747-2146

Visit Berklee Press Online at
www.berkleepress.com

Study music online at
online.berklee.edu

DISTRIBUTED BY

HAL•LEONARD®
7777 W. BLUEMOUND RD. P.O. BOX 13819
MILWAUKEE, WISCONSIN 53213

Visit Hal Leonard Online
www.halleonard.com

Berklee Press, a publishing activity of Berklee College of Music, is a not-for-profit educational publisher.
Available proceeds from the sales of our products are contributed to the scholarship funds of the college.

Copyright © 2012 Berklee Press. All Rights Reserved
No part of this publication may be reproduced in any form or by any means without the prior written permission of the Publisher.

CONTENTS

AUDIO TRACKS	vi
ACKNOWLEDGEMENTS	viii
AUDIO CREDITS	ix
INTRODUCTION	xi
PART I. THE MIRACLE THAT IS YOUR VOICE	**1**
CHAPTER 1. Your Body Is Your Instrument	**3**
Wellness and Music	3
There Are Abundant Opportunities to Sing	4
The Many Benefits of Singing	6
Singing Can Be Life-Changing—Literally	6
Physical Health Benefits	7
The Bliss of Vocal Resonance: Toning	8
Singing in Community	9
The Joy of Performing—or, It's Okay Not to Perform, Too	10
Your Body Is Your Instrument	10
Anatomy: Understand Your Vocal Instrument	10
Breathing: Managing What You Already Know	21
Physical Wellness: Healthy Habits	31
CHAPTER 2. The Whole Singer	**41**
Holistic Approaches to Full Mind and Body Health and Wellness	42
The Self	42
Creativity	43
Authenticity	44
Your Mind: The Power of Thought in Singing	46
Activity 2.1. What I Believe Is True or False	48
Activity 2.2. Daily Affirmations	51
Activity 2.3. Energy Grid: Map Your Daily Biorhythm	52
Vocal Study	52
Your Voice Is Unique	53
Relying on Your Teacher, Relying on Yourself	53
Learn Your Limits and Your Potential	54
Is There "Right" and "Wrong" Singing?	55
Style and Habits	56
Registers and Placement	57
The Five Commonly Defined Registers	57
Vowel, Volume, Pitch, and Diction	59
The Break	60
Resonance, Tone, and Style	61
How We Hear Tone	62
Conditioning	63
Vocal Concepts and Visualizations	63
How You Practice	68
Healthy Mental Thoughts and Practice	69

CHAPTER 3. Embodying Rhythm and Movement — 72

    Feel the Backbeat — 74
    Time Slashes — 74
    Rhythmic Subdivisions — 75
    What Is Swing? — 77
    Scat Syllables, Improvisation, and Rhythm: Making It Interesting — 78
    The Role of the Rhythm Section — 79
    Time Feel Variations — 81
    Rhythms to Reference When Identifying A Tune's Groove — 81
    Embodying Rhythm: Sound Is Movement, Improv Is Movement, Singing Is Movement — 85
        My Arms Look Stupid! — 85
        Pedestrian, Athletic, Dance, and Authentic Movements — 86
        Moving as One with the Phrase — 87

CHAPTER 4. Performing — 88

    "Thank You," She Said, Waking Up A Young Performer — 88
    What Is Your Intention? — 90
    Nine Steps to Creating Extraordinary Performances — 91
    What Do Extraordinary Performers Have in Common? — 92
        Authenticity and a Healthy Ego — 94
        Understanding Your Artistic and Energetic Presence — 96
        Being Present; Learning about Yourself on Stage — 98
    Artist Statement — 100
    Expectations — 101
        Cultural Goals and Influences — 103
        Managing Performance Anxiety — 103
        Activity 4.1. Being Seen, in Three Parts — 104
    Song Choices — 105
        Vocal and Emotional Range — 105
        Style, Key, and Technical Range — 105
    Performance Space: Technical Aspects — 107
        Mic Technique — 107
        Creating the Ideal Performance Environment — 109
    What Audiences Want and Need — 110
        Audience Survey — 110
    Working with Your Band — 112
    Ten Performing Tips — 113
    Understanding Your Energy in Performance: Chakras and Reiki — 114
        What Is Reiki? What Are Chakras? How Does Energy Awareness Impact Performing? What's the Connection? — 115
        Being Aware of Your Energy — 116
        Activity 4.2. Energy Awareness 1: Feeling Your Energy — 118
        Activity 4.3. Energy Awareness 2: With Two People — 118
        Using Reiki at Home and Elsewhere — 119
    Performing: Simply Stated… — 120

PART II. EXERCISES — 121

CHAPTER 5. Pointers and Warm-Ups	**123**
Shifting from Classical to Contemporary Styles	124
Vowel and Consonant Keys: U.S. English Pronunciation	126
Vowel Key	126
Consonant Key	127
About Consonants	128
Body Warm-Ups	128
Body Warm-Ups 1–2: Stretching	129
Body Warm-Ups 3–4: Sounding	130
CHAPTER 6. The Exercises	**133**
Starting Out Easy: Warming Up Your Voice	134
Exercises 1–4	134
Agility and Rhythm	138
Exercises 5–12	138
Flexibility Exercises for Blues and R&B Runs and Jazz Improvisation	146
Exercises 13–20	146
Power	154
Exercises 21–22	154
Belting	157
Exercises 23–24	158
Intervals, Chromatic Movement, and Scat	161
Exercises 25–30	161
Ear Candy	166
Exercises 31–34	166
CHAPTER 7. Tunes from My House to Yours	**169**
Intended for instructional use only.	
Tune 1. Backyard Bop	170
Tune 2. Dreamin'	172
Tune 3. Look Inside for Love	173
Tune 4. Every Little Thing You Do	174
PART III. WISDOM FROM EXPERIENCE: CONVERSATIONS WITH EXTRAORDINARY ARTISTS, MUSICIANS, AND TEACHERS	**179**
CHAPTER 8. Patti Austin	**181**
CHAPTER 9. Ysaye M. Barnwell	**191**
CHAPTER 10. Mark Baxter	**201**
CHAPTER 11. Joey Blake and Christiane Karam	**213**
CHAPTER 12. William Allaudin Mathieu	**219**
CODA: CHOICES	**229**
APPENDIX A Bibliography and Recommended Reading	**231**
APPENDIX B Glossary: Contemporary Rhythm Vocabulary	**237**
APPENDIX C Online Resources	**241**
APPENDIX D Excerpt from 5Realms for Artists: An Investigative Awareness Practice	**244**
ABOUT THE AUTHOR	**246**
INDEX	**248**

AUDIO TRACKS

Track		Page
1	Introduction	121
2	Warm-Up 3. Single Tone	131
3	Warm-Up 4. Slow Movement and Health Check	132

STARTING OUT EASY. WARMING UP YOUR VOICE, TRACKS 4–7

4	Exercise 1. Lip Trills—Relaxed and Easy	134
5	Exercise 2. Movement and Fifths	135
6	Exercise 3. A Bit More Movement	136
7	Exercise 4. Smooth Glissando to the 9th	137

AGILITY AND RHYTHM. TRACKS 8–15

8	Exercise 5. Syncopation	138
9	Exercise 6. Flexibility with Relaxation	139
10	Exercise 7. Calm, Clear Tones, with Breath Support	140
11	Exercise 8. Stretch Range with Bright Vowel, Major/Minor	141
12	Exercise 9. Rearticulation without Glottal Attack	142
13	Exercise 10. Traditional Exercise for Agility with Accuracy	143
14	Exercise 11. Elastic Band, Alternating Major/Minor	144
15	Exercise 12. Creating Melodic Spaces without Adding Breaths	145

FLEXIBILITY EXERCISES FOR BLUES AND R&B RUNS AND JAZZ IMPROVISATION. TRACKS 16–25

16	Exercise 13. Movement and Flexibility	146
17	Exercise 14. Minor Pentatonic Runs for Agility and Note Choice	147
18	Exercise 15. Major Pentatonic Movement and Agility	149
19	Exercise 16. Cat ("C@t") Vowel Using Minor Pentatonic Mode	150
20	Exercise 17. Lydian Mode	150
21	Exercise 18a. Scat Syllables Using Major/Minor. Straight 8ths	151
22	Exercise 18b. Scat Syllables Using Major/Minor. Swing 8ths	151
23	Exercise 19a. Bossa (Latin) Rhythm Exercise	152
24	Exercise 19b. Bossa (Latin) Rhythm Exercise, No Vocal	152
25	Exercise 20. Swinging a Classic	153

POWER AND BELTING. TRACKS 26–32

26	Exercise 21. Power Exercise Volume Swell. Soft to Loud, then Loud to Soft	155
27	Exercise 22. Open Pharynx (Throat)	156
28	Exercise 23. Loud Open Long Tones	158
29	Exercise 24a. 12-Bar Blues, Rock Feel—Higher Voices, Sing with Jeff Ramsey	159
30	Exercise 24b. 12-Bar Blues, Rock Feel—Higher Voices, No Vocal	159
31	Exercise 24c. 12-Bar Blues, 12/8 Feel—Lower Voices, Sing with Jeannie	160
32	Exercise 24d. 12-Bar Blues, 12/8 Feel—Lower Voices, No Vocal	160

INTERVALS, CHROMATIC MOVEMENT, AND SCAT. TRACKS 33–40

33	Exercise 25. Intervals	161
34	Exercise 26. Chromatic and Rhythmic Detail	162
35	Exercise 27. Tritones	162
36	Exercise 28a. Scat Syllables with Intervals—Bossa Feel, Straight 8ths Subdivision	163
37	Exercise 28b. Scat Syllables with Intervals. Jazz Swing Feel, Swing 8ths Subdivision	163
38	Exercise 29. Soul and Intervals	164
39	Exercise 30-L. Swing 16ths Hip-Hop Groove	165
40	Exercise 30-H. Swing 16ths Hip-Hop Groove	166

EAR CANDY. TRACKS 41–44

41	Exercise 31. Arpeggio with #5	166
42	Exercise 32. Full Diminished Arpeggio	167
43	Exercise 33. Major/Minor Thirds	167
44	Exercise 34. Chromatic Scale Do to Do	167

TUNES FROM MY HOUSE TO YOURS. TRACKS 45–52

45	Tune 1a. Backyard Bop, Sing with Jeannie and Jeff Ramsey	170
46	Tune 1b. Backyard Bop, Track without Lead Vocal	170
47	Tune 2a. Dreamin', Sing with Jeannie	172
48	Tune 2b. Dreamin', Track without Lead Vocal	172
49	Tune 3a. Look Inside for Love, Sing with Jeannie	173
50	Tune 3b. Look Inside for Love, Track without Lead Vocal	173
51	Tune 4a. Every Little Thing You Do, Sing with Jeff Ramsey	174
52	Tune 4b. Every Little Thing You Do, Track without Lead Vocal	174

RHYTHM AND COUNTOFF EXERCISES. TRACKS 53–57

53	Rhythm Examples with Drum Set	82
54	Swing Sixteenths, Drums and Bass Example (Reggae and Hip-Hop)	84
55	Jazz Swing, Drums and Bass Example	84
56	Two-Feel Samba Groove, Drums and Bass Example	84
57	5/4 Groove, Jazz Trio Example	84

ACKNOWLEDGEMENTS

I am grateful to my students, mentors, and colleagues, whose immeasurable creativity and enthusiasm inspired me to write this book. Special thanks to my mother Molly Low, for her midnight candle and priceless and loving dedication to detail; to Mary McDonald Klimek MM, MS-CCC/SLP, for her invaluable input; to my family Mark Stallings, Dylan Wolff, and Arianna Wolff; to Jonathan Feist, David Sparr of Little Dog Studios, Suzanne Hanser, Marion Nesbit, and Karen Zorn; to my voice colleagues at Berklee College of Music who continue to inspire me, year after year; and to the musicians who brought their skill and joyful enthusiasm to the accompanying recording.

I am indebted to the artists, musicians, and teachers who contributed their time, humor, and wisdom to speak with me for this book: Patti Austin, Ysaye Marie Barnwell, Mark Baxter, Joey Blake, Christiane Karam, and W. Allaudin Mathieu.

AUDIO CREDITS

VOCALS: Jeannie Gagné (www.jeanniegagne.com)
Jeff Ramsey (www.jefframseymusic.com)

GUITAR: Thaddeus Hogarth (www.thaddeushogarth.com)

BASS: Danny Morris (go.berkleemusic.com/DMorris1)

PIANO: Jiri Nedoma (www.myspace.com/jirinedoma)

DRUMS: Giancarlo de Trizio (www.myspace.com/giancarlodetrizio)

PIANO, PROGRAMMING, SYNTHESIZERS: Jeannie Gagné (www.jeanniegagne.com)

to Dylan and Arianna

INTRODUCTION

Illustrated by Jeannie Gagné

*We are the flute,
and the music in us is from thee*

*We are the mountain,
and the echo in us is from thee*

—Rumi, Sufi Poet

This book is a comprehensive wellness approach for developing and maintaining a healthy, productive, and well-balanced vocal instrument. Whether you are a beginning or advanced singer, this approach will help you build your singing technique for contemporary music styles. The book provides many techniques and activities for balancing your singing practice in body, mind, and spirit; practical information about your vocal anatomy; and methods for developing into a strong and confident performer.

In these chapters, you will:

- Learn how your voice functions

- Be guided through self-reflection, vocal exploration, rhythm, movement, and exercises to support your personal empowerment through singing

- Develop healthy performance habits, understand your impact onstage, and learn how to connect with an audience

- Practice vocal exercises designed for strong and flexible contemporary singing

- Explore how to embody rhythm and become comfortable with movement

- Manage performance anxiety, explore your personal energy, and learn new techniques for relaxation using Reiki, toning, and other methods of self-care

- Learn how to shift from traditional classical technique to contemporary singing

- Nurture and deepen your personal creativity and authenticity in contemporary styles

HOW THE BOOK IS ORGANIZED

In these pages, I share with you my method for studying contemporary singing that enables you to become a healthy, powerful vocalist. You will learn to bring together different aspects of your life with your own inner music.

The seven main chapters give you tools for building and strengthening a wellness approach to being a contemporary singer. The book is organized so that you can turn to the chapter that best serves your needs today.

In part I, "The Miracle That Is Your Voice," four chapters take you through a detailed exploration of the amazing human voice, looking at it holistically through the interconnection of body, mind, and spirit. Chapter 1 tells you how singing and music can benefit you and everything you need to know about how your voice works. Chapter 2 discusses vocal wellness, vocal study, explores your creativity, and looks at skills for managing the power of your mind. Chapter 3 teaches rhythms that are essential for the contemporary singer to embody, and how to get comfortable with movement. Chapter 4 provides tools for becoming an extraordinary performer.

In part II, "The Exercises," three chapters give you practical tools for vocal study. Chapter 5 gives you pointers, warm-ups, and pronunciation guides. Chapter 6 contains the exercises you should sing every day to develop, expand, and strengthen your voice. The audio that comes with this book includes accompaniment and demonstrations for the exercises. Chapter 7 gives you four tunes for you to practice with, from my house to yours.

Part III contains five conversations with celebrated vocal artists, musicians, and teachers who have great wisdom about creativity, staying healthy, and about their life experiences as working musicians. I hope these straightforward, sometimes hilarious, and always poignant voices of experience will give you fresh perspective on being a contemporary singer.

| HOW THE BOOK IS ORGANIZED | xiii |

A holistic study of voice looks at the complete picture: your voice, your body, your intention, your performance desires, your spirit, your hang-ups and fears, and your expectations of yourself. There is a lot of information within these pages; don't try to absorb it all at once. You can jump right to the exercises in chapter 6 and start singing. Or you can begin by reading the interviews in part III to find inspiration in the words of great artists and teachers. Of course, you might prefer to start with chapter 1 and follow the progression through health and wellness, voice study and practices, rhythm, moving, performing, vocal exercises, and great advice.

Throughout the book, you'll come across sidebars with additional information, such as how-to tips, nuggets of advice, and visualizations. Each includes a small icon that indicates its general topic:

 Glowing figure: Wellness and vocal technique

 Singer: Performance health and tips

 Yin Yang: Balance between mind, body, and spirit

 Djembe Drum: Rhythm

 Mic: Planning and preparation

 Music Symbols: Exercises and theory

WHY I WROTE THIS BOOK

During my twenty-plus years teaching voice, I have noticed that people often lose trust in themselves and their voices. It is one thing to practice and improve technically; it is quite another to learn to doubt your internal music. Helping singers to develop more technical skill and artistic expression, while supporting each person's uniqueness, has become a personal mission. It requires a balance between body, mind, and spirit. That is wholeness.

I have spent many years writing this book, though I didn't realize it at first. I researched the works of many thinkers, healers, scientists, musicians, aesthetic philosophers, and sociologists. I interviewed phenomenal artists to find out how they approach performance and how they stay healthy themselves. I conducted an online survey to find out straight from the mouths of live audiences what pulls them in. I sang, I performed, I taught. I learned.

Singing has always done something amazing for me. It affects me at the cellular level. At least, it feels that way. If I don't sing regularly, I don't feel right. Singing, for me, is part of being alive—part of my experience of "I am." It's as important to me as exercising or getting outside to see the moon or hugging my children. But in my early years, *performing* was about executing acrobatic-like riffs, looking good, getting the gig. There was also always a deep desire to be giving, to connect with people through my music, but I did not know how to bring my real self into commercial performance with trust and confidence. With time and experience, I learned to release myself from that trap. As W.A. Mathieu points out in our conversation in part III, we need to ask ourselves, is the music we are singing or playing truly an expression of our life's purpose?

In these chapters, I will share with you ways to help you connect your singing and your spirit.

As a singer, you have the ability—if you choose to use it—to move not only yourself but your audience, profoundly. When you see people's faces glistening with tears after you have sung a song with all your heart and soul, what do you make of it? How do you repeat that moment? It is certainly a wonderful—even blissful—experience to lose yourself in the moment of a song. And feeling an audience's appreciation strokes the ego, definitely.

But singing is more than that. Music is everywhere. It is powerful. Singing comes before speech in the coos of a baby. If you listen closely, you can hear music in a waterfall, in bird song, even in the tempo of a ticking clock. People get married to music, have surgery while listening to it, survive coal mine cave-ins with it. Music has been a part of our human existence even before recorded time, as evidenced by simple instruments found by anthropologists that date as far back as 35,000 years ago. What was likely the first form of music? Singing.

People need music. We go to hear live music to be moved, to have an experience, to step out of the everyday and be part of something extraordinary. It is our responsibility as musicians to rise to the occasion, to be held accountable for the music we create, and to decide who we are and what we are putting out there.

Singing is really good for us. When a person sings, the whole body resonates with the notes that originate on the breath and in the throat. Projecting that song outward, the sound can affect everyone who hears it, as well as ourselves. We have the miraculous ability to direct this effect of the song. We can affect how it touches ourselves or our audiences. It is challenging to keep the personal ego quiet enough to get out of the way of this effect, but when we succeed, the rewards to the audience and the ripples back to ourselves are profound.

Your voice is more than the sum of its parts. *Your Singing Voice: Contemporary Style, Expression, and Spirit* offers guidance through vocal techniques and exercises that will gently nudge you closer to your delightfully unique resonance as a singer and artist. This book invites you into a journey of personal discovery about singing, authenticity, and expression in performance. Let's get singing!

Jeannie Gagné

PART I

The Miracle That Is Your Voice

The voice is truly miraculous. It is infinitely variable, responding to subtle thoughts and emotions, capable of a wide variety of colors, tones, volumes, and pitches that can change in an instant. Vocal technique gives the singer control over how the voice responds, enabling choices for intention, style, and artistry. Healthy practices help to maintain a singer's voice over a lifetime. In part I, we take a detailed look at how the voice and breathing work; wellness practices for body, mind, and spirit; embodying contemporary rhythms; and embracing performing.

CHAPTER 1

Your Body Is Your Instrument

If I were not a physicist, I would probably be a musician. I often think in music. I live my daydreams in music. I see my life in terms of music.

—Albert Einstein, Physicist

WELLNESS AND MUSIC

It is an incredible feeling to sing well. Do you ever think about how singing affects you, in your body, in your mind, or in your heart? If you're reading this book, the answer is probably, "Yes, of course!"

Singing, playing, and listening to music have always been ways in which people touch and move one another. Music inspires. It enlightens. It touches deep parts of us that words alone cannot describe. In the 1960s, songs raised passionate emotions on key issues of the time, arguably spearheading much of the civil rights movement. In worship settings, music is often just as important as the spoken word. Music is often *the* reason why people select a place of worship.

Music enraptures us. It can be very cathartic. It is used successfully as a healing modality to speed up recovery and to reduce stress. Music is so popular because creating it and listening to it transports us away from our day-to-day thoughts and the trappings of our busy lives.

Whether or not music is cathartic, aggressive, celebratory, suggestive, moving, numbing, or has any number of other emotional or spiritual effects on us depends upon each artist's intention and vision. (In recorded music, the producer also has a lot to do with a song's impact.) Artists decide how to channel their creativity into their music. If your aim as an artist is to create a positive environment, you must first take care of yourself. The artist's state of wellness is reflected in his or her work. In the competitive environment of commercial music, not to mention in our fast-paced, instant-food, instant-gratification culture, taking good care of oneself can be a challenge. It is, however, essential.

An artist is someone whose self-discovery from everyday life is shared in a creative way—someone who takes the normal and makes it fresh. It is essential to discover who we truly are as artists in order to learn what makes our music stand out. This takes time to uncover, and our music—like our personal growth—will change and evolve. It's like peeling away the leaves of an artichoke one at a time to reveal the spiny, silky, tasty heart inside that is both tender and prickly. When we are honest with ourselves, this process of self-observation filters into our daily living and drifts seamlessly back into our art. It is a circular process to cherish.

Commercial music seems to have forgotten that it can be much more than a highly successful industry. Today's artist is not supported as in the past, when record labels would stick with their artists over years and build careers. Nurturing an artist or a band through the complex process of developing a unique voice sometimes meant albums that didn't sell well while an act was being developed. All artists who have longevity will experience lean years, especially if they stay consistent with what makes them unique rather than trying to morph themselves to fit the latest trend. This is normal. Public tastes ebb and flow, as we have seen in fashion with the return of bell-bottom pants from the 1970s and brightly colored hair and clothing from the 1980s. Musical acts that stay artistically consistent usually survive the up and down cycles of popular musical tastes. The market will circle back to them.

THERE ARE ABUNDANT OPPORTUNITIES TO SING

There's an African proverb that goes like this: "If you can walk, you can dance; if you can talk, you can sing." Yes, some people sing "better" than others, just as some dance better than others. That's true with everything. Does that mean you shouldn't work at it? Of course not. There are so many places where people sing—on big stages, in coffee houses, on television, at a karaoke bar, in worship, in the shower, on the Internet, on tour, at a party, in the car, on song demos, at weddings and funerals, at auditions, at a ballgame, in a lesson. Where you *perform*

> **"Everyone is born with a voice."**

boils down to hard work, technique and practice, good song selection, your self-confidence—and luck, too. The more professional the situation, the more is expected of you.

Regardless of where you sing, there is one universal truth that never changes: human beings want and need to be moved. Music fulfills this need. Music makes life rich; it validates who we are, it gives a name and a community to our life's struggles. The good news is, because of the ubiquity of the Internet, artists can now share their music worldwide on their own and even develop an impressive following. New, constantly improving, and affordable recording technology offers easy access to excellent recording quality on a home computer with minimal gear. This enables a well-produced, homegrown song to burst onto the scene with hundreds of thousands of hits on YouTube, Facebook, and Twitter. Scores of music sites like MySpace, CD Baby, and ReverbNation provide an outlet for the self-promoting artist. The commercial success of a song is now determined by an audience that is composed of the whole world interconnecting online. There is an audience for every style, every taste, and every musical genre.

> "Sing! Let your voice be heard.
> Dance! Let your life be seen.
> Drum! Let the rhythm fill your soul.
> May our combined voices, and dances, and rhythms, and love, make us whole."

> "There is a reenergized movement to bring empowerment, humanity, and peace into our global community through music."

Music with this intention can *literally* move people. This happens at the cellular level, in the emotional body, in the heartbeat, through the release of endorphins, and in the spiritual body. Music facilitates a deep experience that elevates us to a higher state. *Music is motion.*

This bourgeoning is bringing much of the true essence of music back into contemporary styles. Why? Music that is written and performed from a place of connection to the indescribable, from honesty—from an *authentic*, genuine expression by the artist—returns us to art. Art was never about sales, though making money to support oneself with one's music is important. Artists need to be free to explore the human condition, to explore what inspires them, to question, to be themselves.

Modern composer John Cage once said that artists have a responsibility to bring importance to their work—to create art that is *good* for people—because artists are special ambassadors whose work reaches people very deeply. Many thinkers, including Cage, believe that musicians embody information directly from a higher source into the physical form of their music. It is up to the artist to put the experiences of being a human being into words and music.

We all have hopes, make mistakes, dream big dreams, become paralyzed by fear, and harbor secret longings. To express these experiences through music is both an artist's strength and also a privilege. It is a service. We are in service to our gift of music.

THE MANY BENEFITS OF SINGING

Singing is motion. Vocalists have a unique opportunity—perhaps, a duty—to connect with their audiences. Standing center stage directly before the audience, vocalists have lyrics that express meaning and tell stories in short, carefully crafted, poetic lines. Their faces and body language express the human condition in all of its complexity. They can create powerful experiences not only for the audience but for themselves too, and together with the other musicians on stage, in the spirit of teamwork. This is a gift to the listener. It provides the listener with an opportunity to sing vicariously, to feel what the singer expresses. It creates community.

Singing Can Be Life-Changing—Literally

Sound is vibration; vibration is movement. Our bodies are composed of energy; energy is also movement. Atoms in our cells include electrons that are constantly moving. Electromagnetic wave frequencies in cells with similar rates combine the cells, making structures. As music therapist Louise Montello points out, with all this activity happening within our bodies, it can be said that *our bodies* are *sound*.[1]

Music can literally transform our physical state. Its vibrations stir our cells. Our emotional bodies can be stirred by music, too. "That singing was really moving," we say. Music can nurture personal transformation. Music puts the listener into a receptive state, touching people at a deep level. It has the power to create experiences that are profoundly inspiring for the listener, who might be motivated by it even to the point of taking action with whatever he or she is passionate about. *Music can change lives.*

---

[1] Montello, L. *Essential Musical Intelligence: Using Music as Your Path to Healing, Creativity, and Radiant Wholeness.* Wheaton, IL: Theosophical Publishing House, 2002.

> *Jo parivartan aap sansaar me chahte hai,*
> *veh pehele swayam me layiye.*
> *"You must be the change you want to see in the world."*
>
> —Mahatma Gandhi

Transformation happens when we are able to step away from the day-to-day thoughts that are limiting, becoming open to new ways of understanding our lives and our purposes. Writer Toni Morrison describes music as a mirror that shows us clearly who we are. This is especially true in the voice studio where the student's body becomes the instrument, allowing him or her to become profoundly physically, emotionally, and spiritually receptive to learning.

By using focused intention, a singer can create popular performances that also result in positive and even healing effects upon both the singer and the audience. This engenders a strengthened sense of community, heightened experience, and general wellbeing. It is a bit simplistic to say that music can make the world a better place. Music is, after all, not going to feed hungry children or stop a war. However, it does have the power to inspire those who hear it. Music is powerful.

Physical Health Benefits

The health benefits from singing are many. People often speak of how much better they feel after they sing, which is probably a big reason why attendance in choruses is way up in the U.S. In one study that swabbed saliva of singers before and after their chorus rehearsal, the level of immunoglobulin A increased 150 percent. Immunoglobulin A is a protein antibody that lowers stress and helps maintain immunity to infection.[2] You sing, you improve your health. Simple.

It has long been known that music is good for your health, and it doesn't take a study to demonstrate this fact. It is a common experience all around the world. Every day, music is used to assist healing in hospitals, to help cancer patients, to empower troubled youth, and to help seniors in nursing homes stay active and happy. Music is used with massage therapy to help release muscle tension, in medical treatment to help reduce pain, and in therapy to help lessen anxiety. Mothers sing softly to help their babies fall asleep, and babies even sing to themselves, too. Drumming and singing are traditional aspects of shamanic ritual, where these healers treat ailments by attending to the soul, connecting the spiritual and physical worlds. Music is used during meditation and yoga. Chanting is used as a practice to quiet the mind, to release the grip of the never-ending chatty consciousness, and to center oneself. Meditation reduces stress, and reducing stress improves health.

---

[2] Robert Beck et al, *Music perception*, Fall 2000: 18(1):87–106.]

What about contemporary styles? Can you really sing these without hurting your voice? Absolutely. This book is full of healthy techniques to show you how. Your vocal instrument relies on muscles, breathing, and resonance, regardless of the style of music you are singing. What varies most between styles is how you shape the vowels, how you use vibrato, how you articulate the text, and how loudly you sing. We'll discuss that in chapter 2. Virtually every sound that you can sing can be done healthfully. You may not *like* every sound you make; you may have been taught that this tone is "bad" and that tone is "correct," but that's a different story.

The Bliss of Vocal Resonance: Toning

Toning is a very powerful meditation practice. Unlike singing a song, toning uses the voice specifically to resonate an area of the body in healing. It is a practice of sustaining a note, usually on a vowel, while directing the tone to an area of the body that needs attention. Matching pitch or using vocal technique are not important aspects of toning. Toning is not singing.

Similar to toning is chanting "om" during meditation, where one note is sustained repeatedly on the word "om" for several minutes or longer. While chanting "om" helps quiet the mind, during toning, the objective is to direct the body's healing energy consciously to an area that needs it, in the moment. Is it your shoulder, your stomach, a cramp in your leg? Or perhaps life has thrown you a curve ball and your heart is heavy? Do you have a headache, a neck ache? Or maybe you feel fine, though a bit over-stimulated thinking about all the things you need to get done today. Toning can help lessen your sensation of pain, relax your thoughts, and relax your muscles.

To begin toning, simply hum or sing one note at a soft or moderate volume. Take a breath as needed to create a long, sustained sound. As you tone, listen. Listen to yourself, to your body. Listen to the sound or sounds you make. Let your body guide you to produce the right sound that is the most helpful at that moment. Don't worry about sounding "good" or not. It's not about that. Listen inside. Let your thoughts quiet. Listen inside again. Listen outside yourself, too. Keep this going for a few minutes, tolerating thoughts that may question if what you're doing is of any use.

Usually, toning notes are pitched lower in a vocal range. Move the pitch around on a hum, until the vibration of it feels right. It's like sending a gentle, relaxing, electric current to an area of the body. If you are not sure what area needs it most, just start on any note. Sustain a tone. Feel your body's reaction. Is an area of tension showing up? Try changing the pitch or the sound. Listen to your body some more. With practice, even for just a few minutes daily, you will find that toning is a wonderful stress reducer. When you are done toning, you will feel refreshed and relaxed.

Try toning together with friends, letting the combined resonance of your voices seep into your bodies. It can be an amazing experience.

Singing in Community

Community singing offers a much-needed, strong dose of wellness. Positive, loving elements from making music together balance the overwhelming negativity and despair that often pervade our culture. Singing is a perfect vehicle for this. It can serve by inspiring us to take helpful action in the greater community. It can serve by inspiring us to bring positive intentions to others.

Something wonderful happens when people gather to sing together. The sound of combined voices stirs something very deep within us. I remember the first chorus I sang in, in college, at age eighteen or nineteen. I still recall my wonder at the experience of being inside a group of resonant voices. Men and women, singing together, created a full spectrum of sound that you could *feel*. I remember thinking, "*This* is humanity at its best." I couldn't get enough of it. I couldn't wait for the next rehearsal to experience harmonies of our combined unity, for the blending of individuals combining into one beautiful reverberation. Though I'd sung my whole life, I fell in love with singing in a new way. I fell in love with that group of people in the chorus, too. Singing together brought us love.

When you are standing within a chorus, you hear the voices near you in your section. You hear their individuality, while you also hear the voices blending. You hear yourself, though less than when you sing solo. You feel the vibrations of everyone singing together resonating in your chest, in your abdomen, even in your feet. There might be a piano playing with you, or an orchestra, or a flute soloist, or a rhythm section. You hear these instruments, too. You can watch everyone's deep concentration as they all play and sing together. You can feel the pleasure of all the musicians who have chosen to come together to make music as one. For some people, including myself, it is also possible to *see* the heightened energy as swirling colors around the heads and torsos of everyone who is participating, their energies enhanced in musical expression. In choral singing, you experience being a part of something much larger than yourself, while still expressing who you are.

Joining a chorus or choir is one way to sing without needing to feel the spotlight, and that works well for a lot of people. There are volunteer choirs that invite people to sing even if you think you don't have a great voice, and there are professional choruses for the trained singer. There is a wide variety of music being sung too, from classical works to gospel to contemporary styles to world music. Search your local community for the choir or chorus that fits.

The Joy of Performing—or, It's Okay Not to Perform, Too

The truth is, not everyone enjoys performing. Singing doesn't have to be only about that.

Although in this book, live performing of contemporary music is a featured topic, there is a lot of information here that's just about singing. Sometimes it's important to sing simply for the joy of it, and for no other reason. In fact, if you *only* sing in preparation for performance and skip the part about singing for no particular reason at all besides enjoying yourself, you might be missing out on some really good music!

Singing in performance is one of my greatest joys on this earth. I also enjoy singing alone at my piano when there is no one around to hear me but the cat. (That is, after all, how it all started, way back in childhood.) I have students who will never perform yet study voice because it is therapeutic, because singing uplifts them and they leave the lesson each week with a broad smile. They love that. My mother started taking voice lessons for the fun of it at age sixty. It is never too late!

"You must be the change you want to see in the world." It all begins with you, one note at a time. I hope within these pages you find the inspiration and technique to be the change in the world you want to see, whatever that is for you.

The first step: learning how your voice works.

YOUR BODY IS YOUR INSTRUMENT

Anatomy: Understand Your Vocal Instrument

This section provides anatomical detail describing how your vocal instrument works. It is important to keep in mind how integrated your voice is within your body. Because your voice responds to even the most subtle of thoughts, it is very useful for you to be well informed about the moving parts inside you. Just as an athlete gains muscle control over specific areas of the body, a well-educated singer learns to direct precise movements for optimum results. When you can picture how your vocal body works, it makes it easier to gain mastery over tiny and complex muscle movements that you can't see working.

Voice production has three components: air source, tone generator, and resonating spaces.

Your voice is a wind instrument. When you sing, many parts of the body work collaboratively to take in air, to generate tone, and to resonate and color that sound. Your *whole body* is your vocal instrument.

First, you need an air source. Without breath you cannot sing. The lungs take in air and expel it, acting as a kind of bellows (see "Breathing," page 21).

Second, this airflow generates tone by vibrating the vocal folds (also called vocal "cords").[3] These are located in your larynx, or "voice box."

Third, the tone made in your larynx resonates. It is amplified, colored, and contoured by your throat, your mouth, and sometimes, the cavities in your nose. The brightness or darkness of your tone changes. It is with this resonance that vowels are shaped. Vowels are the singer's primary tonal quality.

Again, sound is movement. Air molecules that are set into motion by an energy source—in this case, by your voice—move small structures in our ears. That movement is filtered and modified inside the ear, allowing it to be interpreted by our brains as tone or noise.

What Happens When I Sing?

What we call the "voice" requires systems in several areas of your body to work together. Everyday movements become intentional instrumental movements and postures. Your torso becomes the main structure of your instrument, supported by your legs. Your neck and mouth become your instrument's tonal chambers. Your breath becomes the power or source of your instrument. Your energy, your movements, and your facial expressions project and communicate with your instrument.

When you breathe in, muscles in the *larynx* open a passageway into your *trachea* (windpipe). On exhalation, the air passes back up through the trachea and travels out through your larynx. Your vocal folds are located there, just behind and slightly below the level of your "adam's apple" (the prominence of the *thyroid* cartilage in your neck). Your vocal folds are part of what opens to let air in during inhalation.

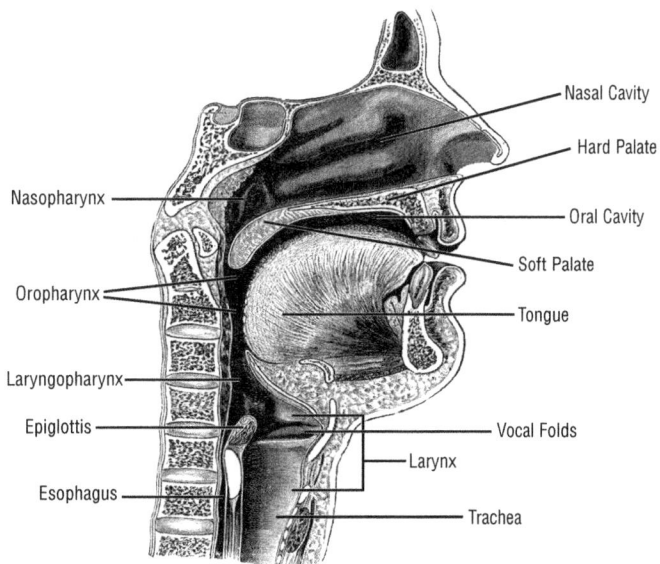

Fig. 1.1. Areas of the Vocal Process

---

[3] The vocal cords are the very edges of the area of tissue called *vocal folds:* these are the actual parts that touch in vibration. In vocal pedagogy, however, the terms have become synonymous. Because the distinction is not important for our purposes, I am only using the term "folds."

When you sing, the vocal folds vibrate against one another, acting like a kind of reed. Muscles within your larynx bring the vocal folds together. Suction and pressure from the air you took into your lungs help in the process, while the elasticity of the vocal fold edges permits the vibrations to happen.

The vocal folds also serve as a component of the valve that closes your windpipe when you swallow or hold your breath. In fact, your larynx's most important function is its participation in the respiratory system. The larynx facilitates breathing and protects your lungs. It is so important that the largest area of the brain's cerebral cortex, which controls motor functions, is devoted to the larynx—even more so than to the complex facial muscles. Amazing!

ANXIETY AND SINGING

Because respiration is the larynx's primary function, any fearful thoughts will cause the body to protect itself and contract muscles in defense, making singing much more difficult. Singing is less important to the body than staying alive; when the body defends itself, it does not analyze why. It just reacts. That's why your thoughts play such a vital role. If your thoughts are anxious, for example, your breathing and singing will become compromised. (See "Breathing" on page 21, and "Your Mind: The Power of Thought in Singing" on page 46 for detailed discussions.)

The sound generated in the larynx is amplified in the cavities of the vocal tract, primarily in the *pharynx* (back of your throat) where your *soft palate* is located. The soft palate is a flexible structure behind your hard palate and above your larynx. It lifts when we speak or sing, most of the time (except when we use nasal consonants: M, N, or NG). It also lifts when you swallow, yawn, or are about to sneeze. Resonance is created as the sound produced in the larynx is colored and shaped by the activities of the tongue, lips, soft palate, and the walls of the pharynx. The teeth, jaw, tongue, and lips articulate and impose consonants on the resonating tones, creating what we recognize as speech or singing.

Except for the hard palate, each of these structures can change shape to affect your voice's tonal colorations. You can lift your soft palate intentionally, which is important to increase the resonant space at the top of the throat. (To feel your soft palate lifting, yawn on purpose.) Think of it like a concert hall opening in your mouth, or like the spacious dome of a cathedral. If your mouth is closed down, the tone has a harder time ringing and projecting, and your muscles may tighten to compensate and to push out sound. The arched space in the top of your mouth under your hard palate, being a part of your mouth's "resonator," also adds to tonal color.

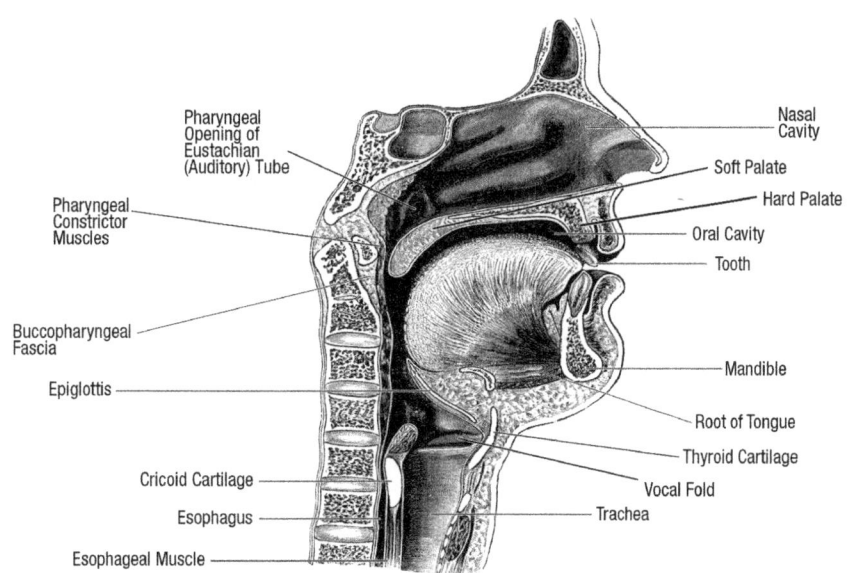

Fig. 1.2. Side View of Vocal Mechanism, Face, and Neck

In figure 1.2, we see a cutaway view of the head and neck. In this illustration, we can see the boney hard palate behind the teeth and the pliable soft palate at the back of the throat. The glottis is the space in between your vocal folds when they are open ("abducted"). The epiglottis is the flap of elastic cartilage tissue, attached to the top of the thyroid cartilage. It covers your windpipe when you swallow, to keep food from getting into your lungs.

In figure 1.2, the mouth is closed and so the vocal space is limited. The space enlarges considerably when you open the mouth and lift the soft palate. You only need to open your mouth naturally when you sing, as if you're saying, "aaah" (as in "Aaah, I get it"). If it is opened too widely, you might stress your jaw muscles and risk tiring out the system. (Furthermore, a mouth that is too agape may make your audience uncomfortable because it looks strained.) Although sometimes we may choose to produce a closed sound such as a hum, during normal singing, if your mouth stays closed, sound cannot resonate effectively.

The Vocal Folds and Larynx

The quality of the voice also depends upon the layered structure of the vocal folds and how they vibrate together. These folds are incredibly malleable, made of soft tissue in layers that can act independently. There is a meaty structure of muscle and ligament deep within each fold, and a soft gel-like layer just below the "skin" makes up the edges that touch in vibration. The muscles within the larynx can act together or in opposition to one another, to thin, thicken, shrink, expand, tighten, and relax the vibrating edges of the vocal folds.

When the "true"[4] vocal folds come together during speech or singing, they vibrate against one another very quickly. To give you an idea of the speed of this

---

[4] The "true" vocal folds are the edges that vibrate together; the "false" vocal folds are the two sides of the meaty tissue that support these edges.

movement, when you sing the A above middle C ("A3" on a keyboard, or 440 hertz), your voice vibrates at 440 times per second. The vibration rate is the same as with any instrument on the same pitch, regardless of whether it is produced by a flute, piano string, or voice. Go up an octave, the rate doubles to 880 Hz. Go down an octave, the rate is half as fast at 220 Hz, and so on. (When your voice is scoped by an otolaryngologist—a medical doctor who specializes in the larynx—a strobe light is necessary in order to see the voice working. The strobe slows the visual rate of vibration for the doctor.) When you imagine the speed with which the vocal folds come together, and then add the force of additional neck muscles potentially over-working or straining, you can understand how quickly vocal damage can occur.

LEARN MORE ABOUT YOUR LARYNX

There is a large amount of material online about the larynx, including pictures and videos. Google it. Just as you would learn about the mechanics of how your guitar or piano works, you will be armed with better knowledge of your vocal instrument if you study its anatomical function. That knowledge makes it easier for your brain to understand how to control the right muscles when you study vocal technique, and to translate that understanding into movements you can control. You don't have to be in medical school to get this stuff. Learn a little, for now. It can take awhile to understand how the larynx functions for singing because of its complexity. But when you have even a working knowledge of the larynx, you are much better off.

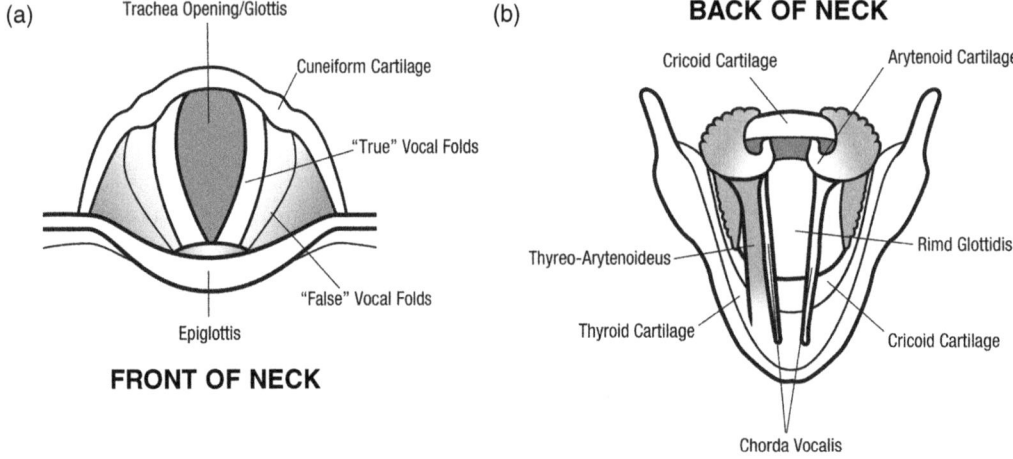

Fig. 1.3. Representation of (a) Laryngoscopic View of Larynx Interior, (b) Cricoarytenoid Joint and Arytenoid Cartilages

Inside the larynx are many tiny moving parts; it is extremely complex. Laryngeal muscles bring the vocal folds together, take them apart, and stretch (or tense) them. There are also nine cartilages in the larynx that move (three single cartilages: *thyroid, cricoid,* and *epiglottic* and three in pairs: *arytenoid, corniculate,* and *cuneiform*). The hyoid bone sits at the top of the larynx, though it is not connected to it. The hyoid bone also moves when we speak or sing.

The most interesting and important structure might be the *cricoarytenoid* joint that opens and closes the vocal folds in different ways (see figure 1.3b). This lubricated joint, which lies on a steeply sloping angle along the backside of the *cricoid* cartilage, allows the two small *arytenoid* cartilages that attach to the back end of the vocal folds to slide, rock, and pivot. This action modifies the distance between the vocal fold edges, altering the space between them (the glottis). This change is key to vocal production.

When we sing higher notes, the notes are not actually "high" in our bodies. (There is no gravity involved here ☺.) They are stretched longer and thinner by the cricothyroid muscle. It contracts to lengthen and tighten the vocal folds, like pulling on a rubber band. The thyroid cartilage also pivots forward during this motion. Then, when we sing lower notes the vocal folds are shortened as the cricothyroid muscle releases its pull, and as the *thyroarytenoid* muscles within the vocal folds contract instead. A similar balance of activity is used to make the edges thicker as we get louder, thinner as we get softer.

When you growl, be careful of creating too much tension and squeezing the "false" folds together too tightly. These meaty structures outside of the "true" vocal folds are not normally part of phonation.

Thin or Thick Fold Edges

If you are singing high and light and descend into your lower voice without letting your voice thicken, your tone will get very light and seem to disappear. There needs to be more substance to the fold to produce full tone at lower pitches. (Imagine lower-pitched instruments: they are larger in size than higher-pitched ones.) The reverse is also true: when you are singing in speech-level tones lower in your range and go higher in your range, if you don't allow your voice to thin as you ascend, you will strain. This familiar feeling happens if you belt to the highest note you can until you must flip into a thin and breathy tone. (See "Power Singing," page 19.) This is avoidable!

The edges of your voice—the vocal folds—change density where they come together, depending on how loudly you are singing. They also stiffen or relax. When one muscle in the vocal process moves, it affects another. When you sing louder, the vocal tissue gets thicker with action of the *thyroarytenoid* muscle.

With study and practice, you learn to *allow* these changes in the larynx to happen relatively seamlessly. Although you will feel shifts occurring within your voice, your audience probably won't hear them.

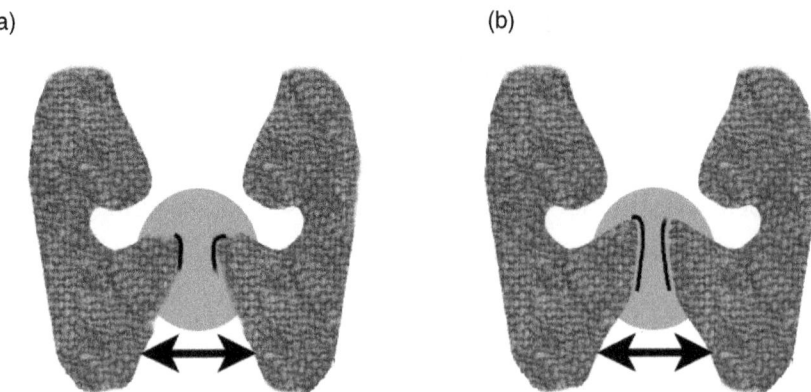

Fig. 1.4. Vocal Folds Meeting During Phonation (Side View). (a) Less vocal tissue coming together, highlighted by the grey circle. Thinner means softer. (b) A thicker fold. Thicker means louder.

Muscle movements in the larynx:

- The PCAs (posterior cricoarytenoid muscles) open the vocal folds.

- The LCA and IA (lateral cricoarytenoid, interarytenoid muscles) work together to close the folds.

- The TA (thyroarytenoid) is the main muscle, in which the *vocalis* muscle is located. It shortens the folds and helps to close them. When the TA contracts, it lowers the pitch.

It is common for females to have a gap even when the full folds come together. This is at the back, around the arytenoids. Some voice teachers call this the "chink." This can make the voice more breathy.

Your Vocal Tract Also Changes

As we've discussed, sound produced in the larynx is shaped into a wide variety of timbres and colors by action of the pharynx, lips, jaw, tongue, and soft palate. Your vocal tract—the spaces and housing above and around your pharynx—also changes in both length and contour. When you sing lower notes, your vocal tract generally becomes longer; when you sing higher notes, it shortens. The laryngeal cartilages are moving and pivoting to make pitch and tone; the entire larynx is lowering and rising to adjust the resonance of the pitch. In this way, the voice functions something like the slide of a trombone.

The pharynx can also contract, expand, shorten, and lengthen. The opera singer wants a wide pharynx, whereas the R&B singer may narrow it to create a bright tone. Tonal qualities are also modified by changes in the pharynx. For instance, when the pharynx is contracted, its walls get rougher and *absorb* sound frequencies, whereas when it's relaxed, the walls are smooth and *reflect* sound frequencies.

BE CAREFUL OF TENSE NECK MUSCLES

Sometimes, singers over-tense neck muscles while trying to "sound better." This usually creates vocal strain. When you learn to let the desired frequencies project through your sound, without undue squeezing in your neck to get a tone you like, there is an efficiency of motion as the laryngeal muscles learn to work together in better coordination. This helps you to avoid straining. Releasing neck tension while you sing is something to work on with your teacher.

Vibrato

Vibrato comes from movement of the vocal tract. The thyroid cartilage, rocking back and forth quickly while you're holding a note, produces vibrato. You can also create vibrato by rapidly shifting between two close pitches, which is movement of the vocal folds. If the vocal tract is too tense, it can't oscillate. It's like holding a bell while ringing it; the sound is dampened. If you cannot sing with vibrato, it is likely that your vocal tract has tension that is inhibiting movement.

Air Pressure—Resistance

In singing technique, we learn to release the breath with intention, using airflow that travels from the lungs to help bring the vocal folds together into vibration. Focusing on the breath helps to take the burden off the laryngeal and neck muscles, which would tend to over-compensate otherwise. That in turn also helps to avoid strain while improving tone.

The volume of the tone is produced by a coordinated effort between the force of air leaving the body and the *resistance* at the larynx. Said another way:

> **"**Good singing technique relies on coordinating your airflow with the natural resistance happening in your larynx.**"**

This process should not be forced; rather, it is a natural feeling, somewhat like holding your breath. Feeling resistance to air at the site of the folds is essential for the voice to work optimally.

When you take in a breath, your lungs fill with air, and the air pressure in your lungs increases. Then, as you release the air when you sing, the pressure drops as the air stream zips over the rounded edges of the vocal folds. This helps to pull the vocal folds together through a process called the *Bernoulli Effect*, and the folds close. (The same effect around an airplane's wings helps to lift it.) Then, air pressure builds up again, which separates the folds again. All of this is happening extremely rapidly in a continuous wave-like cycle, where little puffs of air are produced by this action at your larynx, hundreds of times a second; the vocal folds open and close repeatedly on one exhalation while you sing a note. (See "Breathing: Managing What You Already Know," page 21.) This is especially important because the laryngeal muscles could not vibrate at this high rate of speed through muscle contractions alone. In fact, when you over-tense muscles in an effort to sing, the *flexibility* that is necessary for coordinated vibration of the vocal folds is compromised.

When we select a note to sing, we not only anticipate its pitch (which affects how rapidly the folds vibrate together), we also decide how loud or soft to make it. The brain sends signals to the larynx to change the relationship of push and pull between different muscle groups, making extremely small alterations in the vocal folds.

Getting skilled at "vocal control" takes time because the body is learning to make tiny and coordinated muscle movements and then repeat them to gain consistency. Practicing technique every day is important. When you're on the gig, you want to sound good! By practicing new skills daily, you will be less likely to resort back to your older and familiar singing habits. You will have gained "muscle memory" for better singing technique. Together with breathing techniques, this is what teachers mean when they say, "support your voice." Even when the stakes are higher—even when you are nervous—your new and improved technique will be there.

LET IT HAPPEN

This process in the larynx is complex. The best approach for control at the larynx is to *let it happen*. Ironically, voice technique is largely about letting go; good technique is often about what you are *not* doing. Yes, the larynx does change. It has to. But ideally, the changes can be so subtle that only you or your voice teacher will be aware of them. When you study voice technique, you learn to maximize your breathing and adjust the shape of your mouth. You visualize pitch, and volume, and tone, staying relaxed yet active. You learn to *let your body respond* to your thought. Rather than trying to *make* your voice work in a certain way, think about the outcome you want. Let your voice work for you. With practice, your body will do the rest. It is creating control, without over-controlling the process!

Is Your Tongue Tight?

Notice the size of the tongue back in figure 1.2. It's huge. It is a strong bundle of muscle that is interconnected with other muscles in your vocal tract. When it pulls back or contracts in your throat, your vocal mechanism is being affected, too. Often a person who experiences a lot of tension while singing has a tight tongue.

The solution: Hold it. Yup. Get a paper towel, or a gauze pad, and hold the tip of your tongue when you sing. Does it want to pull back into your mouth? That's how you know if it is tight. If you hold your tongue while you practice, you can train the muscles to relax. You will absolutely find that the tension in your throat lessens.

Power Singing: Force Isn't Necessary to Sound Great

Many singers misconstrue the excess use of force in belting with creating excitement in a song. Frequently, popular music uses loud and powerful singing, with elaborate runs and acrobatic stunts. Or, it may be expressively raspy, as in rock or blues. Some people can sing this way with "cords of steel" that survive through continuous use. Most people cannot. Unfortunately, popular ways of singing forcefully often result in causing permanent vocal damage. If you want a voice that lasts, be very, very careful of continually over-singing or straining. It will not help you sing better. The key is to build strong technique to get the stylistic result you are after in a *different, healthy way* that works with your individual instrument. *It's not the style that's bad; it's how singers think they're supposed to sing to "sound good" that can lead to problems.*

Straining does *not* mean you are giving your all! If your voice is tired or hoarse after you sing, you are doing something stressful or harmful to it. If your voice feels fine and your speaking voice is normal after singing for an hour or more, you are probably okay. (Remember to warm down after singing, explained in chapter 2, where we explore healthy vocal technique at length.)

Don't force your voice to the edge before you release tension in your throat to let the vocal muscles change. This is pushing. If you are singing loudly, there is a lot of torque involved in the larynx as you take your voice to the top of its full voice range. When you keep ascending with volume, there will be a dramatic change: you *must* shift registers. Your tone may suddenly become wispy and weak. Sound familiar? Furthermore, when you continually force your voice to respond, your vocal edges come together abrasively, over and over again in the same small area. In time, this might cause vocal damage.

Instead of using force, you want to build a *flexible* voice. You want to shift gears *sooner*, before you feel you need to push. When you do, transitions are smoother, even imperceptible. (See "Registers and Placement" in chapter 2.) Imagine a rubber band at rest: it has a certain size and thickness. If you stretch it, it gets longer and thinner. Your voice is like that rubber band. When you ask your voice to stretch longer and thinner for higher notes, while also telling it to stay thick for volume and power, your voice is working at full strength in opposing directions. Something's got to give. (This is why belting lower notes is easier: there is less pull on your voice for pitch!) So instead, you "change registers." The voice muscles stretch and the cartilages pivot, allowing your vocal folds to adjust.

It is important to point out that each voice has limits. All voices cannot produce the same sounds! Problems result when a singer tries to force the voice to be something it is not. Singing should always be comfortable. Eventually, with lots of practice, singing can become invigorating yet feel relatively effortless.

Polyps, Nodes, and Acid Reflux

Some conditions indicate damage to the voice. These can be avoided with good technique and sensible singing habits. Usually, you need to be examined by a laryngologist (or an otolaryngologist who treats singers) to know for sure what's going on. The trained ears of a skilled vocal teacher will help you decide when a medical assessment is appropriate. Let's identify three common conditions:

A *polyp* is an area of damage on the vocal cord, usually on one side. It can look like a blister, a broken blood vessel, or a lump of irritated tissue. It causes the voice to close irregularly during phonation, so your voice sounds hoarse and it's more difficult to sing. A polyp is sometimes caused by a single event, like yelling or yell-singing. The result is a broken blood vessel that bleeds into the tissue, causing swelling; scar tissue may develop. This condition may improve with vocal rest, but usually requires surgery to be repaired, especially if it goes unchecked for a while.

VOCAL SURGEONS

Most ear/nose/throat surgeons do not specialize in the singing voice. Most operate on larynxes damaged by cancer or over-talking, where the patient isn't concerned with preserving a high B♭. Be very careful when considering surgery. It is essential that you do your research and choose a surgeon who is board certified and well-known for his or her work with singers, who understands how to preserve the function of the singing voice. This specialist is called a "phonosurgeon" or "laryngologist." Then, avoid surgery unless it is absolutely necessary. (This holds true for any type of surgery.)

Nodes, or *nodules*, are often described as calluses or cysts (fluid-filled sacs). They tend to come in pairs: one node on each vocal edge, the two of them bumping together. If you repeatedly speak or sing with force, such as talking over the noise in clubs or straining to belt, you can cause nodes. As with polyps, these bumps mean your vocal edges cannot come together cleanly, so it is more difficult to produce tone, and your voice sounds hoarse or breathy. Most of the time, nodes shrink with vocal rest, unless extensive scar tissue has developed at the site, from years of speaking or singing forcefully. If you rest your voice (or have surgery) and then go right back to speaking and singing in the manner that caused the nodes in the first place, you will grow them right back. If you aren't sure how to undo this vicious cycle, see a doctor, and work with a voice therapist to break bad old habits and build good new ones.

Acid reflux is a commonly diagnosed condition these days. It refers to stomach acid that is coming back up your esophagus due to your body's reaction to foods and/or certain activities. The stomach acid irritates the tissue in your throat, even if you don't feel any heartburn. When the vocal fold tissues are exposed to reflux and become irritated, they swell, making singing more difficult. Your throat doctor can see the redness and swelling caused by acid reflux with a simple look down your throat. If you have this condition, you will likely have to change your diet, or perhaps consider prescription medications to calm down the inflammation and irritation. There are numerous resources available on the Internet to guide you away from problem foods that trigger acid reflux. And of course, ask your doctor.

Your vocal folds may also swell for several other reasons, including over-use, fatigue, having a head cold, irritation from postnasal drip, coughing a lot, bronchitis, yelling, asthma, and others. A swollen voice means the tissues are plumped up and cannot vibrate properly. At these times, you should rest your voice, though it does not necessarily indicate a long-term problem. If the swelling subsides quickly, chances are your voice is going to be okay. When done correctly, the gentle exercises in chapter 6 can help sooth a lightly swollen or tired voice.

Breathing: Managing What You Already Know

Like other functions in the body, breathing is flexible. You breathe differently depending on the situation and on your body's need in the moment. When you are standing up, you breathe differently than when you are lying down. When you are running, you breathe faster and deeper than when you are sitting down to eat. As we will see, the muscles that support breathing can operate in different coordinated combinations. When we study vocal technique we learn to direct the outcome of this coordination with increased intention, to manage breathing in a way that best supports singing.

Perhaps because of its flexibility, breathing is the source of stress for many voice students, who often say, "I don't know how to breathe!" Of course you do, you're alive. Think of it simply as consciously directing what you do unconsciously twelve to twenty times per minute when at rest.

Maximizing breath techniques creates healthy pressure for optimum function of the vocal folds. However, I find that the phrase "breath control," commonly used to describe this process, implies limitation or restriction. The term tends to lead students to contract muscles unnecessarily, over-inflate with too much air, tense up chest muscles, and generally clog or tighten up. Think of it instead as breath management. In breath management, you use resistance, coordinated muscle movements, and an overall awareness of the breathing muscle groups for a desired result, rather than restricting or contracting areas of the body.

Awareness breathing is at the heart of deep relaxation practices. It is used in many techniques, such as yoga, Feldenkrais, and Tai Chi, to quiet the mind, to help the body function efficiently, and to slow stress hormone release. Studies (and thousands of years of practice) show that deep breathing—intentionally slowing the rate of breathing as in yoga practice—reduces stress and improves one's health. A fundamental element of yoga practice is to connect the body, mind, and spirit through the breath. You don't need to be a singer to benefit from awareness breathing.

Yoga works with the body's energy. *Prana* means "breath" in Sanskrit; the work of yoga is called *Pranayama*, meaning energy-control by controlling the breath to attain higher states of awareness. Yoga is much more than just exercises. Yoga is about learning to direct concentration, to harmonize with divine consciousness.

One difference between singing and yoga is how air is released. During yoga, inhalations and exhalations may be coordinated to a timed count, yet the goal of exhalation is not to bring the vocal folds together and support a long phrase. When we sing, the exhaled breath must last throughout several words while energizing the vocal folds to produce accurate notes and desired tones.

TIP: IMAGINE EFFORTLESSNESS IN BREATHING

During exhalation, you want to resist collapsing by slowing the release of the breath muscles. Picture a magic carpet rising gently and slowly moving forward as you sing a long note. Imagine how effortless it is, how weightless. You don't have to work as hard when you picture having ample breath for singing. It comes naturally.

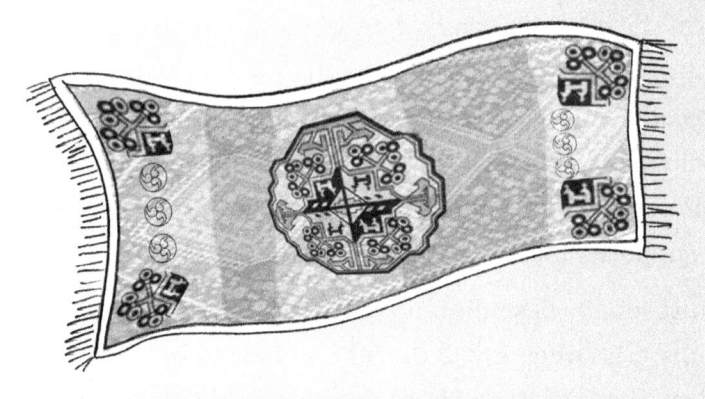

Fig. 1.5. Magic Carpet   Illustrated by Jeannie Gagné

When we are physically active, breathing is energized because the body's cells require more oxygen for enhanced performance. There are many comparisons we can make between vocal technique and physical exercise. When you exercise, you enhance your metabolic rate. Your cells function better. During exercise, your heart rate increases, and breathing speeds up to thirty-five to forty-five breaths per minute.

When we sing, we are athletes internally, even though externally we are usually standing relatively still. This is quite different from being at rest. You learn to energize your core vitality—to take full and sustaining breaths—without actually running. Your heart rate does not need to increase substantially, nor does your breath. For the singer, when we think of ourselves as a kind of athlete, with an optimal use of energy-to-outcome ratio, we are able to elevate the body's functions to support the desired results.

One useful habit is to do your physical workout before you practice your singing. When you've worked out, you've already been moving, so your breathing comes from a deeper, more substantial place in the body. You feel stronger. Though you are standing still to sing, you can picture yourself moving as you have just done in exercise. Your endorphins are charged now, so you probably feel more optimistic. You approach your practice with positive expectations. Your body has been breathing deeply in exercise, so it is already "in the zone" to breathe deeply for singing. Your cells have flushed out toxins, your metabolism is improved. You are approaching singing practice from a place of health.

For the instrumentalist, breathing techniques help reduce stress whether in front of a piano, holding a guitar, or playing a drum set. For the vocalist and any other wind instrument, healthy and sustaining breath management is the key to longevity.

> **TIP: CHECK YOUR POSTURE**
> Practice in front of a mirror. When your posture is slumped, when your jaw is tight or you grimace, or when you are breathing up into your chest instead of fully through your middle, you can see it happening in a mirror. When you are breathing deeply and engaged, but relaxed, you can see that, too. Video recording your practice is also very useful.

How Breathing Works

Air enters the lungs when the volume of the chest cavity increases. The lungs suck in air to fill the enlarged space: you inhale. Next, when the space contracts as muscles relax again, the lungs contract too, expelling air: you exhale. The chest cavity changes size, with work from the muscles of the chest, ribs, abdomen, diaphragm, or clavicles (collar bones). These muscles can work together in different combinations.

The diaphragm muscle sits beneath your lungs, separating them from your digestive organs. It is a large muscle and the primary one for inspiration. You cannot breathe "from it" any more than you can breathe from your belly, which has no lungs. The *intercostal* muscles in between your ribs also stretch your ribcage to enlarge the space around your lungs.

> **MYTH BUSTER: BREATHING FROM YOUR DIAPHRAGM**
>
> You cannot breathe "from your diaphragm" since it's not a lung. Your diaphragm is a large flat muscle, like a curved plate, that contracts and moves down as your lungs inflate and relaxes/releases back up into its dome shape as they deflate. It is one of your breathing muscles. "Diaphragmatic breathing" means the lower muscles in your respiratory system are working effectively, expanding your mid-section, while your upper chest movements are less visible.

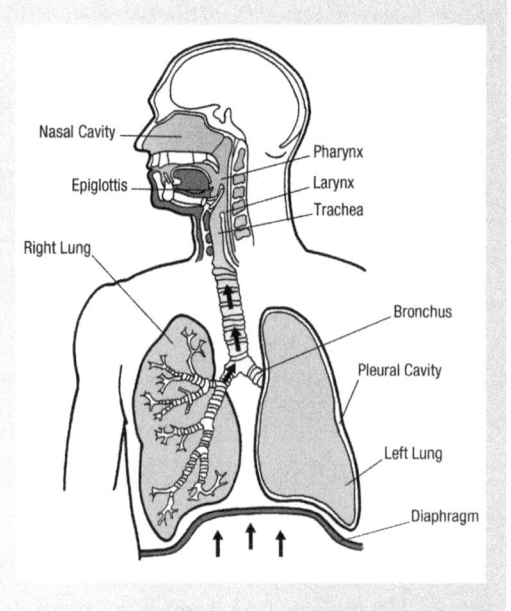

Fig. 1.6. Respiratory System

When you take in a breath, your diaphragm muscle contracts and pulls down, moving your abdominal organs out of the way and stretching the bottom of the ribcage down, while your ribs expand outwardly at the sides. There is a tilt forward of the bottom of the sternum. All sides are not the same: the right side muscle fibers of the diaphragm are usually stronger than the left, to compensate for the greater resistance of the right side that sits directly above the liver. When you exhale, the diaphragm relaxes and returns to its domed shape (see figures 1.7 and 1.8). If we over-contract the chest or abdominal muscles to "control" breathing, the muscles in the larynx will also tighten. This is similar to the normal physiological response we have when we lift something heavy or are physically threatened. (It is difficult to sing with a tense abdomen and can be harmful to the voice.)

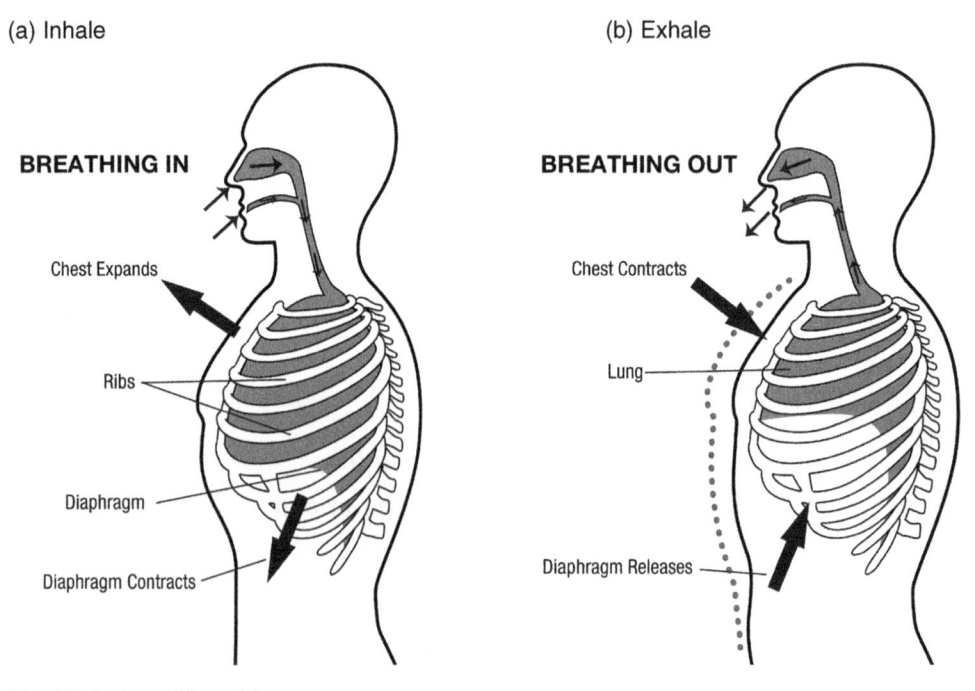

(a) Inhale
(b) Exhale

Fig. 1.7. Action of Breathing

Posture

The diaphragm is at its highest point when the body is supine (lying on one's back), moving the most between relaxed and contracted positions. When the body is standing, the dome of the diaphragm is lower, and respiratory movements are smaller. In x-rays, we see significant changes in the height of the diaphragm with variations in posture. When the body is sitting or slouched, the dome is even lower, with breathing movements the smallest. If the body is lying on one side, the two halves of the diaphragm act independently. The upper half sinks very low, while the lower half rises high in the thorax (upper chest)—even higher than when the body lies supine.

What does this mean? When you slump, you don't breathe as well. If you sing at the piano or while holding a guitar, are you slumping? If so, your breathing will be more shallow. Use good posture to allow for deeper breaths. When you practice breathing on the floor, on your back, you will experience deep breathing naturally. This is very useful. Then, stand up and breathe in deeply, as you did on the floor, to find where it occurs in your body.

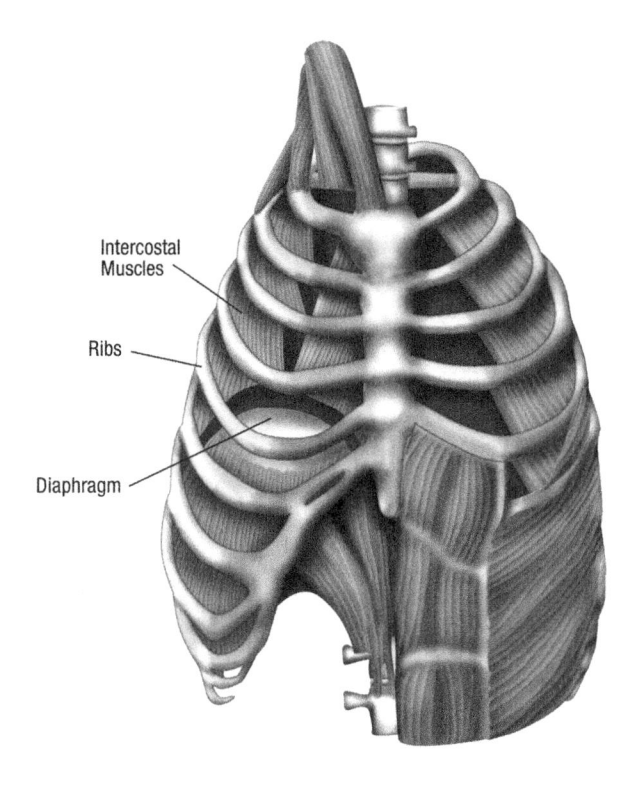

Fig. 1.8. Diaphragm, Ribs, and Intercostal Muscles. Note the dome shape of the diaphragm muscle.

> **WHICH WAY SHOULD YOUR MID-SECTION EXPAND?**
>
> Since breathing muscles can be used in different combinations, the lungs expand in different positions. For instance, if the diaphragm muscle is pulled down low but the ribs don't expand much, the lungs will inflate downwardly yet not fully. If the ribs expand but the diaphragm muscle doesn't descend much, the lungs won't inflate fully either.
>
> Voice teachers sometimes discuss expanding the mid-section like an inner tube. When teachers say "sing from your diaphragm" or "take a belly breath," they are describing taking a fuller breath, allowing the diaphragm muscle to descend deeper into the chest cavity. When you take a deep breath, you allow your ribs to expand, too. If you put your hands on your back on the lower ribs, you should feel them stretching on inhalation. If your upper chest rises a lot, you are probably breathing too high where the lungs are least able to fill. Breathing high in the chest also tightens neck muscles, which press against the larynx and tighten the whole neck system, making singing more tense.
>
> It is not a good idea to add lots of tension to expand your lungs. It is a natural motion that we can learn to monitor. If you find yourself tensing uncomfortably in your effort to breathe properly, or if the feeling in your larynx gets tighter, change your approach.

How Much Air?

You don't always need to breathe to your fullest capacity! Sometimes we over-breathe. The body wants to be efficient; that is why it has options. If you're sitting down, you aren't using a lot of energy, so you don't need to work as hard. If you are standing still, you use less energy (and oxygen) than when you are running. This may go against everything you've been taught, but the truth is some sung phrases simply don't need much air to support the tone. Other singing requires a lot of air pressure. If you take in too much air, you may have the sensation of choking, which tightens the throat.

> **TIP: TRY THIS AT HOME**
>
> Have you ever tried *exhaling* and then singing, just to see what it's like? Or, holding your breath for a second, then singing? Unless a lung is collapsed—a very dangerous and unlikely medical condition—it always contains some air. The key to breath management is how you use the air you have, without worrying about running out.

Students learning breath techniques may experience panic. There is a primordial fear that there will not be enough air, which can cause gasping for more air in between phrases. Remember, the body knows how to breathe. (Can you imagine running for a bus while trying to instruct your diaphragm muscle to descend further, to send enough air to your legs? No, because breathing is an automatic response.) The mind, probably trying to follow a teacher's instruction on better breathing techniques, doesn't trust the body. Or, the body has not experienced intentional deep breathing and coordination and feels awkward, telling the mind it doesn't know how to do it "right," which causes further restriction. Any time we concentrate on learning something new physically, another aspect that was working naturally becomes awkward: two left feet. It's like being at the gym with a trainer, being reminded not to hold your breath while you're working on your triceps.

The other challenge singers face is *losing* the air they take in. The inhalation may be fine, but there's a sort of leak at the site of the larynx like a hole in a balloon. Remember, for the voice to work properly there has to be air pressure helping the vocal folds come together in vibration. Air pressure is generated using resistance within the larynx, and from below it using the breathing muscles. (This process is not the same as tension or laryngeal constriction, which, as we've seen, is not desirable.) Problems result from pushing too much air through, or gulping in a large amount of air and holding onto it by tightening the neck and chest. Or, the under-supported speech habits that are commonplace in contemporary dialects teach the voice muscles to be too relaxed, too weak. When it's time to sing, the same muscles that caused vocal fry during speaking (that 4:00-in-the-morning scratchy inflection) don't know how to coordinate and lack muscle tone. Think about it: the ice skater's thighs don't become flabby when she steps off the ice, the boxer's arms stay buff out of the ring. Why does the singer let her voice sink into lazy vocal fry when she's speaking? The antidote to weak muscles: while you're training your singing voice, be conscious of your speaking voice, too. It uses the same instrument.

One other tendency to avoid is over-contracting abdominal muscles to hold breath in. This holding has a direct connection to tension in the larynx. As mentioned earlier, when you go to lift a box and grunt, your abdomen is contracting along with muscles in the larynx to get the job done. Anytime you contract muscles intensely, you are adding tension to the system. This tension makes flexibility in the voice less available and strain to compensate more likely.

Deep Breathing Helps in Managing Anxiety

A musician's highly complex movements are being monitored by the same brain that supplies primordial instructions for the heart to beat and the lungs to work. The brain, controlling all movement, monitors every effort we make and provides a constant feedback loop. It makes endless adjustments to our movements; touch comes back to the brain from receptors in every muscle, tendon, and joint. Inside the brain are deep hierarchies of activity. There is motion, musical comprehension leading the ear, visual patterns identifying musical notes at a glance. All these aspects of performance are intertwined with every other. There is emotion—perhaps joy, from the experience of singing or a connection to the lyric—while primitive parts of the brain flood the bloodstream with messages preparing the body for action. Stage fright may be present along with the emotion of the music. While the brain is this busy, on top of that, it is fighting its own impulses for survival from deep within the brain stem. The result can be exhausting and cause the performer to make some intense facial expressions.[5]

How can we deal with the anxiety? Slow it down. Breathe in to a count of four, exhale to a count of six. Repeat. You can do this before an audition, a presentation, a lesson. Do this during meditation. Practice yoga. *Listen* to your breath. It is very calming.

Breathing for Wellness

Musician, writer, and Sufi mystic Hazrat Inayat Khan believed that all systems of the body function properly because of breathing, and that all disorders in the body's systems are due to problems with breathing. Mystics see a connection between physical health and the breath. Changes to the body, even including such primal things as blood pressure and heart rate, are affected by rhythmic changes in breathing. Erratic breathing can cause confusion and even emotional upset; concentration often leads to holding the breath. Unconscious breath holding means the mind and body are not well coordinated, and can lead to significant problems. On the other hand, regular rhythmic breathing, relaxation breathing, and similar practices can significantly improve overall wellness. It clears the head and makes space for the intelligence of the soul. Many traditions believe that the breath is at the core of all things. Learning and slowing your breath is the most important practice you can do to enliven your being.[6]

Breathing Exercises

EXERCISE 1.1. "SSS" WITH POSTURE

This is a simple release of air, placing your tongue against the front of your teeth as a valve. The goal is to see how long you can produce a steady flow of air that is consistent. Air pressure is stronger at the beginning of the phrase, so you need to resist using more air then. At the end of your breath, you release more air in order to keep the volume of the "sss" steady through each phrase.

Resist collapsing your chest as the air decreases. Imagine marionette strings gently assisting your posture, connected to your thorax and to the crown of your head. The strings lift you, gently but firmly. Keep your posture consistent throughout: relaxed, but engaged and athletic, never tense.

---

5   Jourdain, Robert. *Music, the Brain, and Ecstasy: How Music Captures Our Imagination* (2nd printing). New York, NY: Avon Books, 2002.
6   Louise Montello, *Essential Musical Intelligence*

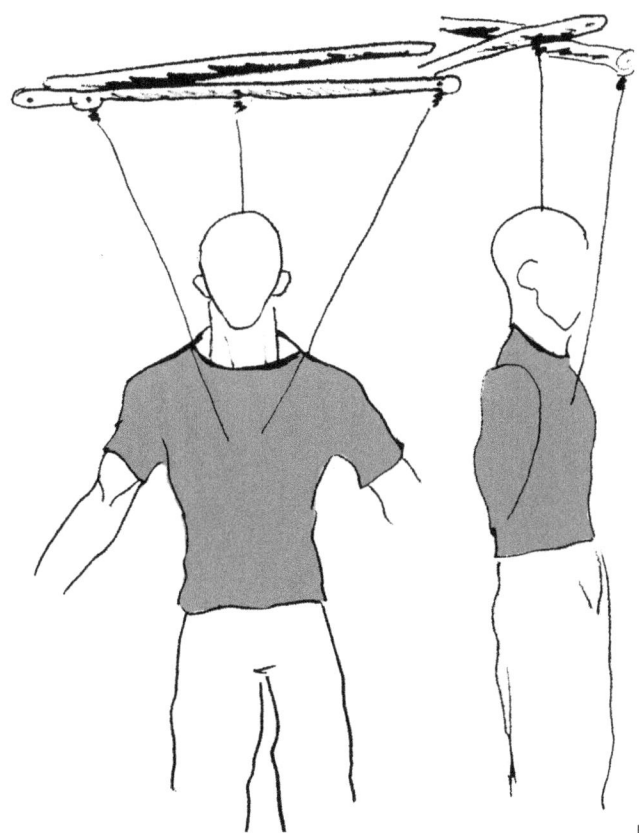

Fig. 1.9. Imagining Marionette Strings

EXERCISE 1.2. AIRFLOW VISUALIZATION

In this exercise, you imagine you have an endless availability of air. Imagine it flowing front to back, down through your abdomen, continuing in a circular motion around your head and torso. When you inhale, you are merely picking up where you left off to continue to cycle. There is a stronger airflow in the front, as the resonance from your singing travels on the air.

Fig. 1.10. Airflow Visualization

EXERCISE 1.3. WINGS

a. Start with relaxed shoulders. Spread your arms outward on your inhalation, letting your ribs expand as your arms open fully to the side.

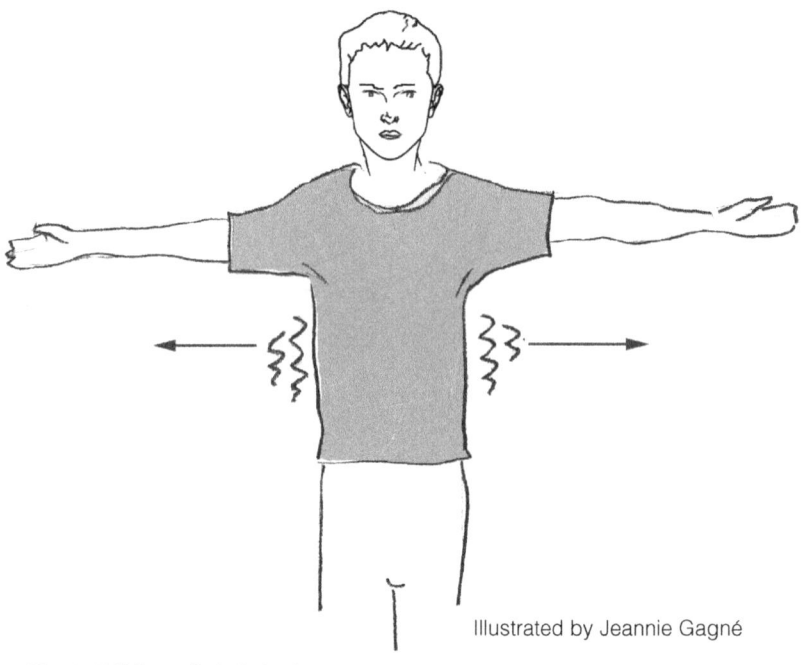

Fig. 1.11. Wings (Inhalation)

b. Then on exhalation, bring your arms slowly together in front of you, sending the breath forward in one continuous stream, being mindful of keeping your posture straight. Without squeezing the breath out, let your air flow steadily as your arms move forward.

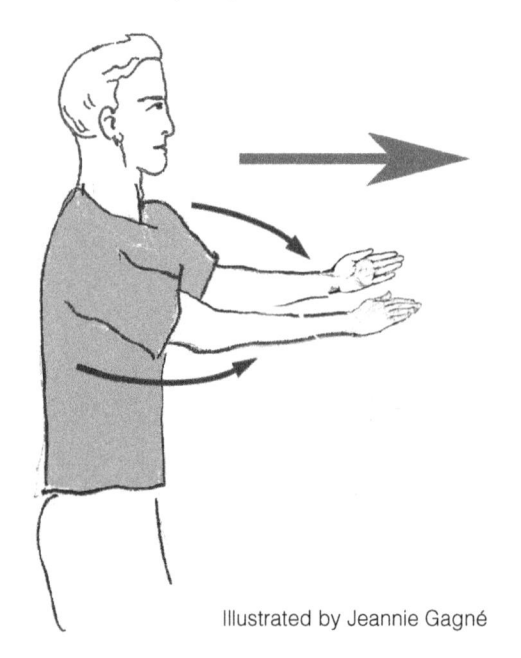

Fig. 1.12. Wings (Exhalation)

EXERCISE 1.4. ON THE FLOOR

Lie on your back, knees bent. Relax your head and neck into the floor. Breathe. Feel a greater expansion of your ribs with each inhalation. Your lungs work the most deeply when you are lying down. Feel the ribs expand into the floor. If there were a layer of paint on you, what pattern would your body make on the floor? Feel your neck and head release tension. Breathe again, in and out. Let tension leave your body. Let it melt into the floor. When you are ready, from this relaxed posture, sing.

Physical Wellness: Healthy Habits

You are your instrument, so you need to take care of yourself to be in good vocal health. The trick is to really *do* it. This section addresses health habits and singing practices for staying in shape. Some of it may surprise you; some of it is good old-fashioned common sense.

The singer's instrument varies daily.

It is reasonable to expect a piano to be relatively the same instrument from day to day. It will go out of tune, it needs humidifying in winter (and maybe occasional dusting), but beyond that, it doesn't change much. How much does your body change? A lot! Your outer layer of skin, part of the largest organ of your body, is replaced every few weeks; your body makes hormones and all sorts of chemicals that course through your bloodstream constantly. You need to keep refueling with food several times a day. Your emotions change regularly, making you excited, or depressed, or blissful, or stressed out. You may be tired or full of energy. We have cycles, and body rhythms, and sleep patterns. Whatever is happening in your body is also happening in your instrument, because your vocal instrument is part of your body.

We know what we need to do to take care of our physical selves, but do we do it? What comes to mind on that health list?

Your Speaking Voice

Your speaking voice is the same as your singing voice. You use it all day. Do you apply the same breath management and awareness of tension when you speak as you do when you sing?

The current American English style of speech is often under-supported, sounding under-energized and full of vocal fry (see page 32). We may speak this way to appear "laid back" or relaxed. It is unreasonable to expect that if you routinely speak with an under-supported voice, you can then turn on a fully functional singing voice without consequence or difficulty. If you were a dancer or athlete who walked around with one leg dragging behind you all day to appear relaxed, you can imagine how your body would train your muscles to adapt to that way of moving. How then could you step into dancing or pitching a major league baseball without challenges? When you see a trained dancer or athlete walk down the street, he or she is still the dancer or athlete, even when using pedestrian movements.

People with vocal issues often get into more trouble from speaking incorrectly than from singing incorrectly! Singers need to find an everyday speaking voice that is comfortable, consistent with singing. You can do this and still sound like *you*.

To speak healthfully:

- Support speaking with your breath, always.

- Take breaths when you need them; don't wait for the end of a long thought to gasp for air.

- Be careful of speaking frequently with too much force. This is tiring on the voice.

- Avoid lazy speech, an under-energized way of speaking that contains a lot of vocal fry, or when the voice drops very low, as if you just awoke. It is very common in our contemporary vernacular, and so it may sound normal to you. When you speak this way regularly, you are teaching your muscles that weak is normal. How can you expect them to jump into singing mode without issues?

- Avoid whispering, which is also fatiguing to the voice. Speak quietly instead.

- Don't scream or shout, especially in anger or in loud places. Yelling at an event is VERY bad for your voice. It is vocal strain and can cause permanent damage. DO NOT speak over loud music. DO NOT lose your voice at a sporting event. DO NOT let your emotions hijack your voice in anger or upset. DO keep your speaking level to a normal volume. DO wait for a moment when you can be heard.

- Healthy scream singing used in heavy metal or alternative music is a misnomer. Done well, scream singing may not be particularly loud and is not pushed. It takes a *lot* of practice to sound aggressive while being careful with your voice, and most voice teachers won't touch it. Melissa Cross' video, *The Zen of Screaming*, is helpful if you wish to study scream singing on your own.

Hydration

The vocal folds are naturally covered by a thin layer of mucus, and need to be moist. To work properly, they must be well lubricated and flexible. They will not work right if they are dried out on the inside or outside. The body will over-produce fluid to compensate for dryness, which causes swelling. (Picture your face in winter with the wind blowing, or how chapped your hands can get if you don't wear gloves.) Dry vocal folds are stiff and unresponsive. Then, when you sing you may overcompensate for the lack of flexibility and cause your voice additional problems.

The mucous membranes in your throat are part of your body's system. You cannot drink water or tea in order to hydrate your voice directly; you must hydrate your entire body in order to supply appropriate moisture to your larynx.

- Drink plenty of room temperature water to keep hydrated. Herbal tea is good too. Drinking six to eight glasses of room temperature water a day is best for this. (Cold beverages cause contraction in the vocal muscles, making singing more difficult.) Carry a water bottle with you, which you can refill at a water fountain. You know you are drinking enough fluids each day when you follow the singer's mantra: hydrate often, pee clear.

- Steam your lungs and vocal cords once a week. A hot shower does the trick. You can also purchase a facial steamer; as long as you keep it super clean, this is good, too. Or, use a pot of hot water with a towel over your head. Steaming is one way to put moisture directly on your vocal folds.

- Sucking on a lozenge can soothe a sore throat, but it will not reduce inflammation or hydrate your voice. Sugary lozenges will coat your teeth with sugar, which causes tooth decay, so opt for sugar-free ones.

- Keep your lips hydrated with lip balm or something similar. This wards off cracking. (Bacteria can grow in those lip cracks.)

Smoking

Smoking is an obvious no-no. Why? Not only does it tar your lungs and potentially shorten your life, it also dries out your voice.

When you smoke, or even when you are around second-hand smoke, the mucus discharge increases on the lining of your sinuses, pharynx, and larynx to protect them from irritation, creating excess gunk. Smoke also dries out your folds. That makes it much harder to sing. If your voice doesn't vibrate well, you will likely strain to compensate and possibly cause permanent damage. Cannabis smoke is even more damaging than cigarettes.

As I am fond of telling my students, you wouldn't pour a glass of water on your friend's guitar… so why would you put smoke in your instrument? You can buy a new guitar or new strings, but you've only got one voice. Some people say, "I like the way my voice gets raspy when I smoke." Sure, you can justify smoking if you want. It's your body. But in fifteen or twenty years, you may wish you'd made a healthier choice.

Drink Me, Don't Eat Me

Some foods create more mucus in the throat than others. It also varies depending on the person. You may find for instance that eating onions triggers acid reflux in you, yet you can eat a cup of yogurt an hour before you sing and be fine. Because the voice *has* to be well hydrated, avoid any food or drink that reduces moisture in your throat (such as caffeine and alcohol) before you sing.

Here is a partial list of common foods, beverages, and medicines that singers should or should not consume:

- **Is dairy okay?** This depends on how your body responds to dairy. Many people develop mucus when they eat dairy; mucus coats the voice, making it harder to sing. If that happens to you, don't eat dairy within a couple hours of singing.

- **Keep caffeine to a minimum.** There is evidence both ways about the risks and benefits of caffeine for the body. The medical experts are *not* saying it's bad for you, but they do say it changes your body chemistry. It may constrict your throat. Does caffeine make you edgy? You need to judge by how you feel. Nonetheless, coffee, tea, and most soft drinks contain caffeine that can dehydrate you. I find that drinking coffee before I sing makes singing more difficult. To be on the safe side, limit your caffeine intake to a reasonable amount.

- **Is chocolate okay?** Some teachers advise avoiding chocolate before you sing, which has a trace amount of caffeine. It may also gunk up your throat. Again, the rule of thumb is how it affects *you*.

- **Acid reflux.** Some people get acid reflux from foods such as onions, spicy foods, coffee, soda, or alcohol. Acid reflux is stomach acid coming up the esophagus and irritating the mucous membranes in the upper tract. If you have this it is likely you have vocal irritation, too. Everything is interconnected in your throat. Spicy or acidic foods may irritate your throat even if you don't have acid reflux. If your voice is frequently hoarse it may very well be acid reflux. To find out, visit an ear, nose, and throat doctor.

- Learn which foods your body reacts to poorly and avoid those. Personally, I avoid onions and wheat products, which upset my stomach. My favorite is dark chocolate, but it coats my throat, so I won't eat any before I sing. The best way to find out what foods bother you is to eliminate one food at a time for a few days; when you reintroduce the food, you'll see if you react to it. If it doesn't bother you, don't worry about it!

- Avoid heavy meals before you sing, but don't go on stage hungry, either. Digestion diverts blood flow and energy away from other areas of your body. It also may make you sleepy. The fullness in your belly after a large meal can adversely affect your breathing technique. On the other hand, if you are hungry you will have less strength to make it through the gig.

- Eat a well-balanced diet, and keep junk food to a minimum. When your overall diet is healthy, you feel better, and your voice responds better.

When You Don't Feel Well

When to sing, when not to sing? The tone of your voice is affected by changes in your larynx, which in turn is affected by changes in your body. When you're under the weather, sometimes it's okay to vocalize, while other times, you should rest your voice.

When you have a headcold: If your nose is stuffy, it will alter how you hear yourself, but it may not change your voice much as others hear it. If your throat is a little sore, it may or may not affect your larynx and vocal folds. If you get a cold and there is extra mucus down the back of your throat, your larynx will have extra mucus, too. The vocal folds won't vibrate satisfactorily with lots of phlegm on them. Postnasal drip can also irritate the larynx and throat.

If you have laryngitis: Laryngitis is a swollen voice, causing you to have trouble speaking. Ironically, your larynx doesn't have the same kinds of nerve endings as your throat, so if it's irritated or swollen, you may not feel it as "sore." It may even feel fine. If you are having trouble speaking, however, this is a clear indicator that it is *not* a good time to sing, and definitely a *bad* time to push your voice through it. You have to use your judgment.

Be careful of clearing your throat abrasively. This further irritates your delicate vocal folds. If you do need to clear your throat, try not to phonate while doing so at all—or, make as light a sound as you can.

In general:

- Be sensible, not frantic. If you're a bit sick and you don't need to sing, don't. If you have a big concert and you're a bit under the weather, weigh your options, take care of yourself, and keep hydrating!

- Avoid medications that are drying, such as antihistamines. Antihistamines dry out the protective mucosal layer covering the vocal folds. If you must take an antihistamine to control your allergies, start with a low dosage and use it as infrequently as possible.

- Avoid taking over-the-counter pain reducers ibuprofen (Motrin) and aspirin. Sometimes you have to take these meds to feel better, but keep these to a minimum. Ibuprofen and aspirin cause the tiny blood vessels in your vocal tissues to rise to the surface, making you more susceptible to vocal injury.

- Ask your doctor or pharmacist which medications singers should avoid. This is an uncommon question and they may not know the answer without looking it up. You can research for yourself online to find out if any meds you are taking adversely affect the voice. There is a long list available at websites like ncvs.org/rx.html.

General Tips for the Healthy Singer

Your voice is part of your body, so take care of it! You've only got one voice. You've only got one body, too!

Should I do sit-ups?

You want to be healthy. Sit-ups are good for you (and good for your self-esteem) by toning your abdominal muscles surrounding your organs. However, if you overwork crunches, you can cause additional strain in your breathing muscles, which is not so good. Be mindful of how you do sit-ups. Try variations lying on the floor to work your lower abs with leg lifts.

What about muscle conditioning?

It is important to be fit, and muscle conditioning is part of a fitness program. If you are weight training, be very careful of causing tension in the neck and shoulders. Don't overdo the training; balance it with stretches, relaxation exercises, and slow, deep breathing work. It's a good idea to schedule a few sessions with a certified personal trainer to get you started safely, or if you're already working out, to check your routine to be sure you're doing it properly. Use a mirror to check your posture.

What exercise is best?

Regular aerobic activity is good because it boosts your metabolism while helping your body to become more accustomed to deep breathing. Swimming is great: it is low-stress aerobic exercise. (Frank Sinatra reportedly swam a lot for his breathing technique.) The key here is regularity. Only doing long, intense sessions now and then will not be that helpful, and may even be harmful if you overdo it. Best practice: regular workouts, three to four times a week, for shorter sessions.

What are TMJ, jaw tension, and tongue tension?

Jaw tension is very common. It can result from grinding or clenching your teeth during sleep. If you think you do this, visit your dentist to have a night guard made to fit your mouth. Jaw tension can also happen during the day. "TMJ" is short for *TMJ disorder*, and means the *temporomandibular* jaw joints are tight. If you hear clicking when you open and shut your mouth, you might have TMJ disorder. Easy stretches are the best way to help alleviate this tension, such as opening and closing your mouth ten times, rest, repeat. Massage is also good: gently press the muscles where your jaw pivots open as you open and close your mouth. You can do this while you are vocalizing, too, to help relax your jaw.

Tongue tension is also common. The tongue is a big muscle. Tongue tension usually shows up as restricted agility when you sing, or as a pinched tone. Singers sometimes tense the tongue to execute detailed riffs, leading to problems in the long run. Or, if you are frequently inhibited about saying what's on your mind, or if you are reluctant to project your voice with volume, you might be overly-contracting your tongue. Try holding your tongue when you sing, to see if it fights you. If it wants to pull backwards, it is tight. Do tongue exercises to help your tongue release its control on your singing. One exercise is stick your tongue way out, hold for one second, then release. Do two sets of ten repetitions with a short rest in between. (See "Is Your Tongue Tight?" on page 18.)

When you are menstruating:

Your voice swells just as other parts of you do each month. Your voice won't work as well as usual when it's swollen. If you are bloated with menstruation, take it easy when you vocalize. (In some opera companies, female singers' monthly schedules are taken into account when planning rehearsals and performances.)

You know your voice is healthy when:

- it resonates easily without strain
- you have very little or no vocal fatigue after you've been singing for awhile
- if your voice does get tired, it bounces back quickly
- your voice works for you the way you'd like it to

Your voice may be strained or injured when:

- the quality of the voice is not what it used to be
- you have to work harder than before for volume or to project your voice
- you clear your throat or cough often
- there is a sense of a lump in your throat
- you have pain or soreness
- when you sing, your voice gets tired easily
- you don't have as many notes in your range as before
- your voice breaks and overall control is lessened

Dos and Don'ts

Do:

- Get plenty of rest

- Use a neti pot. It is available in your local drugstore. This is a way to cleanse your sinuses and pharynx with a warm saline solution, through your nostrils. It's messy! But very worth it. Used properly every day—especially in winter and cold/flu season—a neti pot rinses away extra mucus that causes irritation, as well as small particles that get trapped in the small hairs in the nose and can cause illness. Then, finish off with a gargle with the saline solution. Do it every day to ward off getting sick. It helps! (Warning: Don't use just water. You must use a saline solution. You can buy pre-measured packets of saline powder specially designed for neti pots.) Alternately, you can use a saline spray, also available at any drugstore.

- Exercise regularly. Work on posture. Yoga is great for posture; so is Alexander Technique. When you exercise, your lungs are more active and full than when you are at rest. It is good for the breathing muscles to be in the habit of working. Yoga is excellent for learning to strike a balance between strength and relaxation, two essential ingredients in strong vocal technique. Alexander Technique works on posture and has helped thousands of musicians. There is likely a licensed Alexander practitioner in your area.

- Consider learning practices like Feldenkrais or Tai Chi, which help to maintain a general state of well-being, release stress, and also enhance breathing techniques. (There are links in the Online Resources section of the Appendix.)

- Keep stress to a minimum. Too much "bad" stress releases certain hormones continually into your body, which your body was not made to tolerate. Stress is a major cause of illness. When you are stressed, your muscles become tense, and you are stuck in self-protection mode, masking your creative Self.

- When you can, get a therapeutic massage to help release built-up muscle tension.

- Balance work and play.

- Learn your own natural biorhythm and try to stick to a schedule. Try out the energy grid for a week to map your rhythm (see page 52). Are you always tired around 4 P.M.? There's a good reason for it.

Don't:

- If it hurts, don't do it!

- Avoid self-medicating to excess with food, alcohol, drugs, Xbox, caffeine…

- Don't slump at your computer or over your guitar. Really!

- Don't scream in anger or frustration; you'll fry your folds. You also want to avoid overtalking, especially on the phone or at a location where the ambient noise is loud.

In today's busy world, it can seem impossible to stay strict with the things on this list. Just do your best. You'll be glad you did.

CHAPTER 2

The Whole Singer

**Let your
Open
Voice
Enrich**

Illustrated by Jeannie Gagné

*May your life be as a song,
resounding with the dawn
to sing awake the light,
and softly serenade the stars,
ever dancing circles in the night.*

—Jim Scott

As we've seen in chapter 1, being a singer is powerfully beneficial in many ways. We are complex beings. When we sing, it's not just a physical process; it's also mental and spiritual. Nothing we do is ever one-dimensional. Everything we do is interconnected with who we are: the hats we wear, our emotions, our loved ones, our hopes and dreams, our beliefs, our physical state.

It is about balance. Your inner core is love. Your energy is measured in different ways: biologically, emotionally, stress-wise, metabolically, and as it relates to your personality or temperament. Being alive means you have breath, which your voice uses to express who you are. When you choose compassion, your breath energizes and expresses the love that is at your core.

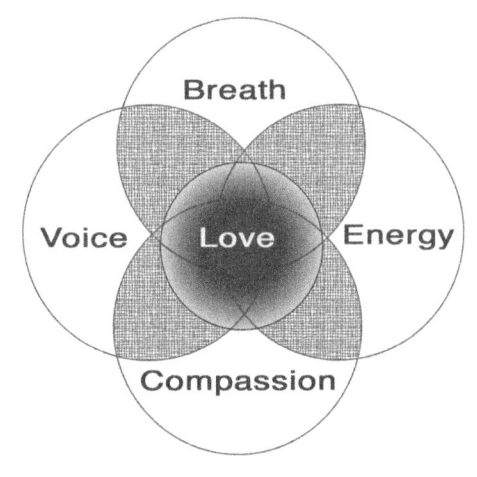

Fig. 2.1. Cycles of Balance

HOLISTIC APPROACHES TO FULL MIND AND BODY HEALTH AND WELLNESS

A *holistic* approach looks at a complete system, made up of individual parts, to understand how the system functions. In health, *holistic* means the mind, body, and sometimes spirit are viewed as part of total *wellness*. A state of wellness is a balance of the various aspects of our lives. When we are in balance, our overall quality of life is positive. When parts of ourselves, such as our social, occupational, emotional, environmental, financial, physical, spiritual, and mental dimensions, are all flowing well and the relationship among these parts of our lives is harmonious, we are well. Any one of these parts can be off kilter and negatively impact the whole.

When we embrace a holistic approach to our lives, we are happier. When, as singers, we recognize that our instruments are part of our overall wellness equation, and we are able to see the wholeness of ourselves, it gives us the information we need to work on any individual parts that may need attention. If you were a saxophone, with it's relatively few components of metal tubing, valves, corks, and reeds, it would be easier to recognize what part needs adjusting to get the best sound out of the instrument. As human beings, fine-tuning our instruments is much more complex and subtle.

> *Music fills the infinite between two souls.*
> —Rabindranath Tagore, beloved Indian writer, Nobel laureate (1913)

The Self

The true Self (capital "S")—the soul—desires peace and contentment. The conscious self (small "s") likes to direct our lives and stay in control. Both selves are useful and important parts of us. The true Self is the subtler of the two; although it is always present, it doesn't yell loudly to be heard. It is the place inside us of pure love. We know the true Self is the voice in our thoughts when judgments are gone, when we feel peaceful, directed, when we experience a loving state—even when facing a challenge.

The smaller self, or the *ego*, is too dominant; it keeps us from listening to our true Selves, which we must do in order to be content.

In musical expression, we have the ability to create magical moments for ourselves, and for those experiencing the music with us, by listening closely to the expression of the Self. That takes practice. Because the ego seeks to protect us from harm, when we feel vulnerable when we sing, we lose conscious connection with the Self. The Self wants to soar on the wings of the bliss of performance, connectivity, and self-expression, while the louder ego is constantly making sure we are safe. That creates an internal conflict. Whenever the ego wins out and the balance is lost, you will likely feel anxiety or failure or less-than or stupid.

Your voice responds to your emotions. Since the foremost objective of the larynx is to maintain life itself, when you are fearful, the body doesn't care if you are also trying to be artistic in song. Even though you are likely not in any real danger, your subconscious will direct your body to defend itself, if your thoughts are fear-based. Your body will contract. It will protect you in any way possible. You will sweat, adrenalin will rise in your system, and your heartbeat will increase. Your breaths will become shallow in preparation for exerting great strength for self-protection. In the process, your vibrato, which is part of the natural vibration of your whole body, will get faster as everything speeds up. All of this makes it much more difficult to sing well! As voice teacher/author Mark Baxter puts it, if one part of you is saying "go ahead and sing" while another is saying "you'd better not!" your voice is going to tighten up.[1]

Each of us has music and creativity deep within that comes from the unconscious mind and imagination, which is different from the conscious mind that likes to control and organize. When you allow your creativity to be active, you can access and communicate this essential musical intelligence. Releasing this inner music can be transformational. The more you allow it to flower, the more you add to your overall wellness, as well as to the harmony of the world around you.[2]

Children do this naturally. The key for mastery comes from learning to trust your internal music, which you express through the technical skill you have developed over years of practice. Explore your childlike freedom with music again. Your singing will become effortless and spontaneous.

Spiritually, you can feel a sense of wonderment when this happens, as if you are a vessel and the universe is singing through you, expressing humanity in some form in that moment, expressing life itself. You resonate with yourself, with your collaborators, with those listening, and it is joyous. It is ecstasy.

Creativity

Creativity is the ability to produce something new using imaginative skill. Where does that something new come from? From inspiration within yourself. You have an idea, you flow in the moment during a riff, you trust your instincts, and you see where the moment takes you. Inspiration comes from the word *inspire*—simply, to breathe in.

---

[1] Baxter, Mark. *The Rock-n-Roll Singer's Survival Manual.* Milwaukee, WI: Hal Leonard, 1990.

[2] Louise Montello, *Essential Musical Intelligence*

Many traditions speak of the energy of the breath, *prana*, or *chi*. *Prana*, from Buddhist traditions, refers to the energy of life, the soul, literally "vital air," which operates the various aspects of the body and also manifests the universal life force within us. It is the subtle, invisible energy we take in along with air when we breathe. When this current is withdrawn, the body dies. *Chi* is the Chinese concept of the vital force believed to be inherent in all things. The *prana* or *chi* in each of us is always there to draw upon, just as we always draw breath.

The more you can observe the self as it works to control a situation, the more you can allow that self to take a rest, enabling the true Self to step forward in creativity.

Encouraging creativity, beyond emphasizing technical mastery, is essential in music education. Technique is important, but so is inspiration. If you are focused on doing it *right* when you study, you may forget *why* you are making music. The essence of your internal music can be easily overshadowed by the rigors of learning technique. Don't forget to keep listening to your essential internal music.

Of course, making music can happen without formal technical training. Powerful music has been made for centuries this way, and many contemporary artists we love have been "untrained." The oral tradition aspect that is imbedded deeply within contemporary styles came out of community music, passed along informally from person to person. A student learning contemporary styles has to *listen* to singers who came before to understand how to stylize them; this is difficult to learn from a book. Nonetheless, there is tremendous potential for artistic expression that comes from combining technique with your own internal music. Good technique provides the singer with tools to express music masterfully and healthfully, which is why vocal technique is a big part of this book. But it's not the "whole tamale," by any means. Regardless of how much training you do have, you have to listen.

As a culture, we have grown accustomed to not listening. We are out of the habit. We are bombarded with music every day, every hour. Elevators, restaurants, department stores, sporting events, doctor offices, even taxicabs provide an endless supply of background music. The good news is there are plenty of opportunities for musicians to make a living playing and recording music. The down side is we have become desensitized to it. The endless availability of music everywhere turns it into background soundscapes, a disposable commodity. It takes patience to create something truly wonderful, timeless, and artistic. Good wine and good cheese take time to age; so, too, does musicianship.

Authenticity

"Authenticity" is one of those words people like to argue about. Can you tell when a person is truly authentic? You cannot help but be influenced by the culture you are immersed in, by the music you have grown up listening to. When you study a great singer like Ella Fitzgerald and learn her jazz scat solo on a tune, is it authentic for you to sing the tune in the same way? Or, are you learning a style and then interpreting it, based on the skill of a master who came before you?

Authenticity is the combination of factors that make you *you*. It is your expression of yourself. When you pretend to be someone else, you are acting. That is not authentic. If you copy Ella's solo, lick for lick, you are copying her, reproducing *her* authenticity. If, however, you learned that solo some time ago and it shows up in a transformed way when you sing the song, now you have *interpreted* it. You have made it yours.

UNDERSTANDING OUR CREATIVITY

The students quoted below let me share with you how they understand their creativity, and what makes artistic expression through music important to them. These quotes were taken early in their careers at music college.

Music is like an arm for me. How am I supposed to describe why I love my arm? I could say what I use my arm for, and how it helps me live my life, but at the end of the day, the arm is simply a part of me, and that's why I love it; that's why I need it. Music is a part of me, and so I love it and need it.

—Joe Berlin

Music is my religion. It taps into an unnamed feeling deep inside of me that is the closest thing I know to the concept of God. For me, it is real magic. It is inexplicable and ethereal and affects humans like no other stimulus. It is the only form of art that can be used to physically move people.

—Joshua Elbaum

When I write songs, it's always from life experiences. I write songs to express the feelings I cannot speak and that others can't as well. Writing comes from my soul and my heart, not from my head. Some songs I hear today seem as if they are just made to become number one hits, and yes, they are fun to listen to, but they aren't written with true meaning behind them.

—Thyra Ford

> *If I'm really lucky and people are really listening, if I sing not only the right notes, but also the right sentiments, I will reach someone in the crowd. Somebody will empathize, relate to me, or maybe just be reminded of an event of their own life. They'll walk out of that place feeling better, understood. And when they tell me what I made them feel a week or a month after the show, I know that what I'm doing is worth it, and I know that no matter what happens in my life and where I end up, I will always sing. I'm an artist because I create and because I express. I have the opportunity to immerse myself in a song and create a universe with my voice. It's not perfect, but it's my own.*
>
> —Fernanda Herrera Domene

Your Mind: The Power of Thought in Singing

> *"Vibrations are the connection between language and music, expression and internal turmoil, reaching people—or not reaching them."*
>
> —Shona Carr (Berklee Student)

Your mind is your conscious and unconscious thinking. Your mind decides how you will respond to a situation or how you feel. It has preconceived notions of what works, or what doesn't work. Some of these ideas are learned through experiences—good and bad. Some of these ideas reflect your tendency to expect a certain result. You can teach your mind to change its patterns of response and expectations. The mind is one part of your highly complex brain.

Your Brain

Your brain controls everything you do. It has automatic responses that control systems in your body, such as your heartbeat and digestion, without any effort on your part. These responses are deep within the "primitive" areas of the brain. The brain also responds to input from your senses: sight, hearing, touch, taste, smell.

Hearing is a process in which your ear transforms sound waves into an electric signal that your brain recognizes as sound or music. First, a sound source creates sound waves, which are vibrating molecules of air. After bouncing on the eardrum, these vibrations pass through to the middle ear, which processes them and transmits them to the inner ear. The sound waves have now become nerve impulses that connect directly to the brain. The impulses are catalogued and identified as "sounds," based on how your brain recognizes them.

The brain also controls motor function. It signals your larynx how to respond when you picture a note to sing—high or low or loud or soft. The laryngeal muscles change in response to tiny signals traveling to and from your brain, in coordination with instructions sent to your breathing muscles to take in and then release pressurized air.

When the brain identifies danger, it sends chemicals such as adrenalin through your body so you can react quickly to it. A little adrenalin can be helpful, giving you increased energy on stage. Stage fright is an exaggerated reaction to perceived danger, with too much adrenalin. Breathing techniques, used when you first feel anxious, can help prevent stage fright from immobilizing you.

Because the brain runs on patterns of energy, we can say it, like sound, is vibrational. Brain wave activity is measured on an *electroencephalogram* test (EEG) that registers electrical activity—energy. Science tells us that energy can neither be created nor destroyed. So too, the vibrations of sound are not created but are instead reshaped and transferred between us through our music. Our brains perceive vibrations as sounds and make patterns of them. Our brains make maps. Brain mapping affects our movements, too—how we believe we should sit at the piano, stand and hold our arms in a voice lesson, or raise our chins in order to reach a high note. There is a wellness technique called *brain mapping* that identifies the body's patterns. A brain-mapping therapist can suggest ways for a person to remap activity, creating new and healthier patterns of movement.

The patterns of thought that develop within the brain affect what we experience. Some scientists say that the world we see is the world we make—that the world is infinitely vast with possibilities we cannot identify. What we perceive is limited only by our own imaginations. We can believe we are limited, or we can believe we are not. When we understand the power of our own beliefs, we can begin the work of shifting our experiences.

Your Loop

Your "loop" is made of the things you say to yourself continually that you have come to believe. If you think studying voice is difficult, it will be. If you think everyone is staring at you and judging you while you perform, you will feel bad doing it. If you think you will mess up and forget the song or the words, or fail to nail a difficult passage, it's likely you will.

In his book *The Music Lesson*, Grammy-winning bassist Victor Wooten reminds us to treat practicing music like a game, to take away the pressure we put on ourselves. Instead of trying hard to be great at it, think of it as *easy*.

The beliefs that make up your loop may have been instilled in you early on, by a parent or school friend, or by a teacher. Or you may have adopted a belief because of an experience. Sometimes, the things you say to yourself are useful: I am a good singer, I will lose weight, I am kind to those in need. Sometimes, they are not useful: I'll probably fail at the audition, I'm afraid I look really awkward when I move my arms, my (fill in the blank) is too big.

ACTIVITY 2.1. WHAT I BELIEVE IS TRUE OR FALSE

Take five minutes to fill each column below with ten things you believe are true and ten things you believe are false, without taking a long time to ponder them. It doesn't matter what they're about, but be honest with yourself. In either column, list both positive and negative things that you believe.

THINGS I BELIEVE ARE TRUE	THINGS I BELIEVE ARE FALSE

Fig. 2.2. True/False Chart

What do you observe from the exercise? Which list was faster to fill? Are your true statements positive affirmations or are they confirmations of negative beliefs? In other words, did your list make you feel good or bad?

Remember, your true "S" Self will not make you feel bad. It is patient and loving and kind. It has all the time in the world. If this exercise leaves you feeling bad, your small "s" self—your ego—is dominating making the lists.

You *can* change the loop. It just takes practice. Try these steps:

Step 1. **Listen to your inner loop; listen to your thoughts.** Check your list again. Do you recognize kinds of statements that you make to yourself? Write down your thoughts and statements in a journal. When you recognize a statement in the loop that you'd like change, identify it in the journal.

Step 2. **Replace negative statements with positive ones that describe the outcome you really want to happen.** The trick is to make the statement positive, trying a new direction. When you frame the idea as negative, such as "Stop straining on that high note," the mind still hears the thing you don't want and keeps focusing on it. That makes changing habits much harder. It's like the old expression, "Don't think about the pink elephant." Too late!

Let's say you are singing constantly sharp in a passage. Do you know why? Rather than thinking, "I don't want to sing this sharp anymore!" think to yourself, instead, something like, "In this passage, my muscles are relaxed yet supportive for my voice, and the tone I sing is perfectly in tune." It may not be precisely true, yet. Perhaps the passage still needs to be worked on. However, your clear thought instructs your muscles how to respond in a way that will support the result you want to achieve, rather than fighting the result you are getting now.

Reframe something you fear as something you'd like to accomplish. For example, rather than saying, "I don't want to fail at the audition," say, "I will do my very best work at the audition. I am focused and ready." Although you can't promise yourself a result that someone else is deciding (i.e., getting the job), you can show up in charge of what *you* bring to the occasion.

Step 3. **Understand how your beliefs affect your decisions.** Keep practicing what you really want to be good at. Did the list exercise identify an area that needs more work? If you simply haven't spent enough time practicing, your negative thoughts may be an honest assessment of your work. That's different than beating yourself up for not being good enough when you truly try your best. You can tell the difference by how you feel. If you feel badly or if you believe you will likely fail, you are judging yourself. Or, expecting to fail, maybe you didn't prepare adequately. Helpful, useful thoughts do not feel bad. Thoughts can either support or undermine your goals.

Step 4. **Keep practicing these techniques.** Keep replacing judgmental criticisms with statements that know how to improve any weak areas. Eventually, the loop will change. Even if a part of the loop changes, that's an improvement!

Step 5. **Remember: Keep practicing.** ☺ The mind is ever-evolving and adaptable.

Your Options: Daily Affirmations

Practice is essential. You can reinforce optimism and determination by practicing affirming beliefs.

It is through repetition, through practice, that you learn. You recognize patterns, which the brain categorizes for future reference. It takes about three weeks of practicing something new to replace an old habit. *Muscle memory* occurs when you practice. It is a term for activities that are stored and reinforced in pathways of the motor areas of the brain. (Many experts believe that "intelligence" and memory are also stored in muscle itself.) You can only think of about seven things at a time; muscle memory is an important way the body accomplishes complex tasks that would require way more than seven things to think about. When you drive, or play a video game—or sing—you have learned to automate these activities.

Correct practice is also essential. Sometimes, you practice something that is not useful until it becomes normal or even feels natural. For instance, I know a woman who presses a pedal with her right foot for eight hours a day in her job. One day last year, she recognized that she had always held her foot crooked on the pedal, and her leg had become "stuck" pointing outward, even while she walked. She wanted to correct that. Her leg was not damaged, though the muscles in her foot and leg had become accustomed to functioning at an unnatural angle. She had to change the angle of her foot on the pedal. This felt wrong at first, but she kept at it every day for a few weeks until her muscles adjusted, her brain remapped, and her right foot and leg returned to normal.

This concept applies to anything physical, including vocal technique. For example, you may have been taught something in a lesson, perhaps a way of forming vowels or using vibrato, that isn't right for a contemporary song, but you don't know how to change it. Part of you resists trying a different approach.

The recommended practice here is to sing the song in a new way while letting your judgments and expectations complain all they want to. (Use the exercises for this in chapter 6.) Ignore these judgments and expectations. As long as you are approaching the new method in a relaxed yet engaged way, and not forcing anything to the point of strain or discomfort, give it a try. Keep at it. You will learn new technique.

Daily affirmations. Every day is an opportunity to reaffirm the beliefs that matter to you and an opportunity to erase beliefs that cause you pain. This is how it works: anything you think about frequently is reinforced in your brain. The brain builds pathways with increased electrical activity that feed connections to frequent thoughts. This is why negative thinking will reinforce an action or belief you wish you could change.

How do you erase unwanted thoughts or beliefs? Change gears. Daily affirmations describe what you truly want, in a positive framework. They come from a place of self-love. Do this even if you don't believe yourself, at first. Then, the energy that had been sent to the first thoughts or beliefs will subside. Eventually, with disuse, that older area of thinking will atrophy. Your unwanted thoughts or beliefs will be gone.

Have you ever watched an unhappy baby? Perhaps she is fussing, her face scrunched up and turning red. If you distract her—make a silly face, sing or play a song, or help her look at something—she will stop fussing immediately. She hasn't learned how to hold onto the fussing yet. She is in the moment. When you redirect your thoughts onto something new, you are distracting yourself, in a good way.

ACTIVITY 2.2. DAILY AFFIRMATIONS

Begin each day by making affirmations for ten or fifteen minutes. These will have the affect of directing how you proceed through your day. Sit quietly, letting your mind become open. Then repeat these affirmations to yourself, even if you don't believe them. Below are some suggestions. Of course, you can make up your own.

- Today is a new day and open to possibility.
- I am whole. I am good enough.
- I can trust the process before me.
- Each breath in is an opportunity to refill my cells with fresh oxygen and fresh light for/from my Self.
- Each breath out is an opportunity to cleanse my cells, to release any toxins or negative thoughts that I have been holding.
- I am building positive expectations. My Self will guide me. My Higher Power will guide me.
- I have what I need.

ACTIVITY 2.3. ENERGY GRID: MAP YOUR DAILY BIORHYTHM

Spend a week tracking your energy on a scale of one to ten, every hour you are awake, where one is tired and ten is your most energetic. Plot the results on the grid along with anything you notice that affects your energy level. The pattern you'll see when you're done is your biorhythm. You'll find out when your energy is low each day and when you are at your best for peak performance. It's important to know what your biorhythm is, and respect it when you make your schedule. Copy this for each day of the week.

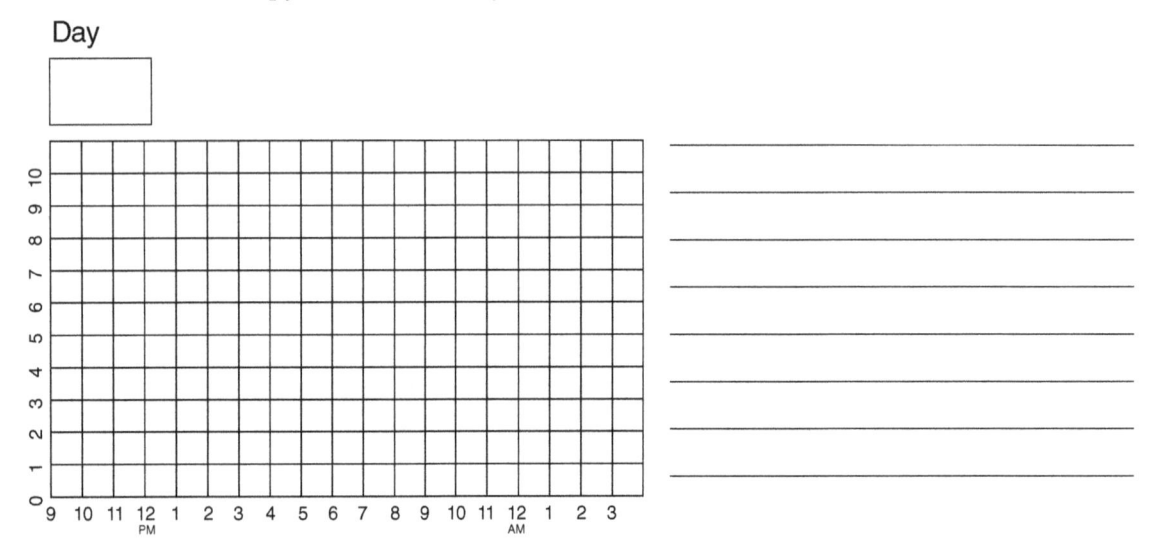

Fig. 2.3. Energy Grid

VOCAL STUDY

Singing is fun. It is miraculous, if you think about it. To be a whole singer, it is important to develop the mind, body, and spirit. Learning excellent vocal technique strengthens the body, releases the mind from worry, and ultimately, gives the spirit room to flourish.

In this section, we look at detailed aspects of vocal study. Vocal study is a very personal experience. For some people, studying singing is a necessity, a practice to maintain mental and physical health. For others, it is an avocation.

My belief is no one should ever be told they cannot sing. Some of the least beautiful voices we've come to love have become iconic artists, alongside those whose voices are so spectacular that you cannot help but weep when you hear them. That being said, when you find the right teacher for you, who is supportive of your goals while being honest with you too, you can grow as a singer. A good teacher will show you techniques, approaches, and attitudes that work with your learning style.

YOUR VOICE IS UNIQUE

There are slight variations from person to person in the vocal anatomical system. The shape of the pharynx and vocal cords, together with the resonant cavities of the head, give each of us a one-of-a-kind instrument.

In traditional (classical) singing pedagogy, we learn diction, placement, tone, and vibrato qualities that are correct for a specific period or genre of music, along with breathing techniques. Traditional singing pedagogy teaches *bel canto* singing—the beauty of the voice, along with exquisite technique. In contemporary music, the individual's personality and sound are favored instead, and there is less emphasis on executing beautiful tones.

In any style, you need to sing in tune and without strain. While developing your individual contemporary singing style, the challenge is to develop a sound that appears casual, or passionate, or smooth—without the technique showing. A contemporary virtuoso makes it *seem* like technique is secondary to phrasing and style. When you listen to other singers, keep in mind that as with any kind of music, there are both skilled and not-so-skilled singers whom we have become familiar with. If you imitate someone with unhealthy or unreliable technique, you could be in for problems down the road.

Relying on Your Teacher, Relying on Yourself

Your teacher is a mirror, a sounding board. He or she provides feedback to help guide you through tiny adjustments in your body that make a big difference in your sound. It's almost impossible to improve your singing voice without studying with a knowledgeable teacher who is guiding you closely. All of the exercises and instruction in this book will be helpful to you, but they cannot replace the value you will get from lessons with a real person.

Typically, voice lessons do not address anatomy in detail. Instead, a teacher guides you through mental images to help your body respond, for the desired sound or technique. A good teacher will caution you if you are straining and show you exercises to strengthen your voice and breathing.

Teachers may disagree on what method is best, even when they are teaching from similar backgrounds. Usually, teachers show students what they know. They teach from how they themselves learn and understand concepts, and from specific techniques they learned that helped them to improve. (That's true about most teachers in any area; it's human nature.)

We don't all learn the same way, though. Because so much of the vocal instrument relies on directing thought, how you learn is important to know about yourself. Some people are more kinesthetic, or visual, or aural, or procedural in how they learn. It's your teacher's job to understand this, to find your learning style, and to honor it. Vocal study puts the body and mind in a somewhat vulnerable position to the teacher's influence. If you find your teacher's style is not working well for you, it's advisable to search for a different teacher. If you leave a lesson in pain, or strained, or feeling unworthy of singing, it's time to start looking.

Everyone has the birthright to sing. Not everyone will be fortunate enough to succeed at performing for others. Not everyone has a musical gift that thousands want to experience. Not everyone has an attractive voice or can sing perfectly in tune. Nonetheless, everyone has the right to sing; it's part of our basic anatomy. Trust your gut. Rely on yourself. Does singing make you happy? If you embrace your limits and appreciate your potential, and if you work hard at your technique, with patience and consistency, your singing *will* improve.

Learn Your Limits and Your Potential

Beyond the right to sing, each of us needs to embrace the physical limitations of the voice we were born with. I always wanted to sound like a deep-toned soul singer, "blowing" impressive riffs like Chaka Khan. But while my pretty soprano voice is very flexible and powerful, and deep-toned when I belt low in my range, I do not sound remotely like Ms. Khan, or anyone else I admire. I will not, I cannot. I sound like me. I have come to appreciate this, and the phrases I can sing that make *me* unique as a singer.

What makes *you* unique?

> "If it hurts, don't do it! Even if it doesn't hurt but your voice becomes hoarse after you sing, you are doing something that is not good for it."

When I was in college, preparing for my final thesis concert, I became ill with the flu. Nonetheless, for two weeks before the concert, I had to rehearse twenty-five musicians through two and a half hours of prepared music. I had planned what became a long, two-act concert. There were opera arias, there were songs I wrote to African drumming ensembles, there was a wind piece I wrote for quintet in which I was the fifth instrument, there were funk tunes with a full rhythm section and horns. I kept rehearsing, through the flu, through exhaustion. If I was going to present my thesis concert and complete my degree, I had no choice.

Three days before the concert, it all caught up with me. I came down with complete laryngitis. No sound emerged from my voice. The day before my concert I led my dress rehearsal without singing. Instead, my best friend translated directions I uttered in her ear for the assembled musicians. I was terrified. I sought medical treatment, I pleaded with my voice teacher to give me a remedy. She suggested tea with honey and lemon and vocal rest. The doctor gave me a steroid to reduce the swelling. (Not something I wish to rely on ever again.) I prayed. I hoped my thesis advisor would forgive the illness and still give me a good grade.

The best part about this unfortunate occurrence was learning that one extremely effective way to rehearse is silently, to oneself. As I lay in bed visualizing the music, without singing a note because I had no choice, what I didn't realize was my brain was processing the actions of singing the concert as if I actually were singing. I have since learned that this is a technique used by athletes and others, and is a very effective way to practice. Brain-imaging technology shows us that the brain lights up when we *imagine* doing an activity, similarly to when you are actually *doing* it.

Another valuable lesson I learned from that experience: when you have a limited time to rehearse, plan a shorter concert!

The good news is that my voice came through, in the end. Save one or two moments where a very high note stopped sounding in an aria, my voice was all there. What else did I learn? I have limits. I need to respect those limits. I am very lucky; my voice is strong. I am determined. Yet, my voice is not infallible. No one's is.

Is There "Right" and "Wrong" Singing?

Yes. And no. Some sounds we make simply *are* bad for the voice and can damage the delicate membranes of the vocal fold edges. Some people's damage alters their voices permanently; these changes may even make speaking more difficult. In particular, styles including rock, gospel, blues, and also opera can be pretty rough on the voice if not done with supportive and careful technique. (Chapter 1 has a great deal of anatomical information that helps you understand why.)

At the end of the day, your goal with singing determines how you should learn to use your voice. If you wish to become accomplished in a certain style, you need to learn the parameters and techniques for that style. If you just want to sing for fun—for your personal enjoyment, for the good feeling singing engenders—technical excellence is less important. If you want your voice to last for years, you need to learn how to take care of it. It all boils down to what you want to get out of singing.

Most people don't want a damaged voice. Your voice teacher is there to teach you technique that supports your vocal goals. Voice therapists work with people to help identify bad speaking or singing habits that have caused problems. Voice surgeons remove or repair damaged areas of the larynx when absolutely necessary.

There is a great deal of misinformation about what is good or bad singing. For example, many teachers believe that belting is bad news, period. This simply is not true. There are ways to support belting that are fine. Perhaps a teacher may not know how to show you the technique you should use for a particularly strong singing style like belting, or believes your voice is not up to the task. Or, maybe a teacher seeks to develop the beauty and agility of each student's voice, and in this case, a non-pretty (non *bel canto*) approach like belting goes against his or her own training and approach.

In general, you should have your own internal barometer with its own indicators for healthy or unhealthy singing. It may surprise you to learn that vocalists who visit a voice specialist most frequently sing opera. For them, specific notes must be available for a career to continue. Rock or jazz singers can go longer without addressing problems, using rephrasing in order to avoid trouble spots. Ultimately, though, bad habits cannot be avoided forever and are going to show up as a problem—maybe a permanent one.

Style and Habits

Style is a very important component of singing, and of all music, for that matter. For contemporary styles, one could argue that style is the most important aspect of singing effectively in a way that draws in the listener.

Simply put, style means aesthetics. Teachers vary widely on their opinion of what is good stylistically. "That's not jazz!" a teacher may say in a critique, or, "That's not *real* country!" "Your r&b riffs don't belong in this tune." Or, "Listen to the great r&b singers, and learn how to improvise over the chord changes."

There are *many, many* varieties of contemporary singing. These days, just about every style is a blend of several influences. In iTunes, there are over forty categories of contemporary music, from jazz to rock to r&b to alternative to hip-hop to house to Latin. There are even more styles of teaching than that.

Everyone has habits that affect singing style. Is your vibrato heavy or thin? Do you tend to slide up to notes? Is your regional accent affecting how you pronounce words when you sing? How loudly do you want to sing that note, that vowel? Is your voice placed in the back in your throat, stuck in your nose, or resonating brightly right behind your front teeth? Do you like that vowel sound, or is the "ee" too bright? Were you told to always pronounce your R's a certain way (or not to pronounce them at all)?

The way I teach, every sound is legitimate as long as the voice is not straining or pounding to get results. If you have *choices* about the sounds you make, with healthy ways to produce those sounds, you have a full palette of vocal colors to work with. When you have technique options, you can use your creative judgment to decide "good" or "not so good." You can choose whether or not your diction and tone work for a given musical style. Then, putting those sounds together into a creative, expressive line is where artistry, technique, and active listening come in. What you bring to it—what you are passionate about—makes it exciting to work with you.

Remember, whereas two instruments of the same kind will sound similar, two human voices will be quite distinct from one another, even on the same note at the same volume. When we hear qualities in other voices we admire, it is tempting to think that we can shift our own settings to mimic those voices we like. This is not so. It is also not important. Simply put, you are not going to sound like Elvis or Madonna or Lady Gaga or Chaka Khan. You may very well be able to sing the same music, but: You sound like *you*.

Registers and Placement

For the vocal instrument, the term *registers* is used to identify some of the complex changes that happen in the larynx during singing. The term may refer to several things for the singer:

- A specific range of pitches (high, low, alto, soprano, tenor, baritone, bass)

- A type of resonance or quality such as "chest voice" or "head voice"

- The process used to create a characteristic timbre

- A region of the voice delineated by a vocal "break" (shifts between falsetto, full voice, etc.)

When we visualize the voice as a set of registers, it can seem that we have a series of separate settings. This is not so. Students often get confused or even misled about this. ("Should I be singing in my chest voice or mix voice here?") In truth, the voice is incredibly flexible and can produce a wide variety of tones, colors, timbres, vowels, and volumes, whether singing a scale or one note. Although laryngeal muscles do contract and release depending on what you're singing, there is not one correct register designation for each note. Some tone and timbre combinations may come more easily low in the range or high in the range. This varies depending on the person. Full voice means singing with strong tones. Belt voice means pushing full voice high; or, singing brightly and loudly. Most of the time, you are singing in mix voice. Mix voice is the singer's secret weapon: blend in a little of this, a little of that. This is what we use most of the time. It depends!

The Five Commonly Defined Registers

1. Vocal fry: loose vocal edges, producing little tone; a common component of current American speech, it sounds "lazy"

2. "Chest" voice: lower pitches, full sounding, thicker vocal fold (speech-level, used in belting and full voice production)

3. "Head" voice: higher pitches, lighter sounding, thinner vocal fold

4. Falsetto: high tones in the male and female voice; the vocal folds do not touch

5. Whistle tone: a super high area of notes, which not all people can produce, made by forcing air through a very taut and thin vocal tract (e.g., Mariah Carey, Adam Lopez)

There are two exceptions to mix voice: when you are singing your highest notes, you are likely in head voice, flute voice, or falsetto; when you are at the bottom of your range, you are likely in chest voice. When you belt with force or yell-sing, you are often in chest voice, too.

In my studio, we use the term "registers" only as a reference point to identify common voice production options, while always reminding ourselves to appreciate and build the ultimate flexibility of the voice. However, because describing the voice in terms of registers is common in vocal pedagogy, the concept is still helpful. Then, how you use your voice becomes a matter of aesthetic or stylistic choice.

Placement of the voice refers to where the voice seems to be coming from in your body, at that moment. You do not have switches inside you that modify your placement. What you do have is a set of complex, ongoing changes in the larynx, as we have seen. For example, when we use the terms "head voice" (high tones that appear to ring in your head) or "chest voice" (low and full placement from the same area as a lower speaking voice), we are really referring to the *sensation* of where sound resonates in your body.

All this boils down to your physical experience and how you learn. Do you learn best by imitation? By experiencing the motions? By watching your teacher? By hearing the tones you want to recreate? Whatever understanding gets you the results you desire is good!

Here's some of the best advice I've heard about learning voice, from teacher extraordinaire Mark Baxter:[3] When you sing, focus on the *result* you want. We cannot go inside your throat to tell each tiny muscle to move consciously, in a particular way, any more than we can tell the muscles in and around your eyeball to contract or expand individually when you are looking at a painting. A skilled singer learns to shift through laryngeal and vocal tract muscle patterns and release tension by thinking about the desired tone and volume, not by analyzing how the registers are working while singing.

---

[3] Baxter, Mark. *The Rock-n-Roll Singer's Survival Manual.* Milwaukee, WI: Hal Leonard, 1990.

Vowel, Volume, Pitch, and Diction

Mark Baxter also explains an effective way to take the concern about registers out of the equation. Focus your intention on three factors: pitch, volume, and vowel. Consider:

- What *pitch* am I singing?
- At what *volume*?
- On what *vowel*?

Pitch, volume, and vowel determine the quality of the singing voice. Your use of diction adds further dimensions to tone and style.

When we shape our mouths to make vowels, such as A (ay), E (ee), I (eye), O (oh), and U (oo), we change the way tone resonates in the mouth. How the singer shapes the vowel influences the quality of the voice.

Stylistically, one of the most significant differences between American contemporary singing and traditional classical technique is the shape of the vowel. (For our discussion here, I am not including traditional folk styles, as they could encompass another book.) Contemporary styles often sound like regular speech sung on pitch. When these styles travel high in the range, there tends to be dramatic singing, belting, riffing; when soft, the tone tends to be breathy. This is not necessarily desirable; it is just the norm at present.

In contrast, in traditional classical singing, the objective is to shape the vowels to achieve an aesthetically "ideal" tone that is beautiful, that has a high tone-to-breath ratio, that conveys a degree of emotion, and that is easily heard over a full orchestra. Of course, in contemporary styles, we are still working with tone and emotion, but the aesthetic qualifier of "that tone is pretty" or "that tone is ugly" is not as important. What is important is maintaining healthy technique—i.e., not straining to get a result, so a career can last—while communicating the emotion or story of the lyric in a compelling way.

There is a simple visualization to understand the difference in vowel placement between traditional and contemporary singing. Traditional vowels are oval in shape, from top to bottom, or north/south. Contemporary vowels turn the oval on its side with a wider mouth, or east/west.

Articulation is essential in singing and is a big part of voice lessons. Language is made clear in the mouth. Where vowels carry the tone, consonants create the clarity of the words. Consonants are like the candy coating on an M&M, and the vowel is the chocolate center. You can sing with only vowels; you cannot sing with only consonants. Of course, you can hum tones with a closed mouth and create resonance, too, though the tonal colors are more limited. You can make percussive sounds with consonants, such as in beat boxing, but you can't produce a resonant tone with them.

"Mask" is a term referring to placement in the front of the face (where you'd wear a small mask). It helps focus placement to the resonant spaces there. When teachers say, "Sing from your mask," they mean picture the sound coming from your nose and mouth area.

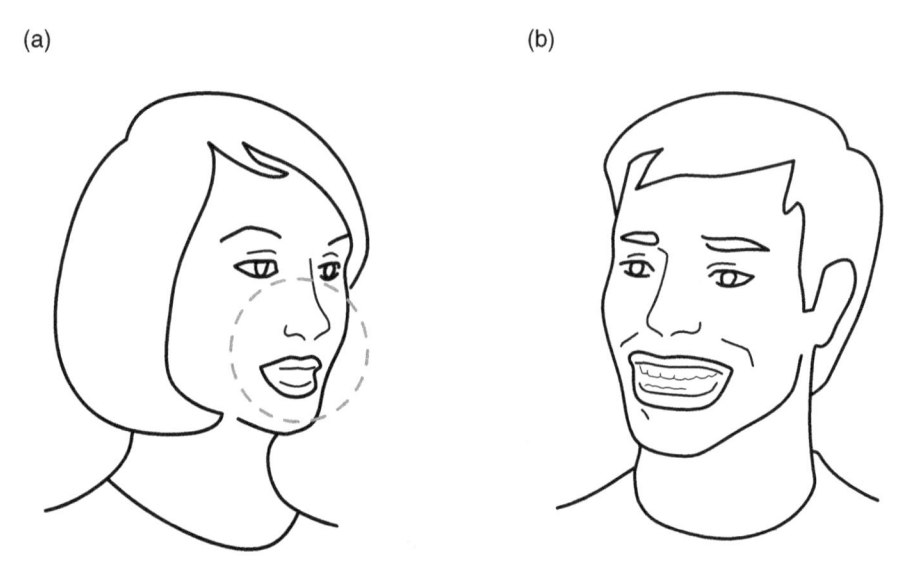

Fig. 2.4. (a) Singing from Your Mask, (b) Singing Too Widely

The figure on the left is singing from the mask with a relaxed, yet engaged, expression. Sometimes we spread the mouth too widely, as in the figure on the right, which can put too much strain on the vocal folds.

The Break

Students always ask me, "Where is my break?" as if there's a place in the voice that has a fault line. Singers are careful to identify and avoid that fabled spot at all costs. The term is a reference to vocal registers. The truth is, you don't have to have a "break." You can strengthen your *passaggio* instead. Vocal pedagogy identifies the *passaggio*—Italian for passage—as a transition area where vocal muscles shift dominance. It is particularly common to use this word to identify the spot in men's voices between the top of full voice and falsetto. Most women also experience an area of transition at the top of the chest voice range, or even lower in the alto range. The use of a yodel flip is a common device in popular singing to utilize the passaggio in order to move in between vocal qualities.

Above or below the passaggio, an ongoing adjustment happens between the muscles and ligaments in the larynx, pharynx, tongue, jaw, and lips (all of which are always moving while you sing). Your goal may be to keep the tone and resonance consistent throughout a section by using one placement in one register. When you move out of the area where this register works best and most comfortably, the voice may become tenuous and weaker. If you are not already blending registers using a mix technique, the voice may strain, if you are forcing it. The voice seems to be telling you that it needs to shift gears in order to keep going up or down the range at this volume.

This so-called change in register, where one set of muscle adjustments transitions to another, generally happens in a small area of notes. The change can happen gradually, smoothly. Only you and your voice teacher may be aware of what is going on, and you may even get to the point where you sing without paying much attention to it. If the change occurs abruptly, you will probably experience this as your break.

Ultimately, where and how obvious your "break" might be depends on how you're singing—the style and range and registers you are using. As you continue to study technique, you may even find a way to make your break disappear.

Remember, to develop a smooth transition between areas in your range, keep your focus on the desired outcome rather than how you are creating it. For example, as you travel up an octave scale on an "ah" vowel, seek to keep the volume constant while letting your voice figure out what muscles and ligaments to shift and stretch. Your voice will, when you let it. This is a much more effective and flexible approach then thinking, "Uh-oh, I'm about to cross the F-above-middle-C threshold, I'd better switch into mix!"

Think instead, "Stay consistent with the 'ah'… release the tension in my neck, let the voice move as needed … keep the volume even." With practice, you will ultimately find a much better result.

Resonance, Tone, and Style

It is common for singers to wish they could do what they hear other singers doing. Can you relate to this? Contemporary music tends to be written low in women's ranges and high in men's, yet most younger women are sopranos (higher), while most men are baritones (lower). Artists we admire bring their unique personalities, vocal qualities, and fabulous senses of style to catchy songwriting. This is appealing, and we want to be able to do that, too! We all learn to sing and to speak through imitation. Listening to skilled artists for learning style is the best place to start. However, it is important to develop your own sound. You may not have the voice of Pink or Ray Charles or Sting, but you may still pull off one of their tunes, in your own way.

It is important to understand that what you hear in recordings (and even in some live performances) may not be totally real. In the recording studio today, techniques are used, like vocal airbrushing, to fix intonation (using pitch correction) and to even out volume (using compression). Some sound engineering "fixes" have themselves become special vocal effects. Real voices don't make all of these sounds. A phrase that seems difficult to recreate in live performance may in fact be two or three passes by the singer that have been spliced together to sound like one. A singer who is breathy yet strong may have even had that breathiness added afterwards by the engineer. In live concerts, when there are many parts on a song, additional vocals are sung by the background singers, or even prerecorded and played back seamlessly by the keyboard player.

The secret sauce is your individual vocal tone. That is what is most compelling. Each type of instrument, like each voice, has a different balance of overtones. That changes the timbre or quality of the note and helps us to identify an instrument—or a voice. What's unique about the human voice is that we can alter our balance of overtones in countless ways—modifying the *quality* of each note—simply by moving the tongue, lifting the soft palate, changing the shape of the throat, or adjusting the vocal fold edges. Amazing!

How We Hear Tone

What makes the tone of an instrument sound unique? If a flute and an alto sax are playing the same pitch, how can we tell one from the other? The answer lies in how our ears and brains process the high frequency components of each instrument's characteristic sound. Every natural tone we hear is actually a composite of a series of frequencies that are part of the note. Each note is really a chord! Most of the time, these *partials, harmonics,* or *overtones* are indistinct (unless you are an overtone singer). Subtle overtones, produced by all natural instruments, add quality to tone. Our brains filter the series of overtones into one recognized pitch, based on the lowest (or primary) frequency by which we identify it, called the "fundamental."

My theory is that sometimes when singers have trouble matching pitch, the brain is confused. These singers not only hear a note's primary pitch, they also hear the subtle overtones of the notes' additional frequencies. This makes it difficult to tell which tone they are hearing is the correct one to sing. Or, while the singer may hear the note correctly, his or her brain has not figured out how to manipulate small changes in the vocal system in order to recreate the note or timbre accurately. The third occurrence that can happen is a singer memorizes a song in its original key: how that melody feels in the voice, where it rings in the body. Then, when the key is changed, the muscles that have memorized the original key have trouble transitioning to different positions for the new key. This is a case where the coordination between hearing and movement is challenged. In all cases, matching pitch can be learned. It is rare for a hearing person to be truly "tone deaf."

Conditioning

We are conditioned to sing in certain ways, whether on our own or in choirs, school, church, while watching television or by imitating artists we admire. Inspiration arises from a mind that is open to exploration and growth. A sensitive teacher guides the student while putting him or her at ease. Similarly, when a conductor knows how to put an orchestra at ease, the musicians play at their best because they are able to focus on the beauty of their sound, on phrasing, and on their synchronicity.

When you understand your body's conditioning process, and when you are aware of your habits, you gain a desire to take control of your life. Conditioning is an automatic behavior, functioning like a switch, in place from years of repetition. Your body adapts to this repetitive behavior, and it becomes normal. That makes change much harder.

So, be patient with yourself. The first step is to learn what conditioning you are undoing in your voice study. Then, repeat *new* patterns, healthy patterns, and techniques. Eventually, these will replace the unhealthy ones and become the new normal.

Vocal Concepts and Visualizations

Following are a few concepts and visualizations that you can try out when you practice. I have found these to be effective throughout my years of teaching for modifying conditioned vocal habits or behaviors. If an idea doesn't make sense at first, don't reject it out of hand; have another go at it. Or, make up one of your own that unravels a conditioned habit, like patiently untying a shoelace knot.

1. Think of opposites. If your vocal line is moving up, think down. Literally bend your knees as you ascend. If your vocal line is moving down, visualize upward expansion. This technique helps your automatic response to gravity release its grip on your vocal muscles.

2. Stay present, but don't direct yourself too much. Too much attention causes tension.

3. The jump rope game Double Dutch is like learning music. In Double Dutch, there are two jump ropes instead of one. Held in both hands of the two people spinning the ropes, the ropes cross over and under one another. You have to learn to find your way into the spaces between the rhythmic arcing of both ropes in order to get into the middle to jump. Once in, it's easier to stay in if you can jump a lot, since the tempo is doubled. Getting out is also challenging. You need to time your exit to align with the spaces made from the rising and falling arcs, without getting caught up in the ropes.

   Not everyone is going to succeed at Double Dutch, even with practice. If you don't get it when you're eight years old on a playground, you may get laughed at, or ignored. Does that matter? Does it mean you shouldn't be on the playground? (When you're eight, it probably seems so.) Some playgrounds don't even know about Double Dutch; it's fairly regional, and there are other playground games.

   If you don't align with the tempo of the two people who are tossing the ropes as one team, you won't be able to jump in or jump out. If the team is supporting you, they'll wait while you learn.

Fig. 2.5. Double Dutch   Illustrated by Jeannie Gagné

   If you really want to join a game already in progress, you'll have to learn the patterns that are in place as you go. You may not succeed. Does that mean you shouldn't be jumping rope? Of course, not. It only means you may not be amazing at Double Dutch without lots of practice. If it is important to you, you will practice it. Your body will figure out how to coordinate your arms and legs to get in and out of the spinning ropes.

And most importantly, if you have fun learning it, other people will enjoy playing with you, too, and the learning will be easier.

4. A grandfather clock has two weights that move up and down while the clock arms move around its face. The weights are in balance with one another. There is a sense of proportionality between them, a relationship. When we study singing, we are also looking to establish balance between the different moving parts in our bodies. If one area is too strong, it will throw off the other areas. A balanced relationship between the moving parts in our vocal body is important.

Fig. 2.6. Grandfather Clock
Illustrated by Jeannie Gagné

5. Sing a slow glissando up, then down. Go through every note, avoiding nothing, let the muscles gradually adjust and shift. Take time as you travel through any weak spots. Keep VOLUME and VOWEL constant.

This is surgical; there is no hiding. We tend to avoid the tricky bits in melodies and phrasing/interpretation. Although it may work out musically, avoiding our trouble spots also avoids truly strengthening the whole instrument and gaining flexibility with it. If you play a flute and one key sticks, you could probably avoid it, but that would be frustrating and limiting, too.

So, practice all the notes, no hiding. There is no style with this exercise, and that is good. Don't expect it to sound like "singing," it is just an exercise, learning the ins and outs of your instrument.

6. Muppet jaw. If you are singing only one vowel, the jaw doesn't need to move. When it moves as you sing a riff, for instance, that means your jaw is tight. Your jaw has to move when you articulate words, and it also needs to drop some to allow your mouth to open. It does not need to "do the muppet."

7. Good technique allows for muscular *isolation*. For example, your tongue muscle is involved in different ways when you say a vowel, but it should not be so involved that it becomes bunched up in tension at the back of the throat. Another area to be aware of is your neck.

8. Fluttering, like the sails on a boat when it's coming about, is the sound of an under-supported or under-energized vocal mechanism. The folds are together but not quite making stable contact with the balance provided between airflow and laryngeal muscular engagement. Avoiding fluttering comes from developing coordination. This is balance, not bulk.

Fig. 2.7. Sailboat
Illustrated by Jeannie Gagné

9. The roof of your mouth is like an upside down sugar bowl. You can press your sound up into the bowl to get additional resonance in your tone. Or, the roof of your mouth is the place where you can press a wad of gum. Carefully press sound into that area, like the gum, to focus your tone and get more ring into it.

10. A garden hose that is turned on has a constant supply of water. When there is no nozzle on it, you can use your finger to direct the flow. If you press the hose opening until it is almost closed, the water will shoot out further with the same amount of pressure. Similarly, the way your vocal folds come together can create more useful air pressure in your larynx. When they are more efficiently closed, the sound will project further.

Imagine you have all the airflow you need, just as the hose has all the water it needs from the faucet.

11. What is a clean tone? The wicked witch, a crow, a puppy's whine. When you do these funny sounds gently, you can experience clean tone without strain.

12. Plan your breathing as you would plan for how much gas you have in your car and how far you have to go on a road trip. If you spend all your air in the beginning of a phrase, it won't be there for the end of it. Spend your air wisely.

13. Energy flows in constant patterns through us. Following the map of the body's primary chakras, we learn that emotion resides in the chest. It is no accident that expression is in the throat. Power is in the mid section. Fear resides low in the gut. Thoughtful awareness is in the third eye, the forehead. The true Self emanates through the crown chakra at the top of the head. When you become aware of the energy in these areas, you have more control of your instrument. (See chapter 4, "Understanding Your Energy in Performance," for a detailed discussion.)

The Chakras

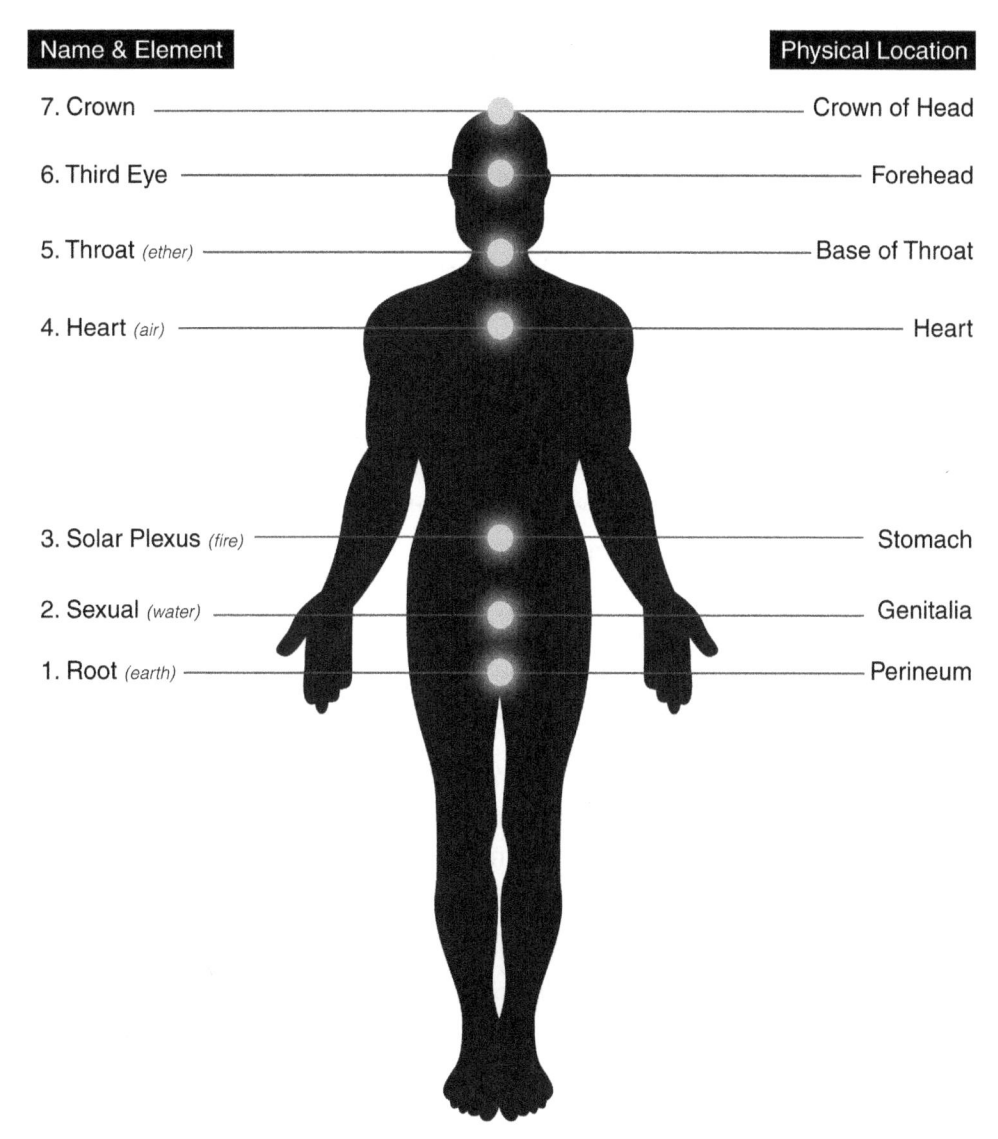

Name & Element	Physical Location
7. Crown	Crown of Head
6. Third Eye	Forehead
5. Throat *(ether)*	Base of Throat
4. Heart *(air)*	Heart
3. Solar Plexus *(fire)*	Stomach
2. Sexual *(water)*	Genitalia
1. Root *(earth)*	Perineum

Fig. 2.8. The Body's Primary Chakras

14. Icing a cake: Imagine the tube filled with icing, with a tip attached to make a design on top of the cake. When light pressure on the tube is constant, the icing flows well, and you can create a smooth line. As the icing goes out of the tip—which is creating resistance—you need to increase pressure on the icing bag gently, so it doesn't glom out and make a mess. Too little pressure is not going to make a design; too much and your design won't come out right.

How You Practice

How Much Should I Practice?

When you are actively working on your voice, you should be practicing every day. Singers practice less per day than other instrumentalists because of the delicate nature of the voice. It is typical for a serious guitarist or pianist to practice for several hours at a time. A vocalist should not do this. When you warm up properly, do at least fifteen minutes of focused vocal exercises, avoid vocal strain like the plague, and also warm down; you may be able to sing for up to three hours in a day. If you practice technique for an hour a day, even better.

Distinguish vocalizing from working on a tune. Be sure you begin your practice session each day with disciplined exercises designed to strengthen your voice. If you are vocalizing five days a week, you are following a good schedule.

Warm Up, Cool Down

To maintain a healthy voice, it is essential to warm up your voice before you sing tunes and cool down after you sing. A warm up should start easily and gently, in the lower middle part of your range. Begin by stretching, focusing on posture and expanding your ribs while engaging your breathing. Massage your jaw and neck as you warm up. You want to release any neck tension. How long you warm up depends on the shape of your voice that day but will range from about fifteen to twenty minutes. A cool down for about five minutes after you sing relaxes your muscles and brings your larynx back into position for normal speaking. To cool down sing a simple phrase, repeating it a step or two lower each time, to bring your voice comfortably back to speaking range.

Determine Your Goal

If you are not preparing for a concert or audition, daily practice of half an hour or an hour is sufficient to keep your voice in shape. When you have an upcoming performance, after warming up, focus your exercises around the type of singing you are preparing for. For example, if you are singing a jazz tune that has higher, quick notes, your warm-up should include lighter-toned exercises for accurate articulation. Or, if you are preparing singer/songwriter tunes that sit lower in your range, emphasize the notes in that range during your warm-up. A fun exercise is to take a short bit from a tune you'll be singing and play around with it, singing it in several keys. It is always advisable to stretch your full range when you warm up, just as you would stretch your legs before running, with more range of motion than you use when you run. Remember, if you don't use it, you lose it. You can also practice breathing, movement, and relaxation-strengthening exercises every day. Study music by singing it lightly or memorizing a score.

Importance of Technique

Learning good technique will give you an instrument that lasts for years. Some people fear that learning technique will make them sound less natural. This is a false concern. Anyone who makes singing look easy has technique that is not showing. There is a wonderful adage that goes something like this: A beginner has unconscious incompetence. As he or she learns, it becomes conscious incompetence. An experienced person has conscious competence. A master has unconscious competence. If you want your voice to last a long time, learning good technique is essential.

Include Just-for-Fun Singing

When we are too serious about something and forget to have fun with it, that is a recipe for stress. It is easy to get worked up over an upcoming audition or concert and then over-prepare to the point of vocal fatigue. Part of preparation is knowing how you respond to stress. If you find yourself getting worked up during your practice, take a breather; sing something just for the fun of it. (Or, take a pause from practicing altogether and take a walk, have a cup of tea, read a chapter in a favorite book, go do your workout—do whatever it is that is a stress-reducer for you.)

Healthy Mental Thoughts and Practice

Compare/Despair

When we compare ourselves to others whom we admire or envy, it is a recipe for feeling bad about ourselves. But we all do it. You can only control yourself, and you don't know what is going on behind the scenes in someone else's life or career. I love this simple adage: Compare means despair. It's a good reminder.

Let Yourself Be Fabulous

The second-hand singing that audiences experience through performers can be profoundly moving. (Have you ever had someone say to you after a show, "That was great, I wish I could do that!") Just as your brain lights up when you practice by *imagining* singing, your audience can have the imagined experience of singing along with you. Studies indicate that when people hear someone else sing, their brains light up as if they are singing, too. When you are fabulous and confident, you put the audience at ease so that they can feel fabulous and confident.

I often remind my students that what is intriguing in contemporary styles is your unique voice and style, your personality, your creativity. Whether you are outgoing or quiet, dramatic or subtle, high-voiced or low-voiced, audiences want to learn about *you*. What do you bring to a known song ("cover tune") that's new? What do *you* have to say?

You are fortunate to be able to express yourself through song. It is something to be grateful for. Take a moment to thank the Universe for giving you this gift. Yes, some voices are more beautiful than yours, some are more expressive, and some are more powerful. So what? Ignore the critical voice in your mind. The voice that criticizes and judges your ability or your talent is a saboteur. Appreciate your gifts. Appreciate your strengths. Every person has the ability to sing—and everyone has the right to.

Practice a Successful Outcome, Not the Mistakes

During the days and weeks leading up to a concert, there is much-anticipated preparation. How you frame this practice will have a large impact on your concert. Visualize each of the songs. Picture how the lyrics feel on the tongue. Imagine what mood is created by the selection of songs. Imagine how the sung and instrumental notes sound and feel in your body. Visualize how everyone on stage will interact together.

Positive practice is essential. Imagine the perfect concert. How do you feel after the last note has finished ringing? How does your voice feel when you've nailed that difficult passage? What is your mood? Put yourself there: *imagine achieving the result you want.* Imagine feeling wonderful and centered in that moment. Then, work backwards.

What to practice, to keep it positive? Uncover what parts of the music you need to rehearse with heightened awareness, being gentle with it. If you always practice the *lead-up* to a problem area, you are practicing the problem and reinforcing it. Instead, start inside the passage, and work backwards. Is there a melody line that hits your passaggio? A fingering that you stumble on in the accompaniment? Untie that knot. Step inside it. Then, unravel the passage, note by note, to analyze, without judgment, why it is challenging. Slow it down. Once you are relaxed with it, and the passage becomes familiar with repetition, you can bring it back up to speed. You have embraced it.

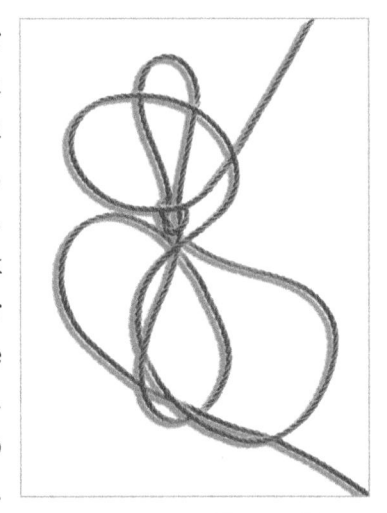

Fig. 2.9. Knots

Learning the lyrics thoroughly will be an important stress-reducer on stage, so you can focus on the joy of being up there. By knowing the lyrics backwards and forwards, they will be available mentally even if there is a distraction in concert, which there always is. Do you tend to forget a section of the lyrics?

Repeat just that section, over and over again in your mind. Or write the words down twenty times. Or make a list of actions that the lyrics convey in your mind, cause and effect. If you are visual, draw a picture of the lyrics. If you are kinesthetic, create a movement to help you remember them. You can practice mentally while walking down the street, while doing dishes, while working out, while driving. Sing a line from the middle of a verse or a bridge section to be sure you can begin anywhere in the song.

Learn your cues to the other musicians, too, such as where the chorus or bridge begins, how instrumentation changes, and where dynamics change. Practice standing and singing into a mic on a stand. Practice your own accompaniment on guitar, piano, djembe drum, shaker, or whatever the instrument is. Practice coordinating your singing while playing, as well as separate practice on the instrument. Your mind cannot focus on both tasks well, so one needs to be more automatic than the other.

Your centering practice continues as you visualize the "pocket," or best tempo, for each groove. Be *inside* the groove when you sing the song.

You may also find you are more centered and relaxed if you memorize your set list. Plan what you will say in between songs, when to be silent, and when to create a musical segue to connect two songs without interruption. Picture the flow throughout the whole set.

> "Strive continually for vocal mastery, while nurturing your ongoing relationship with your source of inspiration."

Excellence, Not Perfection

Recently, a delightful gaggle of my colleagues had a heated debate about musical perfection. Where one musician expected her accompanist to play perfectly, another's blood boiled at the thought. "How can I be expected to be perfect?" he complained. "My goal is *excellence*, not perfection. Hitting every note doesn't make it musical." The general consensus? Perfection is not an important goal; musicianship and expression are. Winston Churchill famously said, "They say that nobody is perfect. Then they tell you practice makes perfect. I wish they'd make up their minds."

This proverb sums it up wisely: A beautiful thing is never perfect.

CHAPTER 3

Embodying Rhythm and Movement

*Dance with me, querido,
into the mystery*

Celebrate! We'll light the flame

*Take my hand, we'll move together
on a journey*

*As we sing the song of love
that calls our name*

—from "Dance with Me"
by Jeannie Gagné
and Jason Shelton

Illustrated by Jeannie Gagné

Rhythm is one of the three primary ingredients of music, along with melody and harmony. In contemporary music, it is an essential and highly complex ingredient, often emphasized more than melody. Contemporary American music is a unique mixture of influences, primarily a blend of Western European and African American music from several centuries. Much of it comes from oral tradition. Oral tradition means communicating verbally, without reading music, by demonstrating feel and groove and by embodying rhythm with movement. In contemporary styles, rhythms are often predominately played by the drums and bass. To sing contemporary music well, it is imperative that the singer understands and embodies rhythm.

Rhythm is in all things. It is a basic part of our biology. It affects our world, our universe—the moon, the tide, sunrise and sunset, seasons, even movement of the planets. Our hearts beat; we breathe in and out. We step to a rhythm when we walk. We have rhythms during sleep. We have rhythmic cycles in a year, in a month, in a day, in an hour, even in a minute. Each breath you take is a rhythm cycle.

> **TIP: DRUMMING**
>
> Take a hand percussion class or join a drumming circle. When you learn to play a hand drum such as a djembe, and especially when you learn to play polyrhythms in an ensemble, you will embody and understand rhythm at a much deeper level. This in turn will help you to sing more complex patterns well, and to articulate rhythms effectively with a band.

Sound is made of waves—particles of moving air that our ears perceive and translate to our brains as electric signals, which we understand as sound. The waves have patterns—rhythms. The structure of life itself is made of patterns, down to the molecule and atom, and smaller even than that. Rhythm is part of that structure.

When we experience the connection between our own personal, biological rhythms and those of the universe, we gain a deeper connection to the rhythms in music, too. By simultaneously observing both ourselves and our environment, by experiencing the push and pull of the rhythm of the moment from the most local aspect to the largest universal and subtle tugs, we are freer to release into the music. When we release into the music, we can also relax into the rhythm, allowing us to feel the groove, or the "pocket." Nothing happens in isolation, including our experience of timing on stage. When the drummer's pulse is in synch with the bass player, when the stabs of the piano and the guitar align, when the singer's phrasing seamlessly weaves through, above and below these elements—this is when rhythm is working for us.

In other words, a band is "tight" and playing "in the pocket" when the rhythms intersect with precision and flow. A singer's phrasing is "solid" when its rhythmic component aligns in collaboration with the groove of the accompaniment. Sometimes, that means *back-phrasing*, or singing with a relaxed feel that lags slightly behind the precision of the groove yet also locks into it from time to time. The great jazz singers are skilled at this. Other times, that means *push-phrasing* or *forward-phrasing*, in which the notes are in with the groove yet pushing slightly ahead of it. Rock and country singers sometimes employ this technique.

FEEL THE BACKBEAT

Usually, the backbeat is on beats 2 and 4. "A ONE, a TWO, a one TWO three FOUR." It is an accent to give the groove energy. When you listen to a rhythm section, identify the sound of the snare drum. It is the drum hitting backbeats 2 and 4 in 4/4 time in many styles, including rock, pop, reggae, country, and blues. In jazz styles, the drum is more improvisatory, with the bass guitar holding down the beat. The jazz drummer may carry the backbeat on a ride cymbal, or imply it with the combination of strokes throughout the drum set.

If you snap your fingers when you count off a groove, be sure you're not snapping on primary beats 1 and 3. The exception to that is two-feel beats such as cut-time country grooves, marching band music, or polkas.

TIME SLASHES

Contemporary song charts often use *time slashes* within each measure, in lieu of melodic notation, over which the chord changes are notated. Time slashes represent the time signature, evenly marking where the primary beats fall within a measure. In figure 3.1, examples of four time signatures are shown.

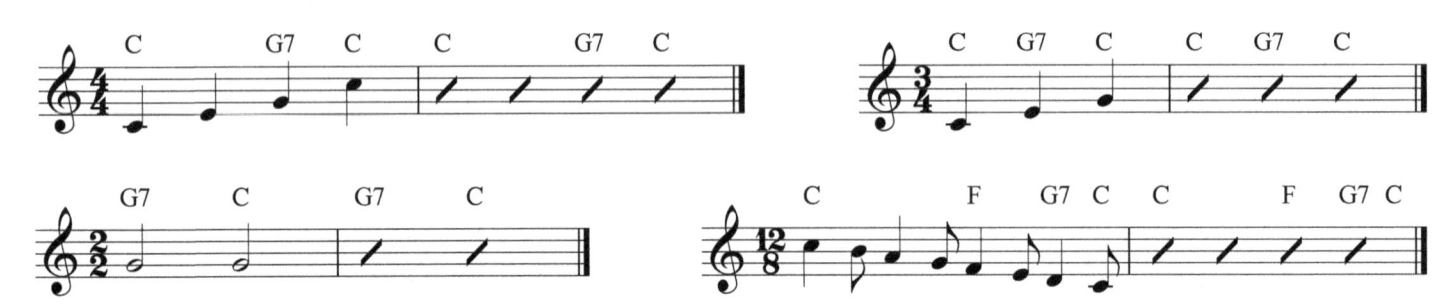

Fig. 3.1. Using Time Slashes

To illustrate how time slashes work, in the first bar of each meter in figure 3.1, a melody has chord symbols above it, corresponding to the precise beats where the chords change. In the second bar of each time signature, the same chords are written above time slashes instead. (A time slash chart would only use slashes.) Notice:

- The number of slashes in a measure equal the *bottom* value of the time signature (or major pulse divisions, such as in 12/8 or 6/8).

- The slashes are evenly spaced between the second and fourth line of the system, as well as horizontally

- In the final measure of figure 3.1, it is difficult to tell when to play the last C chord. This is because there are two chords over one slash in this 12/8 example. Here, it is better to indicate where the chords change using rhythm notation, illustrated in figure 3.2.

Fig. 3.2. Time Slashes and Rhythm Notation

RHYTHMIC SUBDIVISIONS

Regardless of style or genre, the groove can be identified one level deeper than the meter, by specifying the *rhythmic subdivision*. It is extremely helpful for the rhythm section players to have the subdivision articulated in the music, and by the band leader, to help organize the groove between players. A subdivision is the simple math of the groove, the common denominator. For the singer, understanding rhythm in this language will enhance his or her style and phrasing significantly, as well as help to establish a good rapport with the band.

Contemporary styles can be categorized by one of five basic rhythmic subdivisions, or *feels*: straight eighths, swing eighths, straight sixteenths, swing sixteenths, and a triplet feel (12/8 or 6/8 meters), shown in figure 3.3). The primary beat, or pulse, is the strongest rhythm, to which we clap hands, snap fingers, bob heads, tap, or dance. This is also called the count, time, or the downbeat. The note value of the primary beat is indicated by the time signature, or meter. A subdivision divides that primary beat into smaller values, which are played within the rhythmic patterns of a groove.

Beat subdivisions with style examples:

- Straight eighths (even): pop/rock, r&b, country, bossa

- Swing eighths (based on triplet): jazz, shuffle, country swing, blues, reggae

- Straight sixteenths (even): r&b, funk, fusion, samba, house, disco

- Swing sixteenths (based on triplet): hip-hop, swing, reggae

- 12/8 or 6/8 triplet feel: rock, blues, r&b, gospel, Afro-Cuban

1. Straight Eighths

2. Swing Eighths

(Swing grooves are written as normal eighth notes)

3. Straight Sixteenths

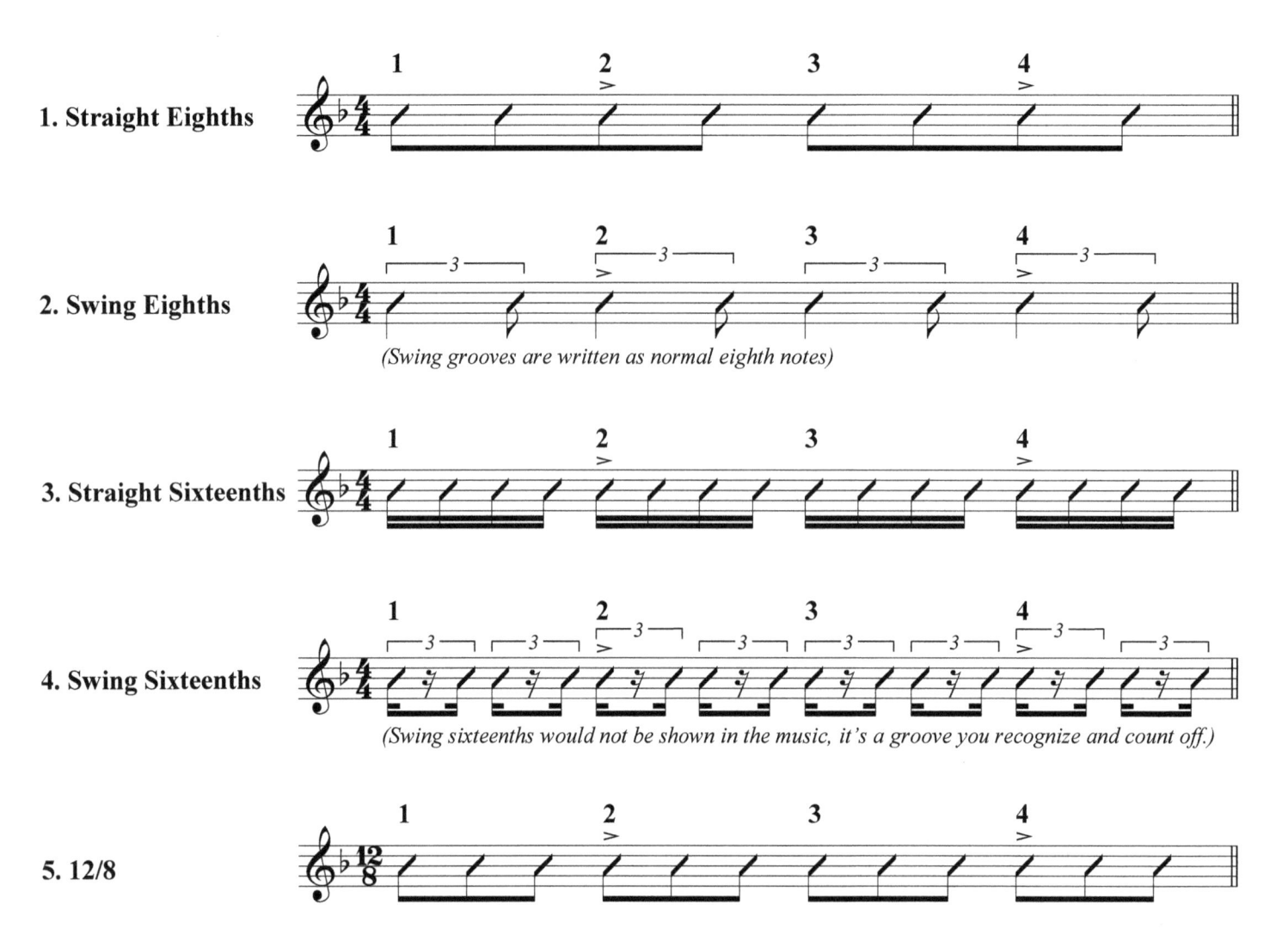

4. Swing Sixteenths

(Swing sixteenths would not be shown in the music, it's a groove you recognize and count off.)

5. 12/8

Fig. 3.3. The Five Subdivisions

> **CLASSIC SONGS IN EACH SUBDIVISION**
>
> **Straight eighths:**
> - "Old Time Rock 'n' Roll" (rock) by Bob Seger
> - "Every Breath You Take" (rock) by the Police
> - "Proud Mary" (rock) by Creedence Clearwater Revival
> - "How Will I Know" (pop) sung by Whitney Houston
>
> **Swing eighths:**
> - "Walkin' After Midnight" (country) sung by Patsy Cline
> - "How Sweet It Is" (pop/r&b/Motown) sung by both Marvin Gaye and James Taylor
> - "Don't Get Around Much Anymore" (jazz) sung by many artists, including Ella Fitzgerald
> - "Some Kind of Wonderful" (medium rock shuffle) sung by Grand Funk Railroad
> - "Is This Love" (reggae) by Bob Marley
>
> **Straight sixteenths:**
> - "Rhythm Is Gonna Get Ya" (Latin pop) by Gloria Estefan
> - "Through the Fire" (r&b) sung by Chaka Khan
> - "You're Still the One" (country ballad) by Shania Twain
> - "I Would Die 4 U" (pop/rock) by Prince
> - "Gotta Be Starting Something" (pop) by Michael Jackson
>
> **Swing sixteenths:**
> - "Rosanna" (rock) by Toto
> - "Have a Heart" (reggae/blues) by Bonnie Raitt
> - "On and On" (r&b) by Erika Badu
> - "What's Goin On" (r&b/soul) by Marvin Gaye
>
> **12/8:**
> - "God Bless the Child" (jazz/rock) sung by Blood, Sweat and Tears
> - "Unchained Melody" (pop) sung by the Righteous Brothers
> - "Minute By Minute" (pop/rock) by the Doobie Brothers
> - "Vision of Love" (r&b), by Mariah Carey

WHAT IS SWING?

Swing is a style of jazz that originated in the 1930s. Beyond that, the term is used to identify a rhythmic subdivision and can be played in any style of music. This is my use of the term here.

Swing is a feel based on a triplet subdivision and is sometimes confused with a dotted eighth/sixteenth figure. Swing feel varies depending on the style and players. It is not a literal or precise triplet subdivision, but that is the best way to notate it. It feels like the gait of a cantering horse, with a longer first beat and shorter second one that takes you back to the first. Swing eighth notes are written as regular straight eighth notes with an indication to swing them.

Swing looks like regular eighth notes:

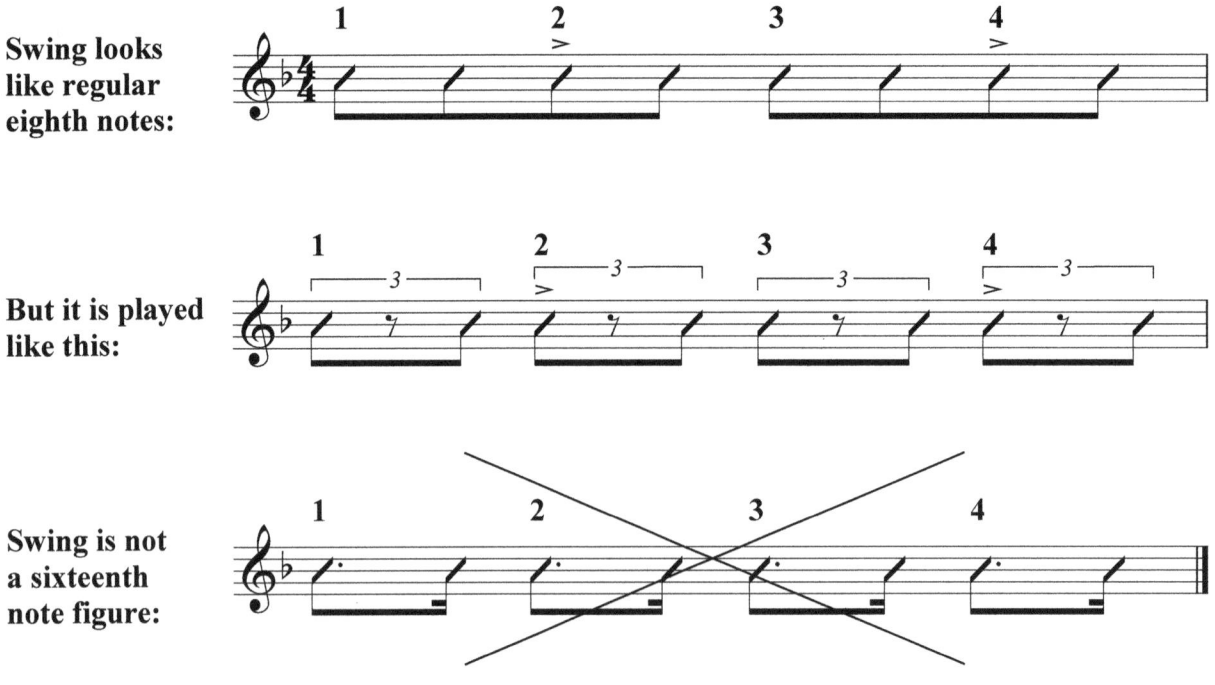

But it is played like this:

Swing is not a sixteenth note figure:

Fig. 3.4. Swing Eighth Notes

In published music, a swing feel is typically identified by this marking:

Fig. 3.5. Swing Feel Marking

In 4/4 time, swing sixteenths means two swings per beat, instead of one. You will hear it in styles such as reggae, hip-hop, and sometimes rock.

SCAT SYLLABLES, IMPROVISATION, AND RHYTHM: MAKING IT INTERESTING

There are books written entirely about scat singing and improvisation, such as Bob Stoloff's wonderful work appropriately titled *Scat*. Gabrielle Goodman's book is also excellent, *Vocal Improvisation: Techniques in Jazz, R&B, Gospel*. We will take but a brief look at scat here. If you wish to learn to scat sing, I recommend investing time into learning it. Most importantly, listen to the great scat singers.

Improvisation means making stuff up. To scat is to improvise, usually quickly, using nonsense syllables. Conceived during the early swing era by Ella Fitzgerald and Louis Armstrong, who improvised imitations of horn players, scat quickly caught on as an art form. Although there are many, many great scat singers, a short list of my personal favorites, besides Ella and Louis, are Jon Hendrix, Sarah Vaughan, Bobby McFerrin, Steven Tyler (Aerosmith), Betty Carter, Dizzy Gillespie, and Kurt Elling.

Because scat is made-up singing on any syllables you like, you can't do it "wrong." But you can be boring, or stylistically "off sides," especially if you keep repeating the same "doo bee doo bee" syllables over and over. So, be inventive. Sing a made up language. Vary the syllables, using at least three or four in a phrase. Scat is energized not only by the notes, but especially by rhythm. If you are singing in a jazz swing feel, for instance, sing swing eighths when you're in 4/4 time; that will get you off to a great start. But, also employ rests—use syncopation and space. It's something you have to listen to and practice often. Eventually, you get a feel for it. Then you get little riffs in your back pocket that you can call upon as you build your repertoire. Every scat singer has licks they use, like stringing beads when you construct a necklace. You can vary the order of the beads, and once you have a bunch, you can make up new ones.

THE ROLE OF THE RHYTHM SECTION

A typical rhythm section is generally an ensemble of three or four players: drum set, bass (upright/acoustic or electric bass guitar), piano, and guitar. Of course, the rhythm section will vary depending on several factors including musical style, artist preference, musical arrangements, even budget. Each instrument has a basic role in the ensemble. How the players expand beyond their roles, or step away from them, is part of the art of creating the arrangements.

Piano and guitar provide improvised harmonic support (called "comping," short for accompanying) by following the chord changes in the score, chart, or lead sheet. They may also support the melody and play solo lines. Comping instruments play rhythm parts or melodic fills in the style of the musical genre. When a piano is electric with a wide variety of instrumental sounds, it is called a "keyboard." A keyboard player plays both acoustic piano and electric keyboard. An electric guitar relies on an amplifier to be heard, with effects pedals to create a wide variety of tonal colors. An acoustic guitar needs to be amplified with a microphone (mic) or pickup mic attached to the body.

The **bass** is either electric or acoustic. In jazz styles, the bass improvises a moving line beneath the melody, connecting the chord changes harmonically, and leading the groove for the ensemble. *Walking* refers to improvised harmonic movement that steps through the chord changes, usually based on the quarter note pulse. In pop and rock styles, the bass often creates a steady repeating pattern (ostinato) that shifts according to the chord changes. Unlike jazz, bass lines are often specified and tend to be more repetitive, with the drummer holding down the groove. In r&b styles, the bass line is often syncopated—perhaps "funky"—and well-coordinated or "tight" with the drums. In all cases, the bass and drums listen closely to one another to lock into the groove.

A **drum set** is comprised of a bass drum (kick drum), snare drum, two or three tom-toms, and a variety of cymbals including hi-hat, ride, and crash. Once called a "trap set" (short for "contraption"), drum sets came into popularity in the early 20th century after the Ludwig brothers designed the first bass drum pedal. For the first time, one musician could use sticks and foot pedals to cover the rhythm of a small ensemble. Drummers create a steady pattern of beats and metric subdivisions that identify the stylistic time feel of the groove. They work closely with the bass player or, if no bass is present, with another instrument fulfilling the bass roll, such as the "left hand" of the pianist who holds down a bass line.

In pop styles, the *bass drum* typically accentuates primary beats plus additional subdivisions. It works in "conversation" with the snare drum in most contemporary styles. In jazz, it may be used freely for spontaneous accents. It is commonly played simultaneously with crash cymbal accents. *To sing a bass drum rhythm, use the vocal syllable "doon."*

The *snare drum* commonly plays the secondary, or consequent, beat (backbeat). It may play primary beats in styles such as hammer beat in rock, or in Motown, Latin, or jazz fusion grooves. In jazz styles, it is used more spontaneously. The snare can be played with brushes, mallets, sticks, or even hands; dramatic articulations include rolls, rim shots, and cross-sticking (rim taps). *Sing the vocal syllable "ka" to represent the snare.*

The *hi-hat* is made of two small cymbals positioned atop one another on a controller stand to the side of the bass drum. When operated by foot, the cymbals close to make a sharp, metallic "chik" sound. They can also be articulated with sticks to produce a closed "t" sound or half-open "tsh" sound, and a range of dramatic articulations are created on the "hat." In jazz, the hi-hat sometimes replaces the snare as the backbeat. *Sing the vocal syllables "tss," "tsh," and "chik" to represent the hi-hat.*

The *ride cymbal* is almost always played with a repeated pattern that indicates a particular stylistic beat subdivision. The *crash cymbal* is used to accent important beats and is usually played simultaneously with the kick drum. It often accents the downbeat of a measure, especially at the beginning or ending of a phrase. *Sing the vocal syllables "tsh" or "wsh" for either of these.*

The *toms* are used primarily for "fills" especially when starting or ending phrases. Sometimes, in styles such as rock, r&b, jungle, or Motown, the toms are played with a heavy pulse pattern. *Sing the vocal syllable "doh" to represent the toms.*

TIME FEEL VARIATIONS

2-beat feel, or two-feel: Although the music is written in 4/4 time, each measure has a sense of two, rather than four, beats. *Cut time*, sometimes written as ₵, is one type of two-feel using a 2/2 meter in which the value of each downbeat is a half note. There are two beats per measure even though the number of beats still adds up the same as in 4/4.

Double-time: The tempo is doubled. For example, the "original time" quarter-note goes by at the rate of what was an eighth note, and measures and chord changes occur twice as fast.

Double-time feel: A variation of the original time feel without changing the beats per measure (bpm). The harmonic rhythm stays the same, but the rhythm section creates the effect of sounding twice as fast by doubling up the subdivision, playing a 2-bar pattern twice as quickly through one measure. The backbeat shifts to four per measure. For example, if the drummer was accenting eighth-note beats on the hi-hat, now he or she is accenting sixteenth-note beats.

Half-time: The tempo is literally cut in half. For example, the "original time" quarter note becomes what was a half note, and measures and chord changes take twice as long to play.

Half-time feel: A variation of the original time feel without changing the bpm. The harmonic rhythm stays the same, but the rhythm section creates the effect of sounding half as fast by reducing the subdivision rate, stretching a 1-bar pattern over two measures of time. The backbeat shifts from two per measure (in 4/4) to one per measure. For example, if the drummer was accenting eighth-note beats on the hi-hat, now he or she is accenting quarter-note beats.

RHYTHMS TO REFERENCE WHEN IDENTIFYING A TUNE'S GROOVE

Find the beat by listening to the rhythm section's integrated groove. Listen below the melody, guitar, and piano parts. Tune out the singer, temporarily. Focus on the bass pattern and on the bass drum and snare patterns. Identify the strongest downbeats. When there is printed music available, compare these downbeats with the music notation to identify the meter and beat subdivision, and for accuracy.

Find the beat subdivisions by focusing on the hi-hat or ride cymbal patterns, bass patterns, and comping (keyboard/guitar) pattern(s). Sometimes, the subdivision is a combination of eighths and sixteenths, with one value more dominant.

The most useful aural cues in the rhythm section with which to identify the groove include the kick and snare drums, accents on the hi-hat, strong beats in the bass line, and strong rhythms played by the guitar or keyboard.

Track 53 takes you through several short rhythmic patterns with solo drum set to demonstrate basic examples of rhythms for different styles and subdivisions, including how to count them off. Figures 3.6 through 3.9 illustrate these examples.

TRACK 53

Straight Eighths Grooves

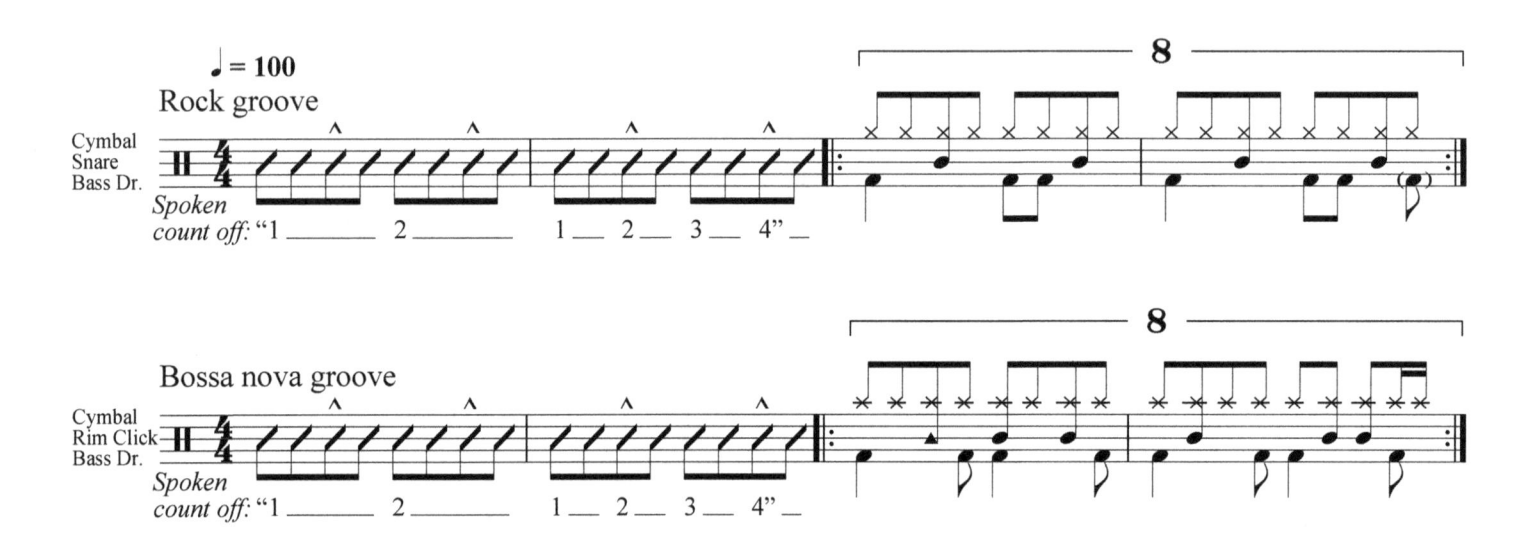

Fig. 3.6. Straight Eighths Grooves

Triplet Grooves

Fig. 3.7. Triplet Grooves

RHYTHMS TO REFERENCE WHEN IDENTIFYING A TUNE'S GROOVE

Swing Eighth Grooves

Jazz Swing example

improvise snare

Shuffle

Fig. 3.8. Swing Eighth Grooves

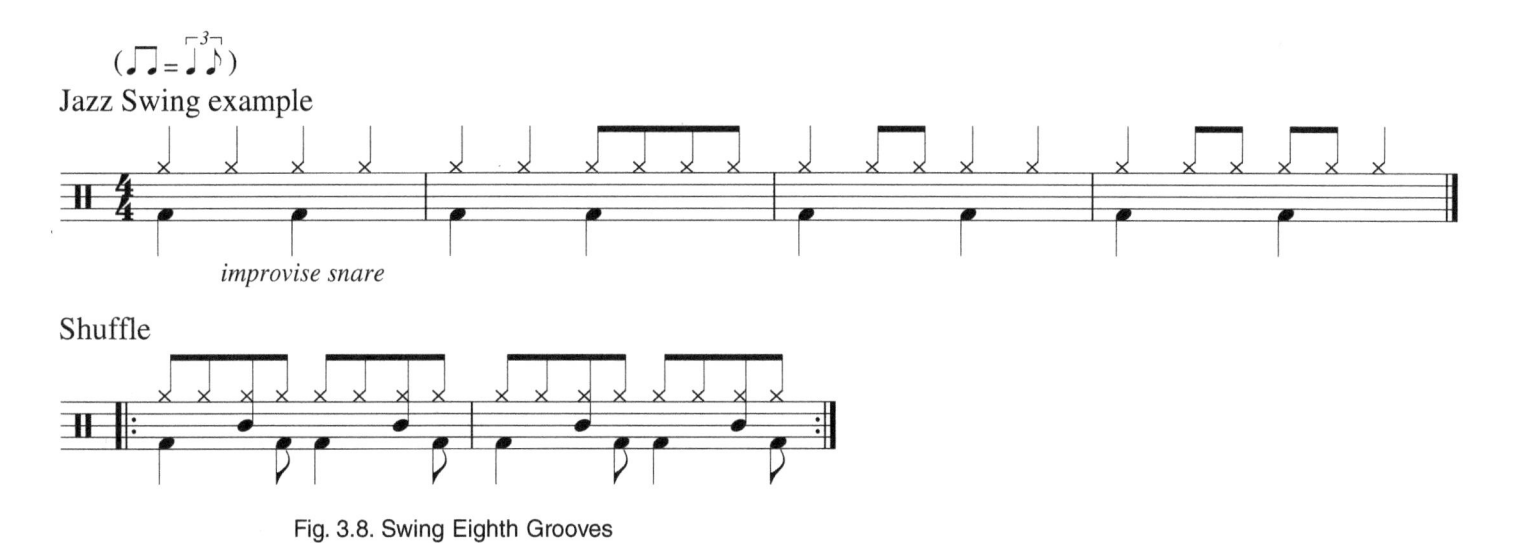

Straight Sixteenth Grooves

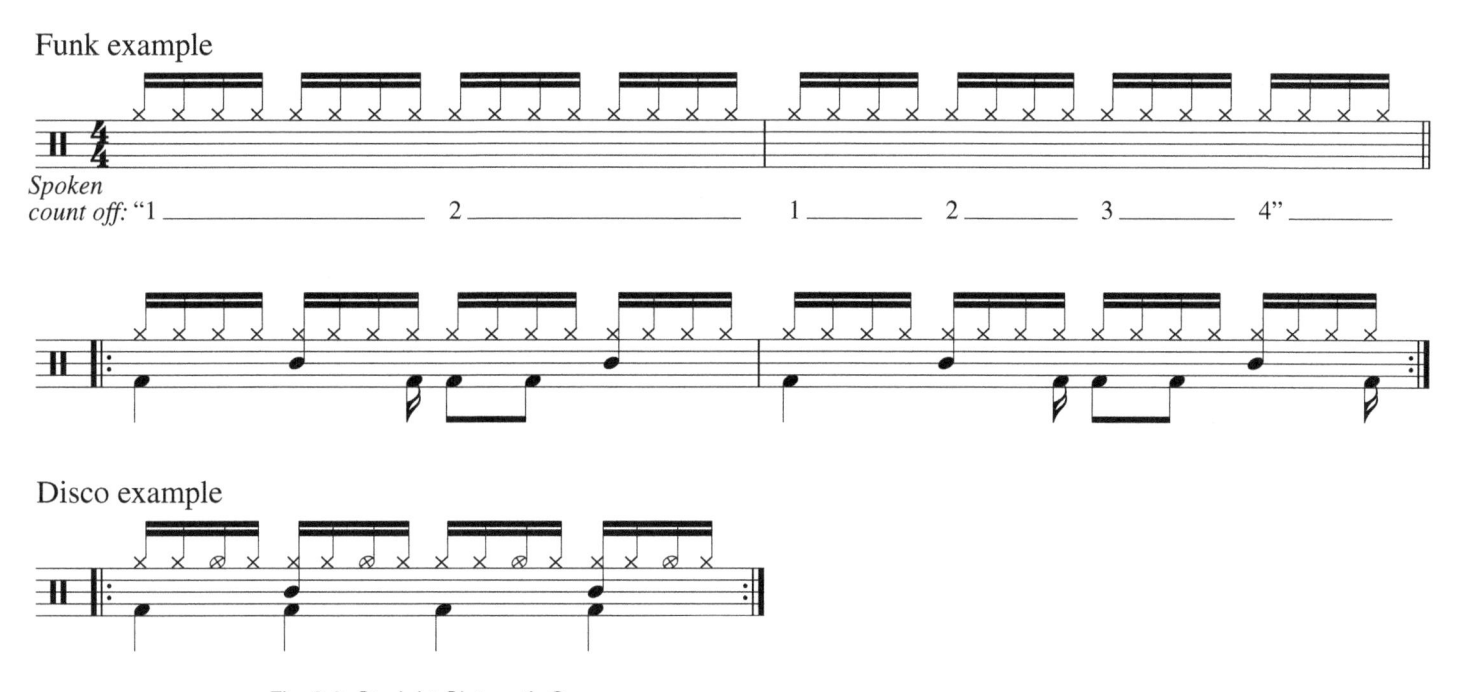

Funk example

Spoken count off: "1 _____ 2 _____ 1 ___ 2 ___ 3 ___ 4" ___

Disco example

Fig. 3.9. Straight Sixteenth Grooves

TRACKS 54–57

Tracks 54–56 take you through several rhythmic patterns with drum set and bass; track 57 adds piano. These also demonstrate basic style examples, including count offs. Figure 3.10 illustrates the swing sixteenths hip-hop pattern played by bass and drum set on track 54.

Swing Sixteenth Hip-Hop Groove:

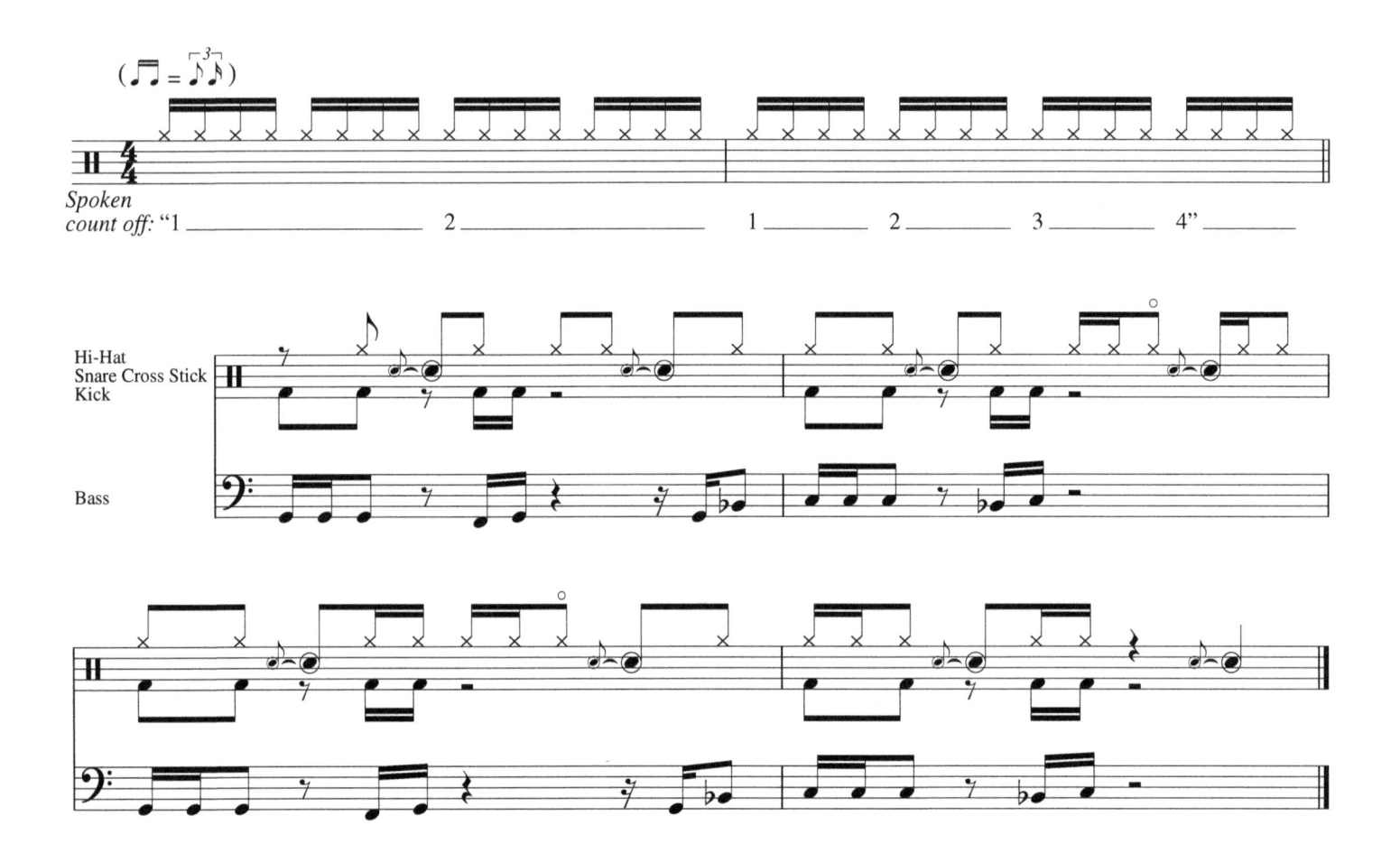

Fig. 3.10. Swing Sixteenths, Hip-Hop, Drums 'n' Bass

EMBODYING RHYTHM: SOUND IS MOVEMENT, IMPROV IS MOVEMENT, SINGING IS MOVEMENT

As we learned earlier in this chapter, when air molecules move our eardrums, our inner ears send a signal to the brain telling us we have heard a sound: Sound is movement. When you sing, your larynx moves. It has to; singing is movement. So, why are *you* holding still?

An important aspect of moving is embodying rhythm. If you are not letting yourself take in the rhythm of the songs you are singing, you are not fully present with them. Your body will tell you how to move, which makes the groove better for the whole band. It just takes practice to trust it.

My Arms Look Stupid!

That's what everyone thinks. Did the drawing of the dancer at the beginning of this chapter fill you with apprehension? You are not alone. Even students who are dancers can feel silly moving their arms while they sing, unless they've been given the green light by their teacher to combine dance movements with singing. Why? Because you feel vulnerable when you stand before people singing. No one wants to look stupid.

But think about it: If you are holding still, not even moving your arms, what else are you holding? Are you holding your breath, holding your abdomen in, holding tension in your shoulders, jaw, and tongue? All of this tension inhibits your ability to sing well. An athlete cannot perform at optimum levels while holding still. Even a gymnast, balanced atop a mere 4-inch wide beam in a handstand with legs in a perfect split, is not holding still. Muscles are contracted, toes are pointed tight, and arms are holding the body's weight. Yet if she twists from that position into a flip, in a state of tension, she will hurt herself. She has to be nimble and flexible, while also strong and balanced.

Singing is obviously way less dangerous than a handstand on a balance beam. (This author can't do that trick, either.) What acrobats and singers have in common is the need to be mentally focused, 100 percent engaged in the activity, well practiced, and *moving*.

So, how can you become comfortable moving and singing? How much should you move? That depends on your personality and your musical style. Traditionally, classical singers are taught to keep movements to a minimum, whereas rock singers move all over the stage. Most genres are somewhere in the middle. There is no right or wrong. It is about giving yourself permission to be you, to become comfortable revealing some degree of vulnerability in front of an audience. That is what is compelling. If you are outgoing by nature, you will probably move more than someone who is more reserved. Either way is all right.

Remember, audiences can't read your mind. Even when you feel you are revealing your innermost self from the stage, no one really knows if it's true. You could be playing a character. More importantly, people in the audience are looking to compare what you are singing about with themselves, finding how they relate to the songs. They are less interested in analyzing what your life is like. Audiences want to enjoy the show. They want you to be great. Think about yourself in the audience. When you really love an artist, aren't you grateful to be there? You forgive a little awkwardness; you might even appreciate it, recognizing that this talented artist is a human being, too. You may not even perceive awkwardness at all in this artist.

How do you get comfortable moving when you sing in front of people? Practice in front of a mirror. Video record yourself. Sing out a lot; it doesn't matter where. When my students watch themselves on video, one question I have them consider is, "How is what I am watching different from what I experienced while I was singing?" Usually what they see is less awkward than they'd thought. If you do make a funny face or move awkwardly, you'll see it on video and have helpful feedback for making adjustments. This process is a tool—not another reason to beat yourself up. As Victor Wooten puts it in *The Music Lesson*, when you have a headache, say a word of gratitude for it. Embrace it. It's trying to tell you something. If you can embrace your headache and find the usefulness in it, you can definitely appreciate the ability to watch yourself on video!

Pedestrian, Athletic, Dance, and Authentic Movements

Pedestrian movements are what we do every day—walking to the bus stop, tying your shoe, putting the dishes away. Athletic movements are how we change our bodies to do sports or exercise. Dance movements are coordinated, intentional forms of expression. It's useful to choose movements intentionally.

Authentic movement is a term for a kind of improvisational movement. After listening to your inner body/mind process, you move in response to it. Your body/mind will tell you what to do in that moment; you move in any way that is right for you in response to what you observe your body needs. Originally termed "movement in depth," authentic movement was started in the 1950s by Mary Starks Whitehouse, a student of the famed dancer/choreographer Martha Graham. Ms. Whitehouse was inspired by Carl Jung's work on the active imagination and combined it with free dance.

If you can find a studio in your area that offers authentic movement, you might want to give it a try. You don't need dance training to try it. When you become comfortable responding in movement to the expressive impulses of your body/mind process—rather than repressing them so as not to look stupid—you become freer. When you are freer, you are more at ease, and you have less tension. It also helps to put your audiences at ease with you, which audiences relish.

Moving as One with the Phrase

As you become more comfortable moving while you sing, what other ways can you explore moving? Think about it: when you sing a lyric, you are stretching carefully selected words into patterns (melody) that are quite different from how you would speak them. Yet, it doesn't seem weird to do this. Likewise, when you move your body while you sing, think about the phrasing *embodied* in the movements. If it takes four full measures to sing, "Summertime and the living is easy," rather than the two seconds it takes to say those words, you can let your gesture take more time, too. The gesture is also a phrase. Try holding out an arm as if you are seeing a vast landscape before you. Can you visualize a movie of the song playing back over the heads of the audience, describing the lyric? Can you imagine the character of the song? What are you describing? Let your body embrace the meaning of the song, and express it, too.

CHAPTER 4

Performing

*Since love prevails in heaven and earth
How can I keep from singing?*

—From the early Quaker song,
  "My Life Flows on in Endless Song"

"THANK YOU," SHE SAID, WAKING UP A YOUNG PERFORMER

When I was starting out as a singer/songwriter in New York City, I worked to earn extra money in the subway and on the streets with my guitar, portable amplifier, and microphone. I learned my physical and vocal strengths and limitations during those days of busking. I learned which songs worked and which songs didn't. The subway was safe. If people didn't like my music, they would pass by, and in a few moments, a new trainload of folks would arrive. If they stayed to listen, I knew I was onto something. This was paid performing with no risk of failure.

One day, I noticed a thin, drawn woman who had joined the commuters who had formed a wide circle around me. She carried a large shoulder bag that seemed as large as her entire side, and it left her unbalanced as she stood there listening to me sing in the subway station. She had a soft smile beneath her dark, close-cropped hair. I noticed her when she cocked her head, as I began to sing the spiritual "Amazing Grace." I was surprised when I looked her way again to see tears sliding down her cheeks.

"THANK YOU," SHE SAID, WAKING UP A YOUNG PERFORMER

Trains on the nearby tracks roared and screeched in and out in typical New York City fashion as passengers walked by steadily in every direction. I hoped my songs would be engaging. Most days, people would stop to listen on their way home from work or school. Tired commuters leaned against the metal bars of the subway fences; others just dropped their briefcases and stood there, watching. Sometimes my subway audience would stick around for an hour, even two—which always astounded me, especially since, by that point, I was definitely repeating songs. Occasionally, a group of girls would pass by in their school uniforms, podding like dolphins. They found it amusing to squeal imitations of my soprano notes and giggle as they walked off. I did my best to be entertaining in those days, grateful as coins and dollar bills were tossed into the guitar case I had laid open in front of me. I was also grateful for those who stayed.

That day, the woman stood in the station with me for a long time, appearing content and patient as I moved into new songs. Eventually she walked over to me, and with a deep smile that creased her young eyes she said, "I want to thank you." She hesitated, then continued, "I have cancer. I am dying. Listening to you has made me feel much better...you have made it easier." She placed her hand on my arm, held it for a moment, smiled as she looked deeply into my astonished gaze, dropped a dollar into my guitar case, turned, and slowly walked away. I never saw her again.

After that day, I recited those words in my mind over and over again like a mantra. "I am dying of cancer. You have made me feel so much better. Thank you."

If she had given me a thousand dollars it wouldn't have been a better gift than her words. Of course, as I sang, I had no idea what she was experiencing while we all stood there on that subway platform. I was just singing. And then, even as I grieved for her, I was amazed and inspired by her composure, her grace, and her courage.

I wonder how long she lived after we met in those brief moments. I hope and pray that she didn't suffer. I wonder if she could possibly have known how profoundly *she* moved *me*. Her unexpected few words transformed my self-awareness as a musician. Meeting her in those few seconds brought forth from me a deep desire to touch people with music. It showed me how powerful music can be to nurture and share love with strangers through the songs we sing.

I imagine the woman must have touched others, too, with her graciousness at the threshold of death. Her kindness in sharing her appreciation of my singing helped me embark upon a musical journey that embraces compassion, spirit, and an open heart. I am forever grateful to her.

The story's coda: My performing has evolved over the years. I have become focused on making every song a chance to communicate, a chance to give and receive the gift of music in community. Just as in love, if we seek our contentment in the arms of another, we are shortchanging ourselves. When we perform mainly from a desire to *receive*, be it fame or money or love or accolades, our music becomes shallow. When we sing for others out of a desire to be helpful, healing, and optimistic in the old cliché, to contribute something positive to the world we share we are happier, and the audience receives a beautiful gift from us. This is wellness, on stage.

WHAT IS YOUR INTENTION?

Do you know why you want to perform? Many musicians say they *have* to do music. It's a vital part of them, and playing music makes them happy. Or, not playing music makes them unhappy. Many also like the feeling of a job well done. They like practicing and rehearsing and studying, and the thrill of having it all come together on stage. Many need, simply, to create. To write songs. To come up with innovative grooves. To sing. Others will admit that it's an opportunity to be seen, maybe even to get a date. ☺ And of course, we all need to make a living.

These reasons are valid, but there is more. Music is communication. It moves us. It creates a feeling of community through shared experience. When we focus solely on intentions to benefit ourselves, we are not as strong on stage as when we consider the audience. Focusing on ourselves usually results in more performance anxiety, too. Veteran performers know that they need to learn their audiences. They are clear about their intention in each and every concert, even if it's "just a gig."

Our intention can be anything we choose it to be. A rock band might have the intention to aggravate people, express frustration and rage, or just party. A jazz musician might be focused on exploring the possibilities contained within a series of modes and challenging how far his or her instrumental skill can go. A singer/songwriter might be focused on telling stories that are personal yet global, in an intimate setting that also feels universal. The members of a choir might strive to join together as one unified voice to express their humanity in their feelings and beliefs through the unique assemblage of their voices. A classical musician might be focused on a combination of technical skill and sublime ecstasy that comes from being lost in the moment of expression. The *what* is not as important as the *why*. (In his interview in part III, Allaudin Mathieu discusses this point with great insight.)

For me, after that subway performance, I decided to let a positive intention be my guide, rather than my ego. At first, it was difficult to *admit* that my ego was bossing me through my career, because I didn't want to be *that* kind of artist. It was even more difficult to understand how to find the right balance between focusing enough on myself on stage and also being selfless with the audience.

I realized that I want to make people happy with music. It has become a calling. This requires a lot of practice, for the ego is a dominant, controlling part of every human being. Each year, I chip away at it a little more, and as a result, my joy in singing has increased manifoldly, and anxiety on stage has disappeared. When the ego's need to be in control lessens, making room for the whole person that we are, that is when the *real* fun begins.

NINE STEPS TO CREATING EXTRAORDINARY PERFORMANCES

1. **Learn what makes you special.** How are you unique? Is it your vocal quality? Your phrasing? Your energy? Your songwriting? A combination of styles? Your dance moves? Your guitar playing? Your band? Your affect on people? This is step number 1, because it is essential.

2. **Learn your audience.** What does the audience experience at your live musical performances? What are you offering them? What is the give and take? What other artists' concerts does your audience attend? What is your market?

3. **Establish a goal—your intention—of offering your audience a profound experience.** Decide to allow the extraordinary to happen, then *let go*. This improves the likelihood that it will. On the flip side, when you expect average results or problems, that is likely what you'll get. It's a self-fulfilling prophecy.

4. **Visualize.** Picture yourself giving a fantastic concert. Imagine you are there, now. Step into those shoes. What feeling do you get when you know you are giving your very best? How do you *want* to feel then? What is your best concert like? What does the lighting look like? What does the concert sound like? Does it earn you money? Who is there? Who is in your band? Do you feel energized afterwards, pumped, proud? If you can't imagine feeling good about it, what do you need to shift to get that result?

5. **Shape each concert.** Structure your performance to get the result you just visualized. Your audience also wants to experience something special. They are hoping upon hope that this night will stand out for them. How can you shape your concert to give them a fantastic experience? (Patti Austin talks about how she does this in part III.)

6. **Stay focused.** On stage, focus on the meaning of the songs. What do they say? Focus your concentration on communicating with your audience instead of on yourself. Focus on communicating with your band. *Focus on this moment. It is all that matters right now. All your other concerns, joys, and problems will still be there when you step off stage.*

7. **Be open to the unexpected.** Flow with the moment. Overall, have fun; love what you do. Share that love with your band on stage. Share that love and gratitude with the audience. There will be an energy exchange between performer and audience, which circles round and round again to impact your performance. When you are open to it, this energy exchange is where the potential for profound experience, healing, and transformation lies.

8. **Keep yourself in good health mentally, physically, and spiritually**. Keep your chops up. Practice, but don't overdo it. Explore your creativity, trusting that you are exactly where you need to be. Practice asking your internal judges to sit down and smile with you if you goof up. Exercise. Eat right. Drink and smoke less or not at all.

9. **Then, let it all go.** Your concert was just one moment. There will be other concerts, other opportunities. What if there were mistakes? Mistakes happen. That bad note, that band goof, will be forgotten, especially if you flow with the whole experience gracefully. You can learn from it for next time.

WHAT DO EXTRAORDINARY PERFORMERS HAVE IN COMMON?

We don't teach musicians enough about performing. Actors get it. Dancers get it. Musical training focuses on technical mastery, on playing or singing correctly, on style. While technique is extremely important, at the end of the day, it is not what *moves* audiences. When someone is amazing at expressing her humanity in concert yet isn't the world's best singer, she can still enthrall her audience. If she *is* the world's best singer technically but doesn't share her heart, we may lose interest. The combination of heart and technique moves audiences.

In our conversation in part III, Patti Austin tells the story of seeing Judy Garland live, perhaps one of the greatest entertainers of the 20th century. Late in her career, Judy Garland's voice was shot from living a self-destructive life. But, ever the actress, she could still deliver a performance that got audiences on their feet cheering for her after just two songs. She had heart. She showed her vulnerability. She laughed and told funny stories. She made each performance seem spontaneous and fresh, even though she worked the same material every time.

When we are at our best in concert, we operate out of a wholeness in which no single aspect of us is overly dominant. The mind is alert and is not sabotaging us with fear-based thoughts. Our emotions are well rounded and grounded. Our bodies are rested, warmed up. Our energy is good. Our spirits embrace the performance because we have chosen to be there.

In yoga philosophy, a person has five levels of being that operate together, known as the *five sheaths*, represented by concentric circles surrounding the core of Self. The most evolved level is the innermost one around the Self, the bliss sheath. The next level is the intellect and intuition. The third level is the mind. The fourth level contains energy and breath. The outermost level is the body.

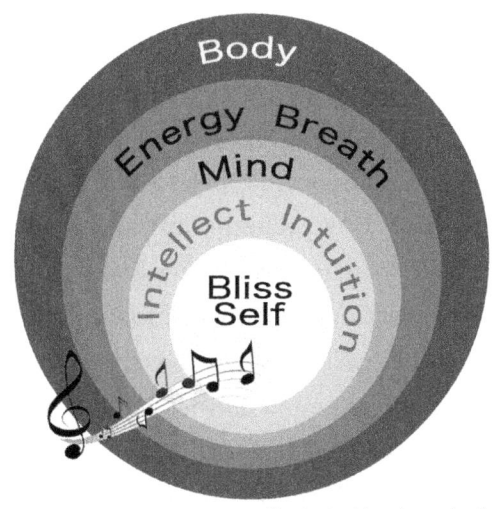

Illustrated by Jeannie Gagné

4.1. Five Sheaths

Music runs through all five sheaths like a river, connecting them. The more you tap into your deepest source of music, the more your true Self can emerge on that river of music. As it emerges, your creativity is freer to be expressed, and you create from that deep place of Real, rather than from a place of Fear. That creativity is genuine and can be very powerful.

The following list names a few key qualities that strong performers have in common. Can you think of more?

Heart	The performer shows emotional connection to the music.
Story telling	Lyrics are important to the performer, and it shows.
Energy	The performer is fully present, awake, and engaged.
Skill	Technical excellence is evident.
Originality	The performer stands out by revealing his or her genuine personality and artistry.
Creativity	Stretching boundaries, the performer puts different elements together in a new way.
Look	The physical presentation (attire, facial expressions, set design) is in alignment with the music.
Connection	The performer makes eye contact with the audience, uses story telling, acknowledges the audience, and reaches out to them often.

Commitment   The performer clearly wants to be there on stage and is giving his or her best.

Heart comes from our emotional realm. It is that intangible something that gives audiences gooseflesh. Heart touches your insides. You can see heart in body language, in facial expressions, in the way the singer moves with the music. When heart is active, the physical and emotional selves are working together. You can *feel* the singer's honesty. The singer is sharing a piece of his or her soul.

Sometimes, the singer is unaware of being disconnected from expression, or is feeling the emotion but cannot (or is afraid to) release it fully. Fancy licks and tricks hide the true Self. Moving an audience happens when you've moved *yourself* first, and it won't happen every time. When your very cells seem to resonate, as joy and love and gratitude rise up from your toes and travel all along your skin and hair, when you perspire and tingle, then you know you have found it. You may even feel connection to a source of divine love. Amazing performances are the result of coordination and openness, when all the elements in yourself and in your performance are harmonious in that suspended, exquisite moment. Be careful, though. If you let yourself be seduced by this experience, you may lose it. It is very often unselfconscious. You may not even realize you went there, until you stop.

> **5REALMS FOR ARTISTS:**
> **AN INVESTIGATIVE AWARENESS PRACTICE**
> Performance poet Caroline Harvey frames the yoga five sheaths or realms of awareness for performing:
> - physical
> - emotional
> - mental
> - subtle energy
> - spiritual or inner wisdom
>
> Harvey's work *5Realms for Artists: An investigative Awareness Practice* teaches the performer how to be more vulnerable and thus genuinely creative, as well as balanced in health and wholeness. See more about the 5Realms in appendix D.

Authenticity and a Healthy Ego

Authenticity is the quality or state of being true and trustworthy, genuine, and original. When the singer is original and genuine in performance, he lets his true Self step forward. He trusts his instincts. He lets go of the grip of his self-consciousness as much as possible, permitting a window into the deeper aspects of his being to shine true into the song. It can be frightening. It takes practice. It is also a tremendous gift to be free enough to go there.

But what if you feel like a fake? What if your thoughts say, "Do this, don't do that. Hey, you look stupid moving like that! What was *that?!* You don't know what you're doing! You sound *awful.*" That is your internal critic, your Judge talking. It is part of your self-consciousness. Your self-consciousness is the endless stream of thoughts you have all the time, every waking moment. It is agreeing or disagreeing with what you're reading right now. It's the bus driver, the ego-self with a small "s." When it speaks from a place of fear, you cannot release yourself into the moment. The fear feeds on itself and spins you up. Sometimes, fear is a good thing; it keeps us out of harm's way. But on stage, where is the danger? The loving Self with a capital "S"—our higher self—lets us see beyond ourselves to enable a meaningful experience making and receiving music.

When a performer is singing from authenticity, she digs deep into true emotions and offers them as a gift to the audience within the artistic vehicle of the song. The song vehicle is also structured. Unlike other instrumentalists, the singer has lyrics. These are crafted to reach people, organized in short phrases. The song is a short story; it has boundaries. The "performance" is only a moment in a singer's life. In that moment, she seeks to share hopes and dreams and fun and fears and challenges and longings and love, depending upon the meaning of the song or the setting of the performance. Well-practiced technique flows without strain, creating the opening to be free in creativity. The performer is comfortable being genuine on stage, presenting an element of her personality and enthrallment with the music to the audience. This takes practice, and trust.

You may be thinking, "I don't want people to see that deeply into me. Performing is a form of acting anyway; it is not real," and that is true, too. Yes, we create onstage personas. In fact, some well-known artists use this as a device to keep their private lives separate from the public persona we have come to love. But many artists focus too heavily on their images and craft, and that makes them come off as artificial. A riveting performance happens when you are sharing—or acting—a piece of your own deeply emotional reality.

We need to be careful not to create authenticity artificially. That seems like a contradiction, doesn't it? The truth is, our self-concept is always connected to the culture we come from. It is unavoidable. Our culture is embedded in our self-definition, whether we are aware of it or not. In the United States, our culture promises freedom and autonomy. It promises that we can recreate ourselves in the ideal image we desire. It promises independence from the ordinary by this act. This, too, is an illusion.

For example, a rock star symbolizes an autonomous, perhaps rebellious, powerful, and sexual leader. That is part of his appeal. He stands apart from any group except the musical "tribe" he leads through his concerts, records, videos, and merchandise. Yet, the irony is, if the rock star does not sell millions of records, he is no star. Therefore, he is codependent with the mass culture he is supposedly apart from. So, even in this case, his authenticity is but a portion of the truth.

The danger lies in believing your own hype. Your "S" Self trusts the music inside you and doesn't need exaggeration to know what is authentic to you. It doesn't need success to be whole. As important as they are for making a living, the marketing strategies we rely on—that promote artists into super human beings—do not identify the true Self.

Understanding Your Artistic and Energetic Presence

So often, we distrust our capacity to generate depth and connection through singing. Students tell me they love to *receive* this connection when seated in the audience, yet they are unsure of how to create it from the stage. Aware that our culture values showmanship—and fearing judgment or failure—performers focus on "How do I look?" "What do they think of my voice?" and "I hope I don't mess up!" without taking in the whole experience. When the focus is on the self (small s), what could be a beautiful reflexive activity becomes stiff, like acting when the focus is on remembering lines instead of *being* the character. We lose touch with the "zone." We think about making mistakes.

In his book *The Music Lesson*, bassist Victor Wooten describes how thinking about mistakes interferes with good playing. When he is playing at his best, music just flows through him. He does not think about the process. When he is playing well, he is not aware of being in the "zone," a place of perfect synchronicity between technique and musicality where you lose track of time and even your self-awareness. He also describes how when a player makes a mistake, it's easy to become self-conscious and to lose the flow. There is a cycle where the mistake causes frustration, and then the frustration causes a mistake. The problem? Poor technique. The remedy? When practicing, first concentrate on the technique. Then, don't think about technique so it can become automatic, concentrating instead on the music. Then, the two types of concentration will fuse together in balance with one another.[1]

The only thing holding you back is you. Remember, no one can read your mind. You are in control of how vulnerable you are, how authentic. You can't hide out on stage, anyway; audiences are very savvy to body language. You *can* become the character of the performer, like an alter ego. You *can* be so focused on the here and now that the other, irrelevant stuff in your mind is pushed to the background. The truth is, the audience is not competing with the performer, even if the performer fears judgment. Audiences are generally pretty forgiving.

---

[1] Wooten, V. *The Music Lesson*. New York, NY: Berkley Books, 2006.

What about you? If an artist sings beautifully but is a wee bit clumsy, do you really care? Probably not. On the other hand, an artist who *apologizes* in word or body language for being less than perfect makes you feel uncomfortable. You squirm in your seat. You wish they'd just get on with it. You admire courage, pluck; you admire someone who doesn't give up even if there is an obstacle. You are also put at ease by humor. When you are the one performing, if you are comfortable making a minor mistake—and mistakes will occur—then the audience is comfortable, too. They probably won't even notice it.

> **TIP: VIDEO RECORD YOURSELF**
> When you practice, video record yourself performing. Set up the mic stand, put on your outfit. Do a performance for the camera as if it were your audience. Then, wait a few days. Watch the video and compare what you see with what you *thought* you did at the time. Is there a difference?

The dynamism we need to develop in order to become confident, and even powerful, on stage is a complex mixture. Authenticity, commitment to one's vision, a strong enough ego to survive the unavoidable disappointments of the music business, and a heart open enough to be aware of others, are all essential for a performer to be extraordinary, regardless of the size of the stage.

It is normal to reflect on an experience while we're having it. The mind is extremely fast at analyzing and coming to conclusions. The trick is to keep that process quiet on our faces, or from interfering with our performing. Otherwise, we can create a kind of self-conscious loop between ourselves and our audiences. When the performer thinks too reflectively about what's happening on stage, the audience sees it and responds to it. The audience response then affects the performer, who becomes even more self-reflective or self-conscious. The loop continues. We get in our own way.

How can you avoid this loop? Work toward unconscious performing. Partly, it takes putting in enough musical practice. Partly, it takes placing trust in oneself. By being aware of all of our parts that are happening at once, movements of the body can be isolated from distracting thoughts. Emotions in the moment can be kept separate from personal issues at home. We can invite the Universe to travel through us in one big, harmonious experience. Like everything, this not only takes practice, but also time to develop.

Being Present; Learning about Yourself on Stage

> **PICTURE THIS: ON STAGE, PRESENT, IN THE MOMENT, AMONG FRIENDS**
>
> You are standing in front of an audience. The energy is palpable. All eyes face forward; all attention anticipates the music you are about to create. As you enter into the pulse of the first song, you feel the room, gauging the dynamics that come from the combined individuals who have chosen that moment to participate by listening together.
>
> Your choice of notes, your energy, your body movements, all come from reading the room. The energy in the room can be affected by the weather, by the time of day or night, by current events. The way you promoted the concert also affects the audience's expectations. What they expect affects how they arrive at the concert—how they are present in the room.
>
> Visualizing the mood you will be in during the different stages of the concert, and the way the spotlight feels on your face, and the shadows that fall upon the audience, creates a picture of the concert weeks before it occurs. Seeing the faces of the audience—those faces that are visible and the outlines of those that are not—brings the presence of strangers into the visualization long before the audience has settled into their seats. It makes them seem like friends. Imagining a joyous interplay of yourself and the other musicians on stage brings a positive expectation into the visualization, which includes the gift of encouragement and playfulness extended to everyone on stage. This is an invitation for all to explore their creativity—hopefully, to have a moment of shared bliss.

Practicing for the gig or concert should include expecting the result you want. Visualize the outcome you desire. What do you need to do to be ready for that outcome? Think about *all* the elements of a performance, including what you say to the audience, and how the songs weave together. How well do you know the lyrics, the chord changes, the length of the guitar solo? When you are prepared, you can visualize being pleased with your efforts and at peace with yourself for the work put in.

Practice what happens when you are distracted. Distractions from the music might include fear about playing and singing well simultaneously, or what the sound will be like through the PA (sound) system, or what shape the voice will be in. Practice being stable and confident in spite of distractions; it makes for a smoother concert.

However, if, while you practice, you expect problems, you are practicing problematic results. It may even lead you not to practice enough. You are subconsciously instilling in your performance the elements that make less than satisfactory results more likely. That's the self-fulfilling prophecy.

Imagine: The day of a concert or gig has arrived. You have a heightened state of awareness, with feelings that range from joy to nervousness, with increased body heat and extra energy. Your adrenaline is pumping. Your personal tempo is likely faster than normal. If your voice is tired or under the weather, doing gentle humming exercises throughout the day helps maintain breath support and a clean tone. Warming up throughout the day at a moderate volume keeps your voice warm and helps to maintain a full palate of vocal tones and colors. This gentler practice is best even if you will be belting some of the songs. Jittery nerves are soothed and slowed by listening to the breath, and by observing the conversation in your mind. See if you can find a trigger there that is causing the jitters. If your mind's conversation is not useful for the job ahead, you can thank it for sharing, and ask for it to step down, so you can focus on other useful topics.

> **PICTURE THIS: CONCERT READINESS**
>
> An hour or two before the concert, I drink plenty of water or maybe hot tea with lemon and honey, move around, and sing briefly to monitor my voice's flexibility.
>
> It is important to check in now with the other musicians to be sure that everyone is clear about the set that night and that everyone has everything they need. As we will be working as a team, each person should feel ready and comfortable when the concert begins. When my team feels acknowledged and appreciated by the leader (me), they enjoy playing together and can relax more on stage. Working together should be fun and rich and inspiring. Everyone wants to do their best; no one wants to be embarrassed by playing in a group that isn't happening. Being the leader is like hosting a party: the players are my guests, and the music is the gourmet meal. I tell myself: this is going to be great.
>
> Stepping out onto the stage, preparations are completed. The things that can create nerves—remembering lyrics and the set list, worrying about appearance, and hoping there is a good audience—are either taken care of, or it's too late anyway. Worry is useless now.
>
> I believe that the people who have come that night are the perfect audience in that moment in space and time. It is as it is supposed to be.

Before the very first note is sung, the performer imagines what will happen to complete the shaping of the concert. This could mean a well-practiced set or creating an environment that invites playful improvisation and transformation.

Every audience is different. The same show on two consecutive nights may be quite different from one another. If the audience is disappointingly small or not engaged, look for the jewels that this audience can share with you to alleviate your disappointment and create a richer experience. If you connect with even one person in the audience, something meaningful has happened. The moment can be as joyous a connection as when the audience is full and energetic. Or, even if the audience is really not connecting with you, remember: this performance is a chance to make music. Nothing more, nothing less.

ARTIST STATEMENT

An artist statement is a useful tool for defining yourself as an artist and for presenting yourself professionally. Borrowed from the visual arts, an artist statement is a document that contains your vision, something about your background, and your education. It will likely change many times during your career. Post it on your artist website, on a CD jacket, in a blog, or within a press package.

By writing an artist statement, you are defining who you are professionally and where you are coming from. It is less about résumé bullet points to list career highlights, and more about the essence of who you are and what makes you tick. It is also different from a bio, which is more like a résumé with a story. An artist statement is an opportunity to put down in words what you are about artistically. It often mentions your creative process, such as describing a song you wrote or how you approach singing a song. It may describe how you view your work in the context of current developments in music. It may describe your aspirations and how you will contribute to the field of music. Or, maybe you're not sure. Can you visualize the future? When you do contribute, what might that look like?

Artist Statement: Jeannie Gagné

My music always originates out of singing. Even when I play piano or guitar, I hear the voice, the song, emanating from it, as if the spirit of it awakens to the resonance of the vibrating strings. Many cultures believe that the voice is the expression of the soul, and it certainly seems that way to me.

Singing is alive for me in a unique way unlike anything else I do. Singing brings a heightened spiritual connection, for me, to everything outside of myself, and that is pure joy.

When I sing, I often feel as if I become a conduit between the universal creative force that is in all of us, myself, and the audience. It's as if my body is just a container, the ego steps aside, the moment comes alive. Everything is heightened then—every dust mote sparkling in the light becomes visible, every piece of wood in the concert hall resonates. I awaken in a way that lets me lose hold of my body, to be 100 percent in the moment. It is effortless.

When I sing, I reach into my inner being to express the truth of the song in that moment. This is true whether the music is solid groove that makes you want to get up and yell and dance, or a sensitive ballad, or a complex jazz composition. I reach into the audience with my intuition to get a sense of where they are. If they are enjoying what we're doing, I keep with it. If I feel resistance, I listen. I feel the room. What can I shift to make the experience flow?

I seek to share a part of myself, representing the human existence, in every song I write or perform. If the audience has benefited from the music, then I have achieved my goal. Of course, I can't know how the music may reach people. So rather than direct an outcome, I direct my intention. My intention is to be joyous and loving, inspired, and real. Some songs are great grooves and make me want to dance. Some of the music is profoundly sad, some is about rocking out, some is funny, some comes from deep philosophical thought that I want to share in song.

Writing songs is also one of the activities I enjoy most. I lose track of time when I write. Each song is a narrative, or a moment in my life where I've learned something that touched me, or an expression of concern for another, or a rhythm that makes me want to move and celebrate being alive. Each piece of music is an opportunity to share life's small moments, to look for a new way of seeing them.

It has been said that the true artist makes something out of nothing. I disagree. I believe all the ingredients are always present to us, and as energy cannot be created nor destroyed, so too is art a reconstruction of what is already there. When it's good, the artist makes combinations of these elements that offer new perspectives. She gets us thinking, she helps us to stretch the imagination. She helps us to see ourselves more clearly. For me, I wish to present the human experience in an optimistic light. I don't aim to fight or argue in music. I aim to uplift, raise hope, motivate, find gratitude. To spread Love.

Love is the foundational element in all things and is the core of our truest essence. When I have written my last song and have sung my last note, I want to be remembered for elevating Love—for bringing people together through the music we share as one.

SUGGESTIONS FOR WRITING A SUCCESSFUL ARTIST STATEMENT

- Stay in narrative form, as if you are writing for a magazine.
- Think about who your audience is.
- Look for interesting phrases, describing what is unique about you. Take time to make the writing distinctive.
- Avoid using clichés and slang, and use good grammar and punctuation.
- Whether you write in the first or third person ("I" or "he/she"), be consistent.
- Remember that this will be viewed widely, especially when you post it on a website. You may even be quoted, so only say what you are comfortable hearing back.

EXPECTATIONS

Feeling pressure to be the best we can be is a normal part of studying music. The challenge lies in being patient if you are dissatisfied with the level you are currently at. It's not dissimilar from developing a new workout routine for losing weight or building up muscle tone. When you first start, you are enthusiastic, but as the days turn into weeks and you don't see significant results right away, you may give up or doubt your ability to achieve your goal. Music lessons are no different. Everything takes practice and time, and patience, and more practice.

For the vocalist, the subtle muscle movements in the larynx are so second nature that we expect to become better technicians rather quickly. But, as with any muscle group, vocal muscles need to be trained through repetition of successful movements in order to respond with a singing voice we like.

Victor Wooten puts studying music into perspective by comparing it with the seamless process of a child learning to speak. Surrounded by masters of the language—the adults around the child who are delighted with her slightest progress—this is a perfect learning environment.[2] Those of us who were similarly supported at home, absorbing a musical instrument through trial and error in the unselfconsciousness of childhood, are fortunate. Did you grow up in an environment abundant with music? Is it second nature to you? Or, do you distrust the music you know you have inside you because it wasn't reinforced early on?

For students to succeed in music college, they must hold onto their passion for music while managing the school's required courses, expectations, and opinions. Teachers may grow impatient because what is obvious to them is perhaps not coming as easily to a student, or because the student appears not to be applying himself or herself. That can demoralize a student, who is probably there because he or she is *called* to study music. The student's moments of inspiration, hopefully, appear in class, alongside a trust in his or her own ability to be successful in the entrepreneurial and challenging business of music, in spite of the teacher's judgments. Some teachers say, "If you can't stand the heat, get out of the kitchen." That is a *lot* of pressure to manage.

Whether in or out of school, we singers expect a lot from ourselves. Our expectations impact our thoughts, which affect our subtle muscle responses, which, in turn, affect how we sing. It is important that our expectations don't get the better of us. Thinking "I don't think I sound good" while you're singing, makes it pretty hard to sound good. That's because the thought interrupts the complex nerve signals between our brains and muscles of the voice, causing the muscles to respond by tightening as if there is danger present. There is a rich array of "self-improvement" books on the market teaching us how to think positively, to visualize the outcome you want to see rather than living in the fear of a different outcome. Changing your thought patterns is absolutely possible. It just takes practice.

---

[2] Victor Wooten, *The Music Lesson*

Cultural Goals and Influences

Each of us comes from somewhere. We grew up speaking at least one language, living in a neighborhood, perhaps with brothers, sisters, mother, father, maybe an extended family. Our family had a style that influenced us. Was it loud? Soft-spoken? Argumentative? Loving? Full of laughter and play? Hard-working? Expecting disappointment or success? We cannot help but be influenced by our backgrounds, likes and dislikes, school, prejudices, families, friends, even the framework of the language we speak.

When we are very young, we learn the music we hear around us. We may embrace it or reject it; we may want to sing music we hear outside of our environment. That is harder because, before you can sing anything, you have to hear it in your head.

What kind of music do you want to sing? Do you love the sound of a strong, scratchy rock vocal? Or, do you prefer the sweet, melodious stylings of a jazz singer? Is your voice naturally low or high? Does your family like your music? What artist most inspired you during your formative years? Is money a factor in your musical choices? These are important questions only you can answer for yourself.

When you step before a microphone with full awareness of your cultural heritage, you know who you are. You have choices now about the influences you choose to embrace. When you understand your influences, you understand how you are relating to a lyric. When you personalize a lyric, you bring it alive for the audience.

Managing Performance Anxiety

If you think about it, performing is weird. After all, standing up in front of a bunch of strangers (or worse, your family) while they all stare at you, hoping for something spectacular to come out of your mouth, is weird. But, it's also exciting and stimulating. It's an opportunity to work hard on skills and have it all come together for one brief, focused, glorious moment.

Consider this: Those in your audience who are experiencing the singing along with you, who are deeply engaged with what you are doing, are in a way, performing with you. It is real for them. They may be getting the same natural high as you. If you are obviously nervous, they will feel nervous with you. No fun. You get the picture.

Here's a group exercise to practice getting comfortable just being you. It can feel really awkward at first! Hopefully, exhilarating, too. The more you practice being seen and being heard, the easier it gets.

ACTIVITY 4.1. BEING SEEN, IN THREE PARTS

This exercise is about doing nothing. It requires only you and a small group of people.

Calling upon the trilogies of *body-mind-spirit* and *yourself-earth-universe*, this exercise is in three parts.

First, define the stage space together. The group will sit facing it. Define the side you will each enter from, the stage area where you will face the audience, and the side you will exit from.

1. Standing in the area you enter from, face the space. Wait. Breathe.

2. Enter the space, standing in front of a group. Do nothing. Plan to be there for about a minute. Keep your eyes open, look around, or be in the moment without trying to do anything, without speaking. Try not to fidget. Just be present. Feel what it is like to be seen, without filling the space with a song or laughter or the need to speak. See if you can stand fairly still. Listen to your inner voice. Do you need to fill the space? Or are you comfortable standing still? What is it like having everyone's eyes focused on you?

   In performance, space is important. Space is a musical rest, permitting form. Remember the phrase, "Less is more." If we are comfortable doing nothing, we can relax into the music without having to fill up every moment. We can use the beauty of space.

   Continue just standing there, observing how you feel. Do you feel naked, vulnerable? In a sense you are. But that is okay.

   See if you are aware of the energy that comes from you and the energy you receive, even doing nothing. Notice the first strong emotion that comes up. What do you get from the people in the room? Scan the faces, one by one. Can you feel their individual energies? Can you sense the vibe around each person?

3. Leave the space. Turn around in the area you have defined as the exit, and face the space. Take a moment of stillness before stopping the exercise. Breathe.

Do you want to draw in your audience and put them at ease? Do you want to put yourself at ease? Do you want to challenge your audience and make them uncomfortable? There is no right or wrong. Is your music a profound spiritual experience, or is it about having fun? You decide. Be sure that whatever choice you make, you are fully present in it. If it becomes an escape from yourself, the audience will know.

You are sharing your most intimate gifts in performance. You are in charge of what you share. No one knows what is inside your head. We can see a lot in your body language, but there is much we cannot know. It is up to you to share, or not.

When you see other performers live, how much of themselves do they share with you? Are you eager to see them again in concert? *Is your own performance compelling?* If you were a member of your own audience, would you want to see yourself again?

SONG CHOICES

Vocal and Emotional Range

Words, when spoken out loud for the sake of performance, are music. They have rhythm, pitch, timbre, and volume. Those are properties of music, and music has the ability to find us and move us and lift us up in ways that literal meaning cannot.

—Anon

The songs you select say a lot about you. When you are a contemporary singer, unless you are singing "for hire," you are free to choose your songs. What is the occasion? Is it a party, a concert, or an open mic? What kind of music is usually played at that venue? What is your accompaniment going to be? Are you accompanying yourself? Does your song work with just a guitar or keyboard? Or, do you need a drum set and bass player, too? Have you changed the key to fit your voice type?

When you put a set of songs together, think about the flow of the set. If you're doing a forty-five minute set, for example, you may want to start with a song that's moderately upbeat, crescendo a little through the first couple of tunes, then bring it down to a ballad around the fourth tune. Then, bring the energy back up and conclude on a rousing high note. Plan an encore, too.

Also, think about who's listening. Is it a big venue or a small one? Is the audience younger or older? Do you know them? Are they fans? Friends? Complete strangers? Also, keep in mind that you want your voice to be healthy by the end of your set. You don't want to blow it out, ever. Balance your songs with how they sit in your voice. Also, balance your songs with how smoothly your accompaniment transitions from song to song.

Style, Key, and Technical Range

Those who wish to sing always find a song.

—Proverb

Many styles of contemporary music can be demanding on the voice. Rock styles, for instance, often come with a powerful and/or scratchy vocal quality. This is usually the result of vocal damage or plain wear and tear. Only occasionally is the singer's voice *naturally* scratchy. Two artists who come to mind with naturally scratchy voices are Melissa Etheridge and Brian Adams. Steven Tyler from Aerosmith acquired his vocal quality over years of singing, followed carefully and judiciously by a vocal therapist or doctor while on the road. Many artists we've come to love have had severe vocal trauma. Decide: Are you willing to risk injuring your voice permanently to get that quality? The answer is probably no.

Another consideration is the PA system. If you are fighting to be heard over the drums, bass guitar, electric guitar, and so on, you're apt to push your voice too hard. Make sure your PA system is working for you and that you've rehearsed what it's like to sing when you're excited. The flow of adrenaline that is a part of being excited also tends to make us push.

As with anything, be sure you are singing within your technical ability. It's important not to push yourself into a song you are not ready for. If the song is very rangy or has a lot of belting or runs, decide if you are ready for it. If your voice feels strained or tired after you sing, that indicates you are not ready. Some styles, such as gospel or rock, involve a large percentage of loud singing. This can be very tiring and cause strain. Other styles are surprisingly sneaky, too. For instance, pop music has a popular breathy quality now, low in the female voice. Often the voice you hear is under-supported, or the breathiness is added afterwards in the studio and isn't real. Folk music is more laid-back than other styles; so is jazz. Whatever style you are singing, be sure you are warmed up.

In contemporary music, we change keys of songs all the time. Every voice is different; we don't have to match our voices to a predefined role. You need to be aware of your accompaniment, such as who is playing with you and on which instrument(s). You'll also need to transpose the music into the right key for your voice.

FINDING THE RIGHT KEY FOR A SONG

To find a song's most comfortable key for you, consider these points:

- What is the highest note in the song? What is the lowest?
- Where does your voice need to be the most powerful in the song? Is it the chorus? The bridge? Place the song in a key where that part of the song is not hitting a weak part of your range.
- In contemporary styles, women's ranges are generally low, while men's are higher. There are, of course, exceptions to this.
- If you're a female doing an old jazz standard, you will probably lower the key.
- It is not important to sing a song in the same key as the original artist.
- It *is* important to sing in a key that is comfortable for your voice, that most complements your voice. Sometimes this is a key change of only a step or two. You want to sound your best, and you want that voice to last for a very, very long time.

PERFORMANCE SPACE: TECHNICAL ASPECTS
Mic Technique

In contemporary styles, you use a microphone. When you are singing with a rhythm section, your voice would not be heard without one. Even in places where your voice would carry, a microphone helps soft notes project and can be used to color your tone.

Using a mic will, indeed, change the quality of your voice, especially because the PA system is affecting your voice with EQ settings. It is important to learn which mic is best for your voice. It is important to invest in a good, professional one. Carry it with you. It is completely legitimate to use your own mic on a gig. (The venue may have a better mic than your own; you can try out both and compare them. You should also know that colds and flus might be spread by sharing a mic.)

Professional microphones have three prongs, called an XLR connection. The base of the mic is "male," meaning it contains the prongs. The XLR cord that connects the mic to the PA system, pictured in figure 4.2, has a "female" end that clicks into your mic and a male end that connects to the sound system.

Fig. 4.2. XLR Mic Cord

A mic is your friend. Don't be afraid of it. It lets you sing as if you are whispering into someone's ear or as loud as you do when you belt from a mountain top. It is all about knowing how to use a mic. It takes practice. Here are some simple tips:

- Hold the mic about one hand's width away from your mouth. If you get really soft, you can hold the mic closer. Don't hold it too far away when you get loud. As you sing, move the mic a little bit closer or farther away, depending on how loudly you are singing.

- Point the mic toward your mouth, not under or over it, as illustrated in figure 4.3. You need to sing *into* the mic for it to pick up the full dynamic range of your voice.

Fig. 4.3. Mic Placement

- Be careful of syllables that "pop" the mic and make an unpleasant sound, such as "b" and "d." To avoid popping the mic, say these syllables a little softer. It sounds a bit weird off mic; on mic, it works.

- Be aware of "feedback." This is what happens when there is an amplification loop between the mic and the speakers causing that horrid, piercing screech that crescendos and hurts the ears. Avoid feedback by not pointing the mic toward the speakers. *Never* cover the ball of the mic with your hand; this only makes it worse.

- Set the mic stand so you are neither stooping nor stretching up to sing.

- If you are self-accompanying, be sure you are not looking down at your instrument so much that the mic is not picking up your voice.

- Work together with the sound engineer to get a volume level. Sing soft tones and sing loud tones to give the engineer the range of dynamics you typically sing with. Saying "mic check 1-2-3" only illustrates your speaking voice, which has a limited dynamic range. Instead, *sing* your volume level check.

- If possible, be sure you have time to do a sound check before you perform (and before the audience arrives!). You need to get a balance between your mic level and the band. Keep in mind: once an audience is in place, the sound will be absorbed by their bodies, so the sound check will sound a bit different from the performance.

- If at all possible, get a good "monitor mix" so that you can hear yourself well on stage. This avoids both over-singing and intonation issues from not hearing yourself well. Sometimes, it means asking the band to play a little softer, depending on the room and on your band. You can also purchase a portable, small monitor that you bring with you to gigs that may not have a monitor.

- Finally, get familiar with the sound of your voice through a PA system. If you only rely on the sound engineer, you are at the mercy of his or her experience. Unless you are bringing along your own engineer, the person "at the board" in the venue that night may have no vested interest in your music! You know your voice; you know the sound you are going for. Although you cannot hear yourself through the "house" speakers when you are singing, by using the monitors for reference, you will be able to make useful, respectful requests of the engineer. This person tweaks your settings on the "mixing board" that controls your EQ and volume settings, and controls how you sound to the audience.

Creating the Ideal Performance Environment

As a performer, it is important to strike a balance between creating a healthy boundary for yourself and sharing intimately with an audience. Authority is established by this boundary, while the sharing makes the performance compelling. The physical space of the venue fills with your presence, with your intention, with your music. When you perform, you are inviting the audience to enter that environment and be part of the experience with you.

Sweet Honey in the Rock comes to mind as a group who succeeds at this balance beautifully. Clearly passionate about their music and current social topics, Sweet Honey chooses their songs for a given concert depending on what is happening in the world that week and on who is singing lead that night.[3] They project confidence, personal authenticity, compassion, and knowledge of their material. They reach out to their audiences musically, in the words they speak in between songs, and by their body language. They fill the venue space with their music, in all of its aspects. They also put the audience at ease while uplifting them.

It is essential that we stay connected to the music within us, even as that music evolves alongside our life journeys. In his inspiring book *Effortless Mastery*, author, pianist, composer, and arranger Kenny Werner relates how the meaning of "music" has evolved during his career. He has learned that singing—hearing the sound of his voice—is a powerful way to be expressive, even though professionally his "voice" is a piano. Music is an extension of Werner's life; his compositions and playing *are* the journey of his life. *Effortless Mastery* helps

---

[3] *Sweet Honey in the Rock*'s Ysaye M. Barnwell is interviewed in part III.

musicians gain access to internal music, while learning how to monitor the internal critic.

For Werner, music is the messenger—not the message. If the point of your music is to show off, the music will get only so deep. But, when you have something to say through your music that no words can describe, music then becomes profound. You establish a dialogue between you, your emotions, and your urges. You listen to your inner voice, and play or sing from that place. The more you do, the stronger your music gets, no matter how well you play technically.[4]

The space we make for ourselves as performers, as artists, as voices, can have a profound impact, not only on our own lives, but on the lives of our audiences. How you fill that space, and even how you decorate it with lighting, stage accoutrements, and the like, will have a lot do with what kind of concert your audience experiences.

WHAT AUDIENCES WANT AND NEED

When you go to hear live music, you often leave feeling better. How can we, as performers, create this experience for ourselves and for our audiences on purpose? That day in the subway, I learned how profound performing can be. I was singing in a *subway station*, for heaven's sake! Yet, that brief moment remains one of my top ten best concert memories.

Singing in the subway was the first of many more profound experiences to come. Over time, I grew curious and began asking people *why* do they go to hear live music? I know why I go. I know why I play. But, are there common experiences that people hope to get out of a live musical performance? After all, it would be easier to stay home and listen to CDs. Why hire a babysitter, go out to dinner, and spend money on tickets and parking to attend a live concert?

Live music is the way musicians earn money these days. Long gone are big record sales, unless you're one of the very lucky few. In addition to songwriting royalties, merchandise and ticket sales are how musicians pay the mortgage. It is business. In business, you need to understand your customer. How can a performer know and understand who the people are who will venture out to see him or her?

Audience Survey

I conducted a small online survey to find out. Five hundred people responded. I asked open-ended questions, rather than multiple-choice questions, giving respondents the space to form their own answers. I asked questions like, how do

---

[4] Werner, Kenny. *Effortless Mastery: Liberating the Master Musician Within*. New Albany, IN: Jamey Aebersold Jazz, 1996.

you usually feel at a concert, or hope or expect to feel? What kind of music draws you to a concert? What kind of music or performance do you find distasteful in concert? What makes you decide to see a musical artist again?

Not surprisingly, almost 100 percent of the survey respondents said they attend concerts to have some kind of experience. They go to be moved. They go to hear excellent playing, to watch musicians at work. They go to see what an artist or band is like live, to "take home" a little piece of the real person through that experience and proximity. They go for the community of shared, loved music. Some go anticipating the feeling of live sound reverberating in their bodies. Some go to be uplifted, to escape their own routines, to have fun.

We can create concerts that are beneficial on many levels. Performing is a way of sharing vulnerable parts of ourselves in a public forum that can bring the musicians and audience to heightened, at times even transcendent, experiences. The word "vulnerable" literally means "able to be wounded." This includes letting yourself be pierced emotionally. You may be so moved by a piece of music that you feel your heart is breaking. A performer who is vulnerable to music, who allows it to penetrate him in this way, can then communicate this power to his audience.[5] What an incredible gift. How amazing it is to be able to share that experience. Do your audiences tell you they receive it from you? Listen to them.

WHY DO PEOPLE ATTEND CONCERTS?

Here are some of the answers to my survey:

- "I attend musical concerts to get 'fed.' Live music excites me, makes me think, makes me feel. The concert experience allows me to connect with others in a totally unique way. I connect with my family or whomever I attend with by sharing a common experience, dancing, tapping, etc. I connect with the musicians. And I connect with the composers/arrangers through their everlasting gift of music."
- "Music feeds me—my heart and my soul—in a way that nothing else can do."
- "I believe people are literally starving for music, and the more we can give them, as performers, the healthier they'll be."
- "My primary reason for attending is the possibility of having a transformative experience as a member of a larger group (rather than alone)."
- "If all goes well, I am able to forget about the tasks of the day and actively meditate through the music. I usually feel better after attending a live music experience...unless the concert was performed badly."
- "I hope to feel that euphoria that comes (occasionally), or at least be proud of what the group has accomplished. I attended a concert a couple of months ago that was absolutely stupendous—the best, musically, of ANYTHING I've EVER heard—that left me high for days. It's much like Kundalini rising in my body (middle), then flooding me (end) and hopefully, staying."

---

5   Bruser, *The Art of Practicing*, p. 9

People in an audience can experience an emotional connection within themselves and to others. Music is movement. Sound waves touch the body to create actual movement within, and physically, music has an effect on the brain. The audience is literally *moved*, into a feeling of community, into a new emotional state. It is powerful stuff. Although you cannot guarantee that you will create this from the stage, if your intention is clear to you, you are increasing the likelihood that you will. *It is a gift to the people who came to see you, and in the giving, we elevate our own experience.* When you have truly reached and touched people, they, in turn, want to express their deep appreciation for what you have brought them.

WORKING WITH YOUR BAND

Whom you select to play with is a very important choice. Not all players are skilled at every style of music. That would be super human! Everyone has strengths and weaknesses. A player may favor one genre of music over another. A player may have the tendency to push the backbeat or lay back on it. He or she may be great at playing jazz but not so good at pop.

Trust your ears. Listen carefully to the musical arrangement of the song you are rehearsing. Look for the *call and response* interaction between the instruments. When you rehearse, listen for that same musical conversation. Also, listen for instrumental choices each player can make. Is the guitar using the same tone that you hear on the original recording of a cover song you're rehearsing? (Assuming that's what you'd like to hear.) For that matter, is it electric or acoustic guitar? Are the bass player and drummer locking into "the pocket," by playing well synchronized together? Should the drummer use sticks or brushes? Is the keyboard player on a synth or an acoustic piano? Is there space left in the arrangement for the melody?

Be sure when you go into rehearsal that you have a complete mental picture of how you want each song to sound, or as close to complete as you can imagine. Do your homework. Know your song *really* well, inside and out. How many bars are there in the chorus? When does the bridge come in? The solo? Who is taking the solo? You need to listen actively to the band and somewhat less to yourself singing. Imagine that you are listening through the other players' ears. Ronnie Jones, a talented student of mine who is both a pianist and singer, put it this way:

> *"Good players know how to open themselves up into someone else's musical ideas, letting those ideas flow through them. I also feel that when you listen through another musician's ears, your spirit connects with that musician. This connection occurs because you take on their feelings and passion that goes into playing, which allows you to understand where they are coming from, musically."*

Then, when you're ready to perform, you can focus more on your own parts.

Finally, be organized. Be on time. Make sure your music is correct. Be respectful. When you create an environment of trust and respect, and mutual enjoyment of the music, your result will be much stronger. Encourage spontaneity and creativity, as well as remembering what you rehearsed. (Recording rehearsals is a good idea.) Remember that even a well-seasoned player may not share your exact vision. When it's your project, you get to make the final decisions. So, listen carefully. Then, trust your instincts.

TEN PERFORMING TIPS

1. Preparation, preparation, preparation. Then, once you're on stage, focus on the music. (Like the old joke says, "Hey Mac, how do I get to Carnegie Hall?" …Practice!)

2. Practice being *distracted*. Can you be interrupted during your song and still pick up where you left off?

3. Do you know your lyrics? Practice them frequently—walking down the street, doing the dishes, working out. Be sure you can begin a lyric anywhere in the song; that's how you know you know it. Then, practice the little bits that you tend to forget or mix up.

4. Learn to recognize the parts to your song, like the verses, chorus, and bridge. Knowing your song's structure really helps you and your band or accompanist to stay well synchronized. Practice knowing the tempo. (Use a metronome.)

5. Once you know a song, stop listening to the original CD. This has aural cues that you could become dependent upon but won't be there live. It also helps you shift away from imitating the original artist's phrasing.

6. When you have changed the key of a song, practice it in that key, not with the original recording or sheet music. You want your "muscle memory" to work on the song in the right key.

7. The concert is more about the audience and less about you. When your focus is on giving them your best, on creating an experience that they'll remember, it helps you get out of your own way. Plus, it's more fun that way.

8. Make eye contact from time to time with your audience. Draw them in. (But don't stare them down, either.) If you have stage fright, it's okay to look over the audience's heads. Resist closing your eyes throughout your songs; it shuts the audience out. Try picturing a music video of the song's story, playing over their heads as you sing, drawing your focus.

9. Sometimes situations arise when there are things you *cannot* control: the PA system, your guitar player's tuning, a rude club manager. How will you handle being disappointed? How can you turn a bad situation around? Don't let it get under your skin. After all, it's just one day in your life. (As I tell my students, if you haven't had a "bad gig," you haven't been riding that horse. Sometimes, you fall off.)

10. That piece of stage is yours during your song. Own it.

UNDERSTANDING YOUR ENERGY IN PERFORMANCE: CHAKRAS AND REIKI

We are our own energy sources, which we create from the food we eat, the air we breathe, the thoughts we hold, and the other people in our lives. Some say there is also a universal energy of which we are all a part. Energy moves in waves. When we project our own energy outward in performance, it moves in waves in collaboration with the audience's energy. When several people come together in a group, their energy merges into one new type of being. This is palpable. A choir becomes one; individuals in a group may do things together they would never risk alone. Understanding this energy in terms you may not normally think about can be very useful, giving you additional awareness of yourself and your interaction with others.

What Is Reiki? What Are Chakras? How Does Energy Awareness Impact Performing? What's the Connection?

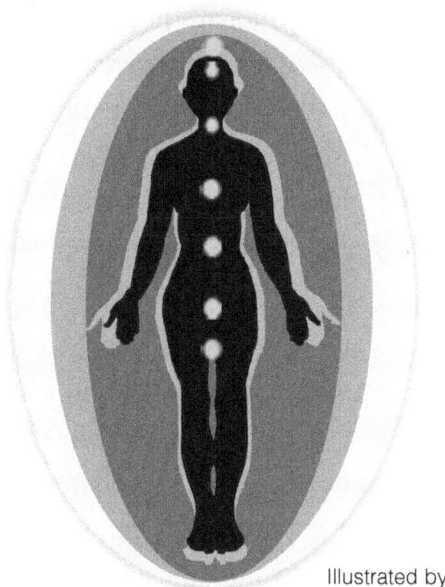

Illustrated by Jeannie Gagné

Fig. 4.4. Aura and Primary Chakras

Reiki is a healing art that originated in Japan. It has become very popular in the United States. It works with the body's energy fields, with our chakras (see figure 4.4). Understanding energy fields that surround people is not normally taught together with performing skills. It is an Eastern concept, often even dismissed in the West. The closest a performance class might get to that connection is emphasizing being aware of the audience, making eye contact, realizing that you are working for the audience and not the other way around. *Reiki* training definitely does *not* teach vocal performance. So, why combine Reiki and performing skills here?

WHAT IS REIKI?

Reiki is a Japanese-based energy healing art. Reiki brings the body back into balance by stimulating the body's own healing ability, using the seven primary *chakras* (energy centers) as focal points. When you train in Reiki, you learn to be sensitive to the energy that is in and around us all the time. Expanding upon the one-on-one treatment standard of Reiki practice by bringing this awareness into performance, the vocalist can become sensitive to the energy flow within and with the audience, and the healing potential of a group setting.

Reiki is taught in several stages. One must learn from a master/teacher who decides if the student has mastered each level of training before moving on to the next. Master level is the third plateau, at which point the student can become a practitioner. Though the concept of using Reiki energy and awareness in a concert setting is unusual, the master/teachers I studied with support it, as long as the intention of the vocalist or other musician is positive and focused on a healing outcome for the audience.

Let's begin by defining what Reiki practitioners mean by "personal energy." That is the flow of energy that is moving in and around you all the time. We generate heat; that is a form of energy. The food we consume gives our cells energy to grow and function. You may not even know there is a flow of energy around you or think this idea is silly. But when you learn how to, you can feel or sense the energy easily. This energy flow is called your *aura*. Some people say they can see auras as layers of colors around your body. In many traditions, including Reiki healing, the body's energy is also described in terms of *chakras*. Chakras are the strongest energy centers in our bodies. Spinning energy wheels that correlate to specific bodily function, thoughts, and emotions, chakras are a normal part of us.

When you let your personal energy rise up—energy that is heightened from being on stage and from the gathering of many people into one place—you gain access to a kind of personal magnetism that all strong performers have in common. Earlier in this chapter, we looked at what most seasoned performers experience in concert. Their focus is on the music, on the audience, and on the other musicians. Less focus is placed on outward appearances or on what people think. (No one can change someone else's thoughts, so why worry about them?) Just being oneself, or authentic, becomes paramount. Being in the moment, letting one's energetic self *expand* into the concert space, is part of that authenticity.

Being Aware of Your Energy

Personal energy is a very individual experience, like our emotions. My own awareness of personal energy began when I was a teenager, when I first became aware of "seeing" colorful energy around people. I could feel it, too. We all feel it, though we may not know it.

Think about it. When you feel someone's anger or love or enthusiasm, it is energetic. We each have different levels of awareness and beliefs about what we perceive. You can call that a kind of spirituality.

> **MEETING TRUE *SELF* FOR THE FIRST TIME**
>
> When I was sixteen, I first experienced a split in my understanding of Self. I will never forget that moment. It was the first time I became aware of a greater, older, "higher self" that supported the efforts of the young woman I was becoming. It occurred in New York City one evening, sitting on the sofa with a close friend in my family's apartment, in the middle of a deep conversation.
>
> I had difficulty making sense of this experience, which was happening as we talked. An older woman resonated from deep within my being, speaking my words along with me. We were one. She watched and listened patiently. Who was she? Was it God? An angel? An older, wiser me?
>
> Even as I explained the experience to my friend, it continued. A sense of bliss overcame me. I felt I was seeing a corner of the fabric of the meaning of life. As I spoke, I heard her voice too, like a deep river, resonating and supporting my own. I observed the thoughts of being sixteen, while in that moment, I also understood love and patience coming from what seemed to be great wisdom. My senses were heightened, and yet they became less important.
>
> Having this profound experience for the first time, I became aware that my sixteen-year-old self had choices. She was living a life that was difficult, emotional, and also rich and joyous. Although she didn't know it, she chose her own actions, and her actions affected her experience of living. Although she could not choose her family, her school, her homework assignments, her body shape, how her friends behaved, and so on, she could choose how she responded to those things.
>
> Since that night, I have never felt alone. I always know there is a great strength that lies within. That is the Self.

One of the leaders in the field of energy healing, Barbara Ann Brennan, describes the auric field and chakras in her phenomenal book *Hands of Light*. She teaches the reader how to learn to see the auric field. You begin to sense these energy fields when you relax. They vibrate at very high frequencies. Many can see auras with the "third eye," a clear sense of something there that is not as obvious as the table or floor before you.

You can easily experience your own energy. You should become aware of it. It affects how you interact with people and how they see you. A good place to start is to feel the energy in your own hands. Hands are a focal point of our energy. Here's a way you can experience the source of your own energy that you carry with you all the time.

ACTIVITY 4.2. ENERGY AWARENESS 1: FEELING YOUR ENERGY

Rub your hands together briskly for a few seconds, then hold them about three feet apart in front of you, palms facing one another, fingers straight and closed. Pay attention to the sensation in your hands. It is subtle; be patient. You may feel heat, prickles, or mild resistance, or perhaps nothing special yet. Slowly bring your hands together until a sensation is noticeable. Does it increase as you bring your hands together? By the time your hands are a few inches apart, most people feel something. It might feel like tingles, or very subtle resistance like a magnetic pull. You are feeling your own energy. It comes outward from your palms, and the sensitivity of your fingers and hands can usually sense it.

Fig. 4.5. Energy

Normally, we keep a comfortable zone of our own energy around us. Many people describe this zone as about two feet wide. Curiously, although all people have an energy field around them, the size of the comfort zone varies somewhat by culture. When a stranger enters that zone, it may feel uncomfortable, or it may feel exciting, especially if we like the person and welcome close connection. Activity 4.3 shows a way to find out what yours is.

ACTIVITY 4.3. ENERGY AWARENESS 2: WITH TWO PEOPLE

Stand facing one another, about six to eight feet apart. Slowly walk toward one another, paying attention to the sensations between you. You might feel tingles, heat, discomfort, or perhaps very subtle pressure increasing as you get closer. Notice how close you are when the comfortable distance between you has reached its limit. If each of you has a two-foot energy bumper, you will be about four feet apart.

See what happens when you get closer. You're in each other's "personal space" now. Does it feel weird? Uncomfortable? Are you giggling? Be in this closeness for a moment, and just experience it. Quiet your mind. Observe.

Now, if you feel comfortable exploring your energy further, try this: one person stands still. The other holds hands over the partner's two-foot boundary and gently "touches" it with palms facing the partner, fingers together. See if either of you can feel this energy touch.

Try to visualize the energy "bubble" that surrounds you all the time (figure 4.4). You can contract it when you want to be less visible, and you can enlarge it when you want attention. It's like a three-way light bulb. You can choose low, medium, or high. Your normal might be low or medium. Consider performing as acting upon your decision to switch your light from low to medium or high. In energy terms, you are deciding to increase the diameter of the energy you emit, from two feet or so on low or medium, to a larger diameter of five or six feet on the high setting. One comfortable and controllable measurement is arms' length. To gauge this parameter, extend your arms out straight from your sides, picturing the line around you that you could draw with the tips of your fingers. When you perform, try filling this larger space with your personal energy. It is manageable, and it helps you to project your personal magnetism.

A compelling performer can project this magnetism by choosing to become somewhat vulnerable and open—letting the audience in. Our energy and vulnerability are a gift to the audience, a gift that enables us to receive energy back from them.

But it can be risky, too. Performers can deplete themselves too much. Healthy performers set a kind of boundary, so they won't "give it all." One rule of thumb is to give 80 percent of yourself to the audience, saving 20 percent for you. Two artists who come to mind as extreme examples of *not* succeeding at this are Kurt Cobain and Judy Garland. Tragically, they could not separate their musical brilliance and gifts from the way they were in the world, and on stage, their complete energetic presence was both electrifying and risky for themselves. Luckily, most of us are not at risk of self-destructing by performing.

The best way to measure this boundary is by experience. You need to be open enough to be authentic and to give and receive with your audience and other musicians. If you feel terrific after a concert, you know you have set the boundary just right. If you feel depleted, consider tightening the boundary next time you perform. If you feel disappointed, you may need to open up more.

Using Reiki at Home and Elsewhere

When my daughter was young, every night I put her to bed with a Reiki bubble. This is a motion I created to tuck her in. After quieting my own mind, I would sweep my hands gently around her aura as I looked to "see" the color she emanated at that moment. My two goals were to relax her and to help her learn to fall asleep on her own. I told her to "bring in light," and then I "massaged" her aura with it.

Focusing on her primary chakras, I looked for any activity that would get in the way of sleep. Was she upset about something? Her heart chakra told me. Was her mind spinning too fast for sleep? Her "third-eye" chakra, at her forehead, told me. This Reiki bubble was instantly comforting to her. She received my loving intention while feeling honored by this action.

Although I was not taught this specific technique in my Reiki training, my teacher has accepted it as a valid use of Reiki healing. By also placing a hand on my daughter's forehead and on her heart for a few moments, she could settle her anxiety and move into a restful state. Within minutes, she was fast asleep.

On occasion, I use the Reiki aura touch when I teach private vocal lessons, with my students' permission. (This spoken permission is important.) If a student is feeling flustered, disconnected, ungrounded, the Reiki touch can be very comforting and calming. It requires a loving intention on my part so that I do not inadvertently communicate negative feelings when I connect at such a close level. I also know how to "shield" myself in a veil of loving light, so I don't absorb the student's negative energy by accident.

You interact with other people's energy all the time, but you may not be consciously aware of it: a "close talker" who makes you uncomfortable, a ride on an overcrowded subway when you can't wait for the pushy strangers to get out, the discomfort of standing before a group who are all looking at you and directing their energy into your space, the comfort of a close friend sitting next to you. The more that you are aware of these dynamics, the more you are able to control how you respond to them.

PERFORMING: SIMPLY STATED...

Effective practice includes working on technical competence as well as preparing mentally. Refer back to "Nine Steps to Creating Extraordinary Performances" earlier in this chapter.

Remember:

- You decide how much of yourself you share with your audience. You are in control.

- Expect performing to be inspiring to you, the other musicians, and the audience.

- Be aware of the energy in and around you that you create and receive.

Expect to have a great concert. Choose what you want to create on stage, and do it. Revel in it. Marvel in it. Share it with your friends. Share it with everyone on stage. Share it with your audience. It might just be amazing.

PART II

Exercises

Part II provides more technical advice for your voice, exercises to help you warm up and develop your voice, and some of my own original songs for you to practice these techniques, and for fun. Most of these exercises have either corresponding audio tracks with accompaniment to sing with, or demonstrations of how to sing them. The text before each exercise gives you a range guideline. You can sing higher or lower than the guideline if that is comfortable and you are not straining. Generally, as you work your voice you are stretching it—kind of like working pizza dough: start in the middle and stretch the edges, a little more each time.

TRACK 1 • INTRODUCTION

CHAPTER 5

Pointers and Warm-Ups

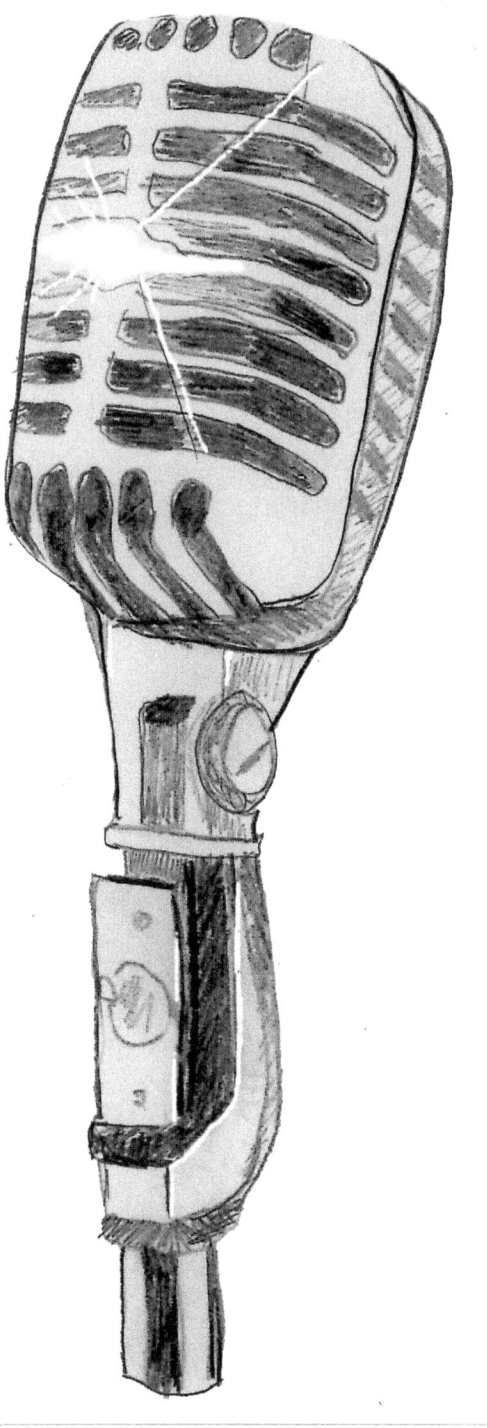

"If music be the food of love, play on."
— William Shakespeare
(*Twelfth Night*)

It may surprise you to know that healthy singing uses much of the same technique in many different styles. Whether you are singing contemporary or classical or folk music styles, you are using the same parts of your anatomy: breathing, larynx, and resonating parts of your head and chest. Just as a piano with eighty-eight keys can accommodate virtually any style of music, so too can the human vocal instrument sing just about anything.

Frequently, students want to learn how to sing like a specific artist. But because no two voices are the same, it is unreasonable to expect yourself to sound exactly like the vocal on a favorite song or to sing a song in its original key. You were not born with that artist's vocal instrument. In fact, although listening to and imitating favorite singers is an important way to learn musical styles, a *performance* that imitates someone is not the goal. (Unless, of course, your performance is specifically about presenting the work and character of a known artist.)

Illustrated by Jeannie Gagné

Let your vocal instrument be available to you to use creatively rather than have it dictate what you can and cannot sing. That being said, remember you cannot sing everything, any more than a guitar can be a piano, flute, or tenor sax. You do have some limitations defined by the physiological structure of your vocal instrument. However, over time, with practice, what you are able to do with your voice will continue to increase and expand.

There are four main goals to these exercises:

1. Gain flexibility and fluidity
2. Gain fine motor control while changing pitch, vowel, and volume
3. Learn the full palette of your voice, your "64 crayons"
4. Travel through register changes smoothly when desired

The overall design of the exercises will help you embody contemporary styles through tone, rhythms, and diction.

So, what exactly makes you *unique?* If you were able to watch yourself from the audience, or when you watch a video of yourself, what qualities do you see that stand out? We know the sound of your voice is yours alone. Beyond that, take some time to think about the question. Journal on it. Notice what way of singing you lean toward naturally, what is most effortless. Notice what fills you with the most joy. What music do you enjoy singing? (We like listening to many styles of music that may not be what we are best motivated to, or suited to, sing.) Notice when audiences respond most favorably to you.

Deciding whether or not you like the sounds you make is highly subjective and part of your artistic choice. Often, we judge ourselves harshly and don't like our voices, especially as we modify technique to new tones and outcomes (see chapter 2, "Your Loop"). *Virtually all sounds your voice can produce can be done in a healthy manner.*

SHIFTING FROM CLASSICAL TO CONTEMPORARY STYLES

If you are a classically (or traditionally) trained singer, these basic concepts will help you sing contemporary styles more authentically.

Include singing that is speech-like. In contemporary singing, diction is more casual than in traditional singing. Melodies are often placed closer to speech range. Singing should sound natural, not over-articulated. For example, words ending in "t" will have no aspiration: traditional "ThaTT" becomes "Thadt." Rather than singing with consistent tonal colors, use the melodic and variable tonal colors of speech instead. In addition, by using less vocal energy than in traditional styles, singing appears to be more relaxed. Even with this approach, vocal technique that is basic for all styles is maintained, including supporting the breath and utilizing the resonant spaces in the mouth.*

Modify vibrato. Vibrato is a vibration of the body's natural rhythm, but it can be modified. In contemporary styles, the use of vibrato can range from none at all to fast. One technique, used frequently in jazz singing, is to hold back vibrato until the end of a note, then release it slowly. A modern r&b use of vibrato is quick and tight, shortly after the note is sounded. In folk rock, there is often no vibrato.

Modify legato. Contemporary styles tend to be very rhythmic, even syncopated, with much less legato. Connect notes less frequently, allowing space to be part of your phrasing.

Avoid musical theater styles. In contemporary musical theater, although diction is more speech-like than classical styles, ends of words are still well articulated, legato is maintained, and vibrato is strong. To sound less like musical theater, soften these qualities.

Lighten or fatten your tone. If you are accustomed to always singing with a clear tone, consider modifying the tone, such as softening it. For men, switching into sweet, falsetto tones is "money in the bank." Strengthening your falsetto is important. For women, develop the full tones in your lower range as part of your overall palette. When you ascend in a riff, keep the tone bright and energized, while slightly flattened (east/west). This is a simple way to visualize the difference in vowel placement between traditional and contemporary singing. Traditional vowels are oval in shape, from top to bottom (north/south). Contemporary vowels commonly turn the oval on its side with a wider mouth (east/west).

---

* There is a specific technique called "speech-level singing" that is somewhat controversial. I am not referencing this specific technique here. Many teachers insist that speech-level singing is the best approach for contemporary styles that great pop and jazz stars have employed for decades, while other teachers believe that this approach is weak technically and can potentially strain or damage the voice. Remember, any style of singing should never cause you vocal strain.

VOWEL AND CONSONANT KEYS: U.S. ENGLISH PRONUNCIATION

These pronunciation keys will help you in a few ways. First, refer back here if you are not certain how to pronounce a word or syllable in the exercises. Second, if you come from classical training, these keys will help you to sound more contemporary. Third, for my readers from around the world, these keys will help you with your U.S. English pronounciation.

Vowel Key

Vowel	As in the words
Aw	awe, jaw (round)
Ah	fa la la, rah (broad)
Ee	see, tree (true "e")
O	sew, go, toe (true "o")
U	you, ewe
Oo	ooh, blue
I	eye, five (true "I")
Ay	day, way, say
Aah or @	cat, sat, mat (very bright)

Consonant Key

CONSONANT	AS IN THE WORDS	QUALITY
B*	boy, baby, bat, scab	Lips seal then burst open with air
Ch	chair, charge, cherry, such	Similar to "SH" but with a harder onset
D	dad, deal, seed	Tongue presses against front teeth with a burst of air
F	flower, fine, scarf	Air blows quickly against bottom lip and top teeth
G or J (soft)	jewel, gem, giant, hedge	Tongue and teeth seal then open quickly with a burst of air
G (hard)	good, great, lug	Back of the tongue comes up to close the pharynx then releases with a burst of air
H	hair, howl, hide	The only open consonant, air is pushed through an open vocal fold (abducted)
K	thick, shack, like, kite	Produced in the back of the throat, tongue presses up against the soft palate with a soft burst of air
L	love, lie, real, royal	Tongue presses up against front of hard palate in phonation
M	mom, may, mighty, same, time	Lips close, sound vibrates in the open space of the pharynx
N	nice, nasty, mine, run	Similar to "M" but the closure is from the tongue against the hard palate and lips don't close
P*	paper, pool, soup, lip	Lips press together and release with a burst of air
R	ready, run, car, star	Tongue is held in contraction in the middle of the mouth, while frequencies ring upwards through the hard palate
S	sexy, see, eyes, saves	Tongue creates a valve near the front teeth as air is pressed through the constricted opening
SH	shut, shout, push, fish	Front of mouth is partially closed as air is pressed forward
T*	time, tell, pout, about	Tongue presses against the front teeth explosively with a burst of air
V	vain, vogue, rave, love	Top teeth buzz lightly against bottom lip
W	why, went, few, how	Lips pucker and release during phonation, sometimes with a small burst of air ("wh")
X	xray, extra, flex, exactly	Produced from the back of the throat, this is actually three sounds blended quickly, "eh" + "K" + "S"
Y	baby, why, sky, may	Sounds as "ee" at ends of words; or, the letter sound, as in "why," is a diphthong: "wah-ee"
Z	zebra, razzle dazzle	Tongue is pressed against hard palate behind teeth during strong phonation

*On a microphone, lessen the sound so it doesn't "pop."

As you say the words, see if you can feel the muscles in your mouth and lips that contract or constrict, then release to produce each consonant.

ABOUT CONSONANTS

Consonants are implosive, non-pitched sounds that, when paired with vowels, help us to shape words. Usually, consonants are formed by pressing the lips together or moving the tongue against hard areas of the mouth, such as the teeth or hard palate. Traditional singing technique teaches us to sing on the vowel, reserving the consonant for the end of the note, or syllable, for clear diction. This is because the vowel provides vocal tone and an open throat, while the consonant creates closure. However, in contemporary styles, it is also common to complete a word while still singing it, extending the consonant. This is only advisable on a low pitch so you don't add stress to the voice.

For example, the musical phrase "I'm singing in the rain" could be sung, "I'm si(. . .)nging in the rai(. . .)n," or, because the melody travels up an octave on the word "singing," "I'm si(. . .)nging in the rainnnn," holding onto the "n" while completing the note. This is a common device in jazz singing.

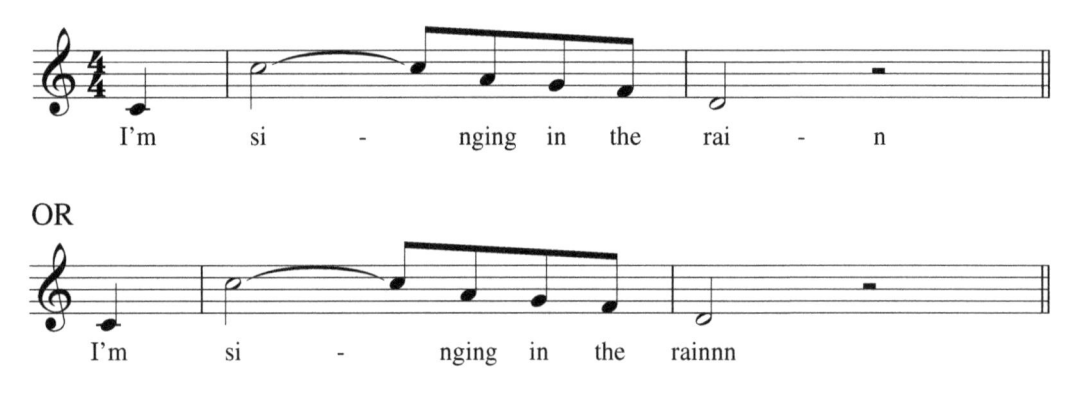

Fig. 5.1. "Singing in the Rain"

BODY WARM-UPS

It is important to begin each practice by warming up your body before you sing, even briefly. If your body is tired or cold or stressed, for example, your singing will be affected, too. Begin by observing your body and general state. Stretch. Take deep, slow breaths, in and out. Are there any tense or tired areas? Allow your mind to help those areas to soften, to release tension. Are you thirsty? Drink some room-temperature water or herbal tea. Can you send extra energy and attention to nurture areas that may need it, without judgment or added tension? Continue to encourage any tight muscles to release as you stretch and warm up your body. Is your overall energy low right now? Do some jumping jacks or swing your arms around to get yourself moving.

> **TIP: STAY HYDRATED**
>
> Remember, drinking water when you are about to sing will not hydrate your voice. Like the rest of your cells, the tissues of your larynx stay moist, indirectly, when your whole body is well-hydrated. Drinking eight eight-ounce glasses of water per day is the standard *minimum* recommendation. Tea or juice is also okay. Caffeinated beverages are diuretics, causing you to urinate; alcoholic beverages are *dehydrating*. If you become extremely thirsty, that means you went too long without getting adequate fluids.

Body Warm-Ups 1–2: Stretching

WARM-UP 1. ROLL DOWN/ROLL UP

This simple exercise should be relaxing. It's a good way to begin each time you vocalize, to help you make the shift from pedestrian movements to your-body-is-your-instrument movements.

First, stand straight, feet hip distance apart, and point your toes forward. Slowly roll down over your feet to hang from your waist, letting your torso, arms, neck, and head relax to release tension, with loose (not locked) knees. (The woman in figure 5.2 is very flexible; hang as comfortably low as you do naturally without worrying about touching the floor.) Let your head swing a little, like a rag doll, being sure you aren't holding your neck. Hang there for about a minute while taking slow, deep breaths. Feel your back expand as you breathe normally. Picture any tension you may be holding, from working at a computer, stress, leaning over your guitar, driving, or any activity. Pour it out of your neck and shoulders to be absorbed by the floor. Take more slow, deep breaths.

Now, *slowly* roll back up, restacking your spine as you do, with your neck and head the last to realign. Try counting to 15 or 20 as you roll up. When you get to the top, be careful not to shake your head to fix your hair; do that with your hands instead, so your neck stays aligned. By rolling up in this manner, you have realigned your posture. Now, you're ready to sing!

Fig. 5.2. Demonstration of (a) Roll Down and (b) Roll Up

WARM-UP 2: LONG STEADY BREATH RELEASE ("SSS")

Take a comfortable and deep inhalation, taking care not to over-stuff yourself with air. As you release the air, create resistance by saying, "Sss," as if you were a valve slowly releasing gas. Listen to the sound, keeping it steady. See how long you can make the sound last: count to 12, then, on your next breath, count to 16; then, try counting to 20. Repeat the exercise, and see if you can make it last longer. At the beginning of the phrase, there is more resistance to the release of air. Then, as your air runs low, you will use more pressure from your abdomen to keep the sound at a steady volume. This breath management exercise uses the same principle as singing a steady tone.

Body Warm-Ups 3–4: Sounding

WARM-UP 3. SINGLE TONE FOR CENTERING

Although you are beginning to produce tone now, this warm up is not a vocal exercise, per se. It is more like a meditation while giving you another way to become mindful of your breath. The warm-up encourages you to begin your singing practice by centering. It is very relaxing. Hold one note throughout four measures, keeping the tone steady, clean, and easy. Take a slow breath in between each phrase. Use this as another opportunity to release stress or negative thoughts. Embrace the vibration of your own voice, letting it calm you. Use the same breath approach as you just did in the "Sss" exercise to maintain a steady flow of air, making sure your tone is not breathy. Being able to produce soft, relaxed, but *clean* tones is the cornerstone of healthy technique.

BODY WARM-UPS 131

🔊 **TRACK 2**

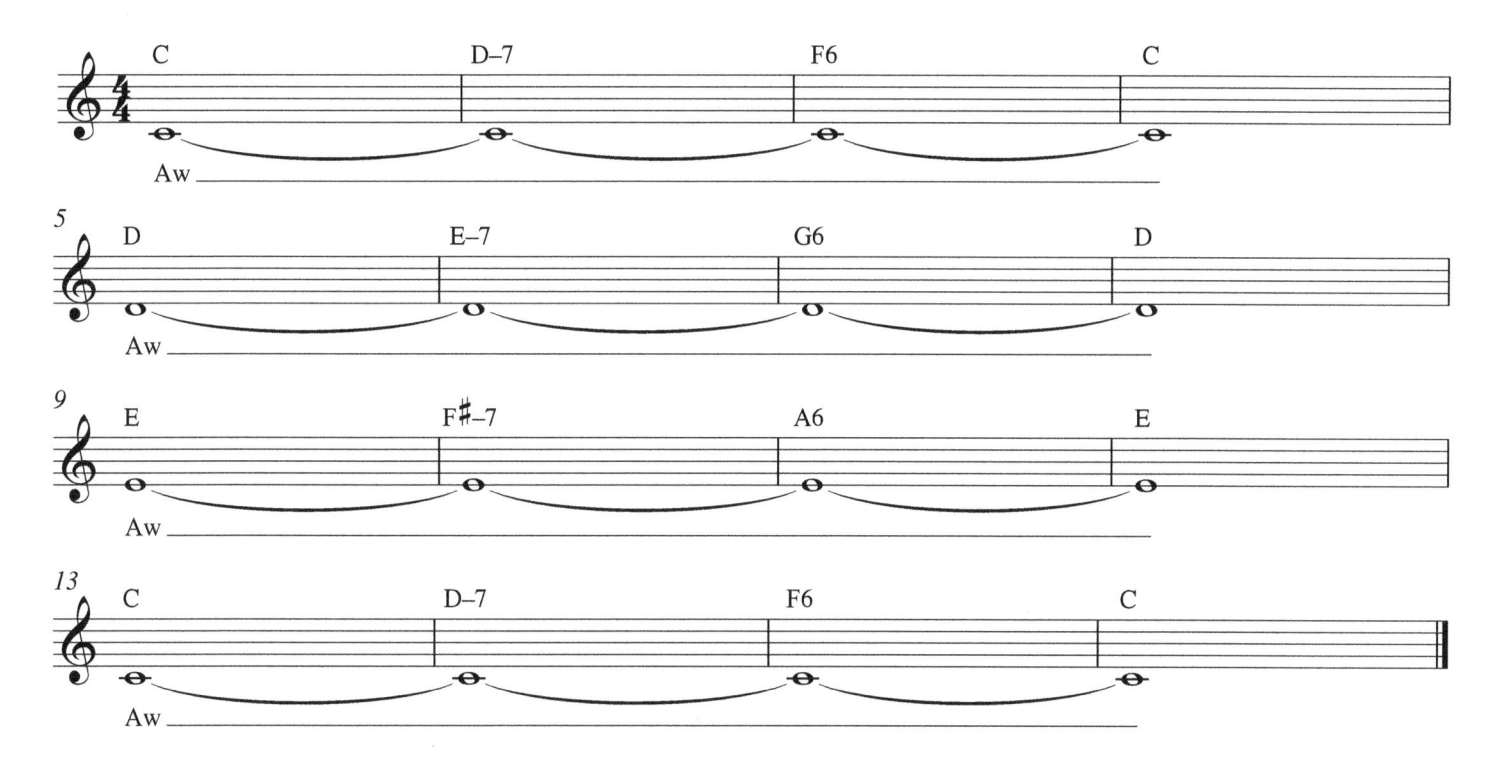

Fig. 5.3. Single Tone Exercise

WARM-UP 4. SLOW MOVEMENT AND HEALTH CHECK

The goal is a soft, clean tone that blends from note to note. Slide slowly between pitches, keeping the tone constant. Be sure to maintain the airflow through the final note of each phrase as if you're going to hold the note longer than you need to. In line with warming up gently, don't travel as high or as low as you can sing, yet. Move through the exercise by half steps.

TRACK 3

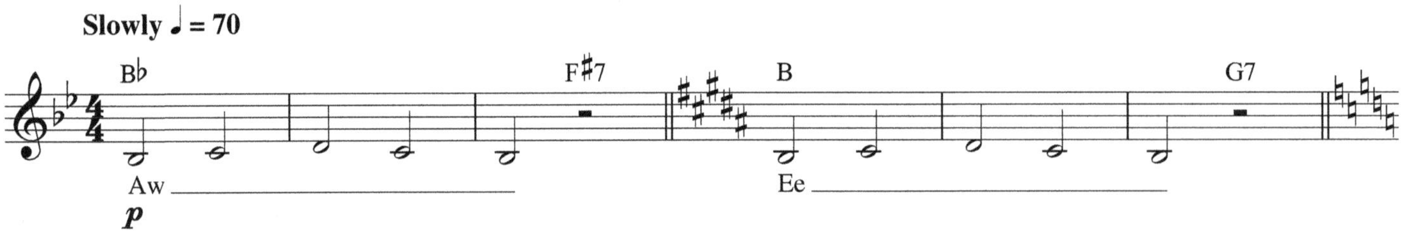
Slowly ♩ = 70
B♭
F♯7
B
G7
Aw
p
Ee

Continue moving up by half steps with each new phrase, keeping the range comfortable as you begin.

Once you reach the key of G below, turn around, traveling back down by half steps.

G
F♯
G♭
F
Aw
Ee

Conclude comfortably, low in your range, relaxed but engaged, tone clean without breathiness.

A♭
Ee

CHAPTER 6

The Exercises

Illustrated by Jeannie Gagné

*There are numerous strings in your lute,
let me add my own among them.*

*Then when you smite your chords,
my heart will break its silence,*

And my heart will be one with your song.

—Rabindranath Tagore, 1861–1941

Now that you are warmed up, we will shift into the vocal exercises. They start slowly and easily, gradually becoming more challenging. I've included some that are more traditional, both because they work well and because strengthening and maintaining basic technique in any style is a must. Others I have written over years of teaching, finding they work well for flexibility, style, and rhythm and pitch accuracy. The goal is a resilient, reliable instrument that you can use creatively for years to come.

When done properly, these exercises are good for your voice, bringing blood to the area, and helping your mind direct healing thoughts where needed. Have you already been speaking a lot today, or is it the start of your day? Is your voice tired or hoarse before you've begun? On a day when your voice is feeling great, you may not need to sing through all of the warm-ups. Use your judgment, and listen to your body. If at any time your voice feels tired or sore, stop.

TIP: HIGH AND LOW

We use words like "high" and "low" to describe pitch and range, when in fact there is no gravity involved! High notes are simply faster frequencies; low notes are slower frequencies. The higher notes on a piano or guitar are to your right; they are not up. Unconsciously, we often tense the body to reach for high notes as if we are climbing, which only adds tension as we sing. When you feel this tension occurring, try bending your knees to trick your body into letting go of gripping onto notes. Conversely, low notes don't require you to press down parts your body. If you feel yourself doing this, try standing on the balls of your feet or raising your arms as you descend.

STARTING OUT EASY: WARMING UP YOUR VOICE

Ranges this section: High: Low:

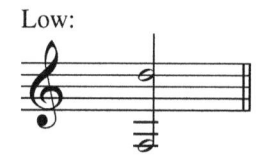

EXERCISE 1. LIP TRILLS: RELAXED AND EASY

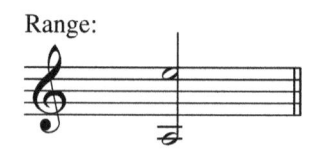

Range:

Lip trills are created by blowing air across your lips to get them to vibrate together, as a child would do when imitating a motorboat. While your lips are vibrating, you are phonating on the exercise.

🔊 TRACK 4

bbb

Continue up by half steps until you reach the top key:

bbb

STARTING OUT EASY: WARMING UP YOUR VOICE

Now travel back down by half steps to where you began, concluding comfortably low in your range.

bbb

TIP: SOFT BUT NOT BREATHY

Soft does not necessarily equal breathy. A breathy tone means there is air escaping in between the vocal folds, or the tone is simply under-supported. Yes, sometimes a breathy tone is used in certain styles; however, while warming up and building technique, using a soft tone that is clean is best for your voice.

EXERCISE 2. CALM, CLEAR TONES, WITH BREATH SUPPORT

Take a relaxing, centering breath in between each set of notes, during the full measure of rest. Use this time to calm the mind. Listen to the sound of your voice, the resonance. Let that sound ground you.

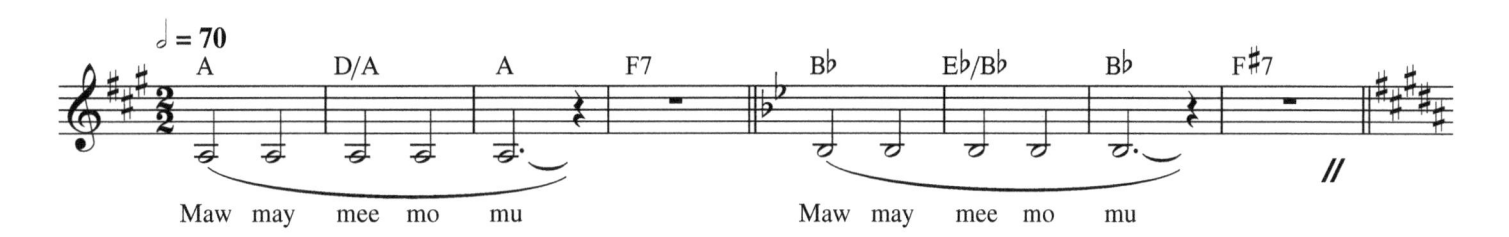

TRACK 5

♩ = 70

Maw may mee mo mu   Maw may mee mo mu

Continue up by half steps.

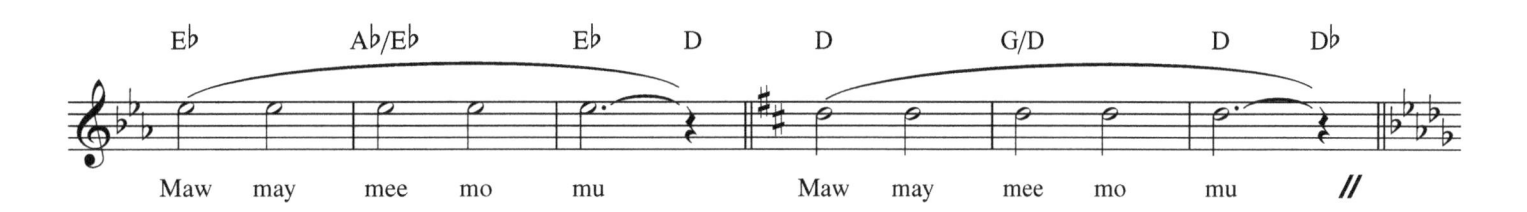

Maw may mee mo mu   Maw may mee mo mu

Now, travel down by half steps, concluding low in your range.

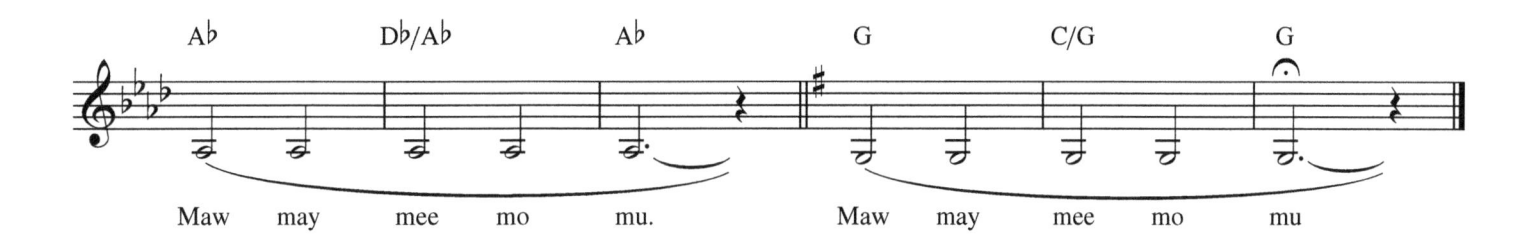

Maw may mee mo mu.   Maw may mee mo mu

EXERCISE 3. MOVEMENT AND FIFTHS

Picture yourself on a level with the upper fifth note, to take away the feeling of reaching for it. Imagine you're already at the note before you begin, like having climbed rungs on a ladder, on a level plane with the note. Then, let the larynx drop for the root note. The voice will pivot gently between these two placements.

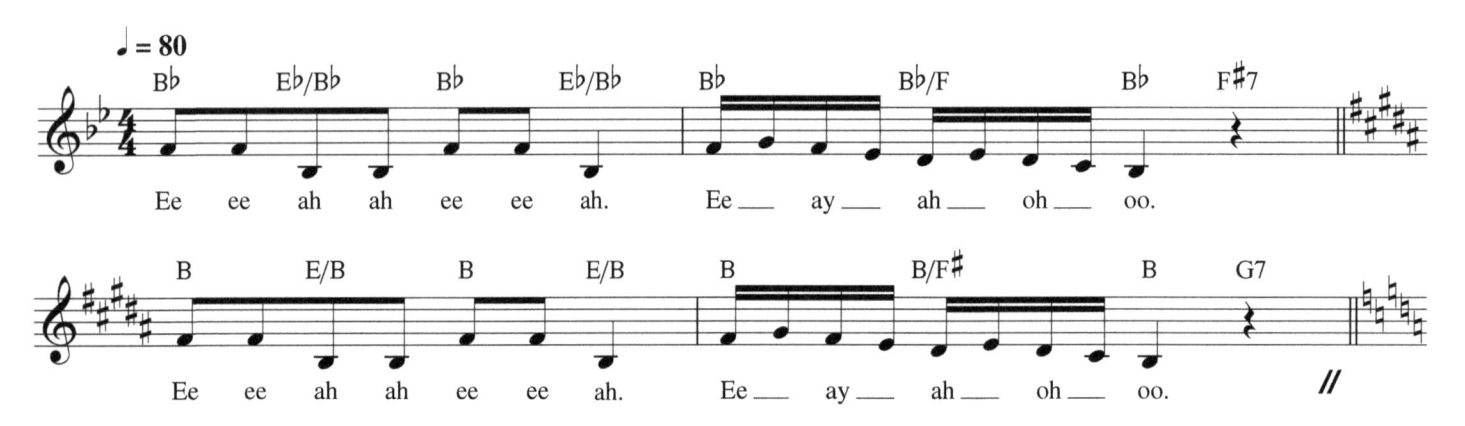

Range:

🔊 **TRACK 6**

Ee ee ah ah ee ee ah. Ee___ ay___ ah___ oh___ oo.

Ee ee ah ah ee ee ah. Ee___ ay___ ah___ oh___ oo.

Continue moving up by half steps until you reach the key of F, below.

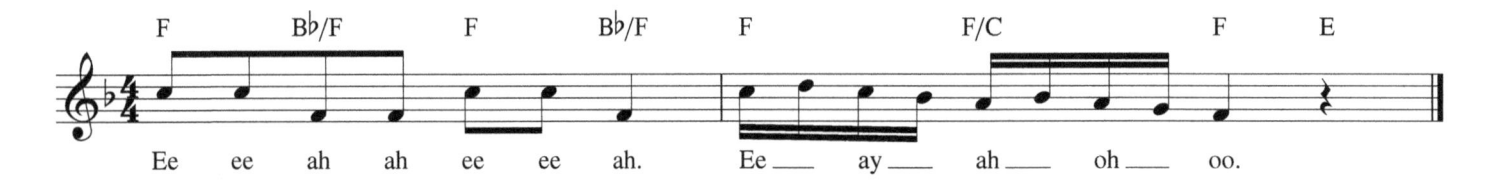

Ee ee ah ah ee ee ah. Ee___ ay___ ah___ oh___ oo.

Now descend by half steps to conclude where you started.

STARTING OUT EASY: WARMING UP YOUR VOICE

EXERCISE 4. A BIT MORE MOVEMENT

Continue to keep your singing fluid and legato while warming up. Connect the notes, and breathe at the rests. Keep the jaw relaxed and the throat open. Don't go too high yet, and end a note or two lower than where you started. The goal is to stay relaxed while becoming more active. This exercise moves quickly, but the notes are articulated loosely.

🔊 **TRACK 7**

Continue moving up by half steps until you reach the top key:

Now go back down by half steps, concluding comfortably low in your range:

Variation, with Staccato

Fig. 6.1. Staccato Variation

VISUAL: ROLLING PIN

Imagine a rolling pin in between your ears that you can adjust with your hands as you ascend or descend in a scale. As you travel up, the roller moves forward, a little bit with each note. Then, it rotates back as you descend. In this way, you are *stretching* your voice to sing "higher" notes comfortably and without force.

Fig. 6.5. The Rolling Pin   Illustrated by Jeannie Gagné

EXERCISE 5. SMOOTH GLISSANDO TO THE 9TH

As you sing this glissando, *mf* volume, blend from one note into the next as if you were using fingers on a charcoal painting, using *melisma*. (A melisma is a smooth, blended connection between notes on one vowel and *very* useful for training your vocal folds to be flexible.) Don't worry about being note-exact; instead, let your voice explore the full range of an octave-plus-1 and back down again. Be mindful not to pull back from a note, but let each note have its full due. If your voice wants to shift registers, let it, while keeping the airflow connected. Use this as an opportunity to observe what happens when you don't back off. **Remember: While the pitch shifts, maintain the vowel, and keep a steady volume.**

Glide your way from pitches 1 to 9 (or Do to Re 8va) and back down, on one breath. Keep it loose but connected to tone, as if you are stretching a band. Imagine you can feel the stretch of your vocal folds as they lengthen for the "higher" tone then relax back to where you started. (Tip: Create a bright tone.)

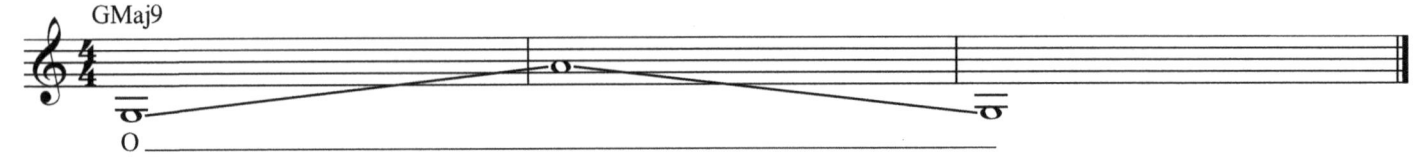

TRACK 8

Fig. 6.2. Glissando to the 9th

AGILITY AND RHYTHM

EXERCISE 6. SYNCOPATION

The exercises are getting more agile now; the goal is increasing flexibility while maintaining clean lines. Listen to how this exercise melody relates to the chord changes as your ear and vocal mechanism coordinate. Strive for a clean tone with the least amount of air sounding through the note.

TRACK 9

Continue up by half steps until you reach the top key.

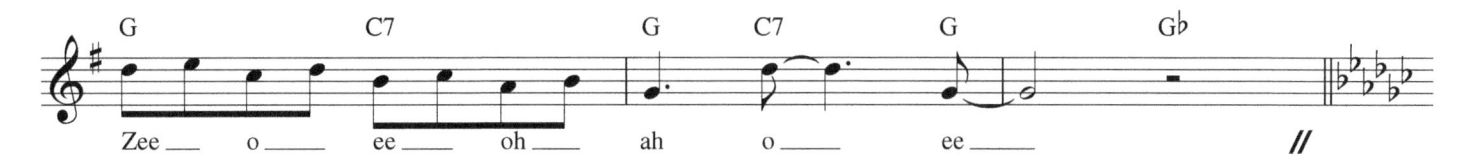

Now, go back down by half steps.

Conclude without reaching the bottom of your range.

EXERCISE 7. FLEXIBILITY WITH RELAXATION

This exercise is sung quickly, with an easy jaw. "O" and "ee" are very close vowels; you don't need to change much inside your mouth to articulate a difference between them. Seek that "sweet spot" where the notes are ringing in the roof of your mouth, almost effortlessly. Notice how similar the sounds are in the physical placement of your palates. The speed of the exercises helps you to change vowels without working too hard at it. Be sure to maintain your breath through the last note of each five-bar phrase. Look in a mirror to be sure you aren't grimacing, yet opening your mouth enough so the sound comes out.

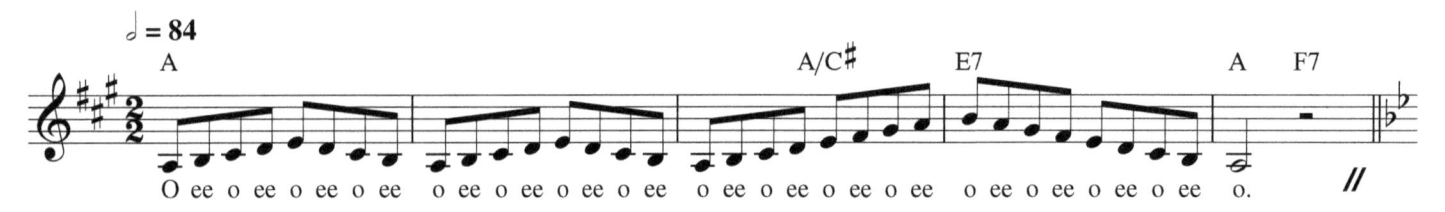

Range:

TRACK 10

Continue up by half steps until you feel a good stretch in the top of your range, but you are definitely not straining. If it feels a little bit "high" on top, bend your knees in an easy plié as you approach the fourth measure; then straighten up for the last note:

Now, travel back down by half *or whole* steps until you end a note or two below where you started:

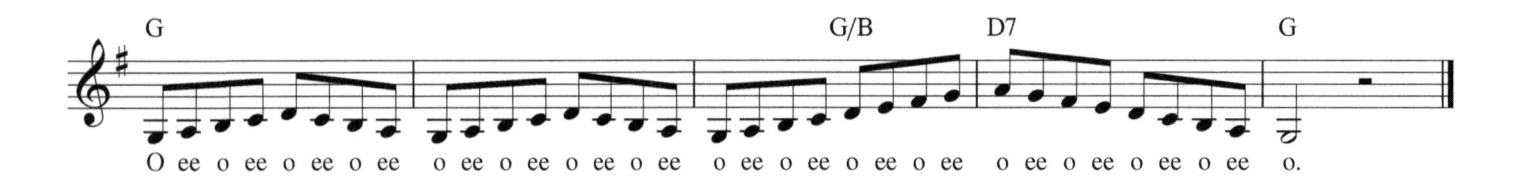

EXERCISE 8. STRETCH RANGE WITH BRIGHT VOWEL, MAJOR/MINOR

Sing this exercise soupy, stretchy, rubbery. Focus your thoughts on aiming for accurate notes in the triad: Do (1), Sol (5), Te (♭7) and Mi or Me (3, ♭3).

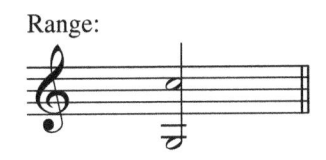

Range:

TRACK 11

Fig. 6.3. Stretch Major/Minor Exercise

You may sing toward the top of your range if that is comfortable. When you do, float the notes, never pushing or straining. Let the bright sound do the work for you. Also, be aware of maintaining a constant volume; notes get louder naturally as you go "higher," so you will need to lighten up as you ascend. It may appear softer to you as you rise and keep a steady volume; you may *feel* as if you are lightening it up. (To check your actual volume, record yourself with a device that has a visual display for audio, such as GarageBand or a sound-level meter.)

Again, finish up the exercise lower than where you started. Travel deeper into your range without pushing down your larynx to get those notes you're after (as a child does who is trying to sound older). Instead, always *allow* the mechanism to move rather than forcing it.

> **TIP: SMILE** ☺
> When you smile naturally, not only does your body send endorphins throughout your system (yes there really is a physiological connection between mood and facial expressions), but it also reinforces bright, "forward" vocal placement, making singing more effortless.

EXERCISE 9. REARTICULATION WITHOUT GLOTTAL ATTACK

Singing twice on one pitch to rearticulate it, without tightening the throat in the process, helps develop detail work without strain. Sing each three-bar phrase on one breath. Low voices begin on A; higher voices begin on C.

Sing it once with straight eighths, then up one half step with a swing feel. Repeat, alternating straight with swing as you ascend by half steps.

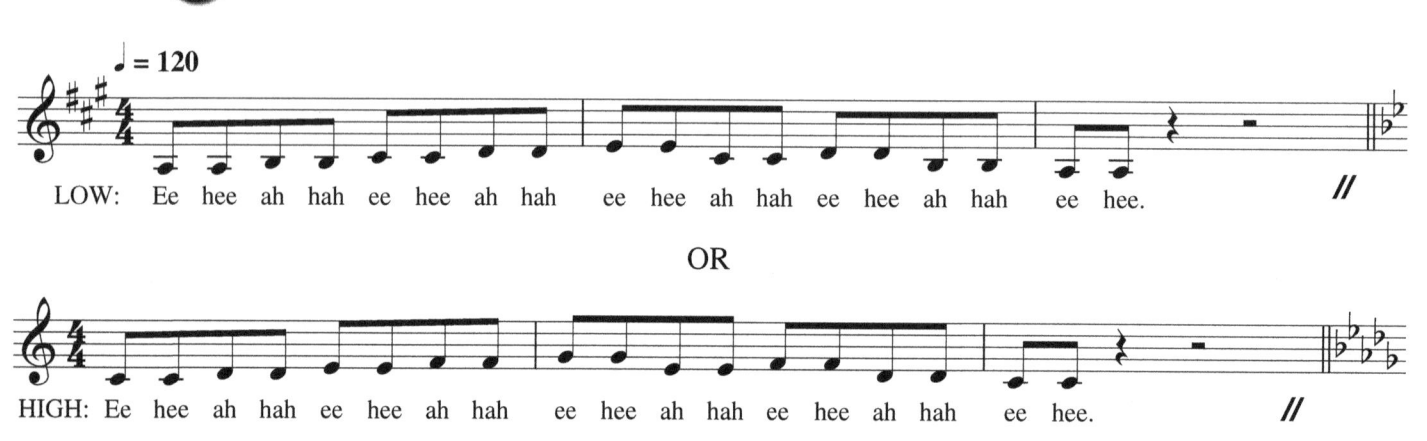

🔊 **TRACK 12**

♩ = 120

LOW: Ee hee ah hah ee hee ah hah ee hee ah hah ee hee ah hah ee hee.

OR

HIGH: Ee hee ah hah ee hee ah hah ee hee ah hah ee hee ah hah ee hee.

Continue up by half steps, then turn around to sing back down by half steps.

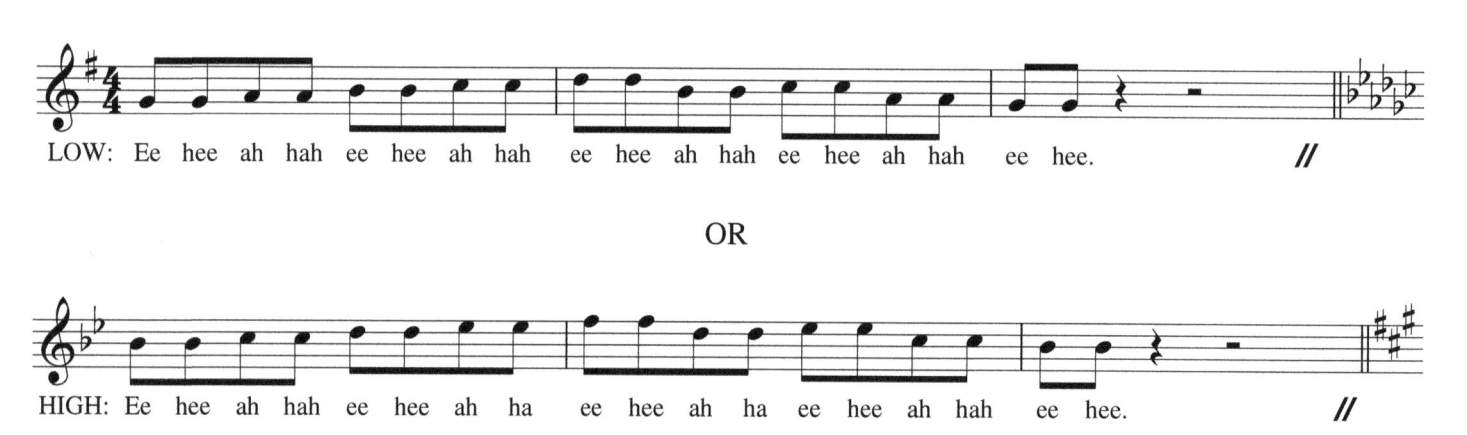

LOW: Ee hee ah hah ee hee ah hah ee hee ah hah ee hee ah hah ee hee.

OR

HIGH: Ee hee ah hah ee hee ah ha ee hee ah ha ee hee ah hah ee hee.

Conclude comfortably low in your range. Because you are warming up your voice, each note can approach your bottom note as long as you don't press the larynx down.

EXERCISE 10. TRADITIONAL EXERCISE FOR AGILITY WITH ACCURACY

This exercise is often used in choir warm-ups. It's simply the word "alleluia." The "le" vowel is pronounced with a short "e" as in "let." Be mindful of the interval between "lu" and "ia" so that as you approach the octave, the top pitch doesn't pop out. Higher voices may keep heading up; both voices, stop ascending before you feel strain.

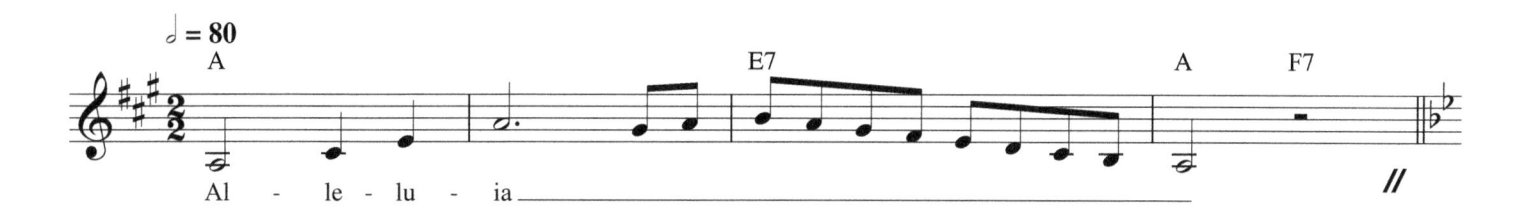

🔊 **TRACK 13**

Continue moving up by half steps.

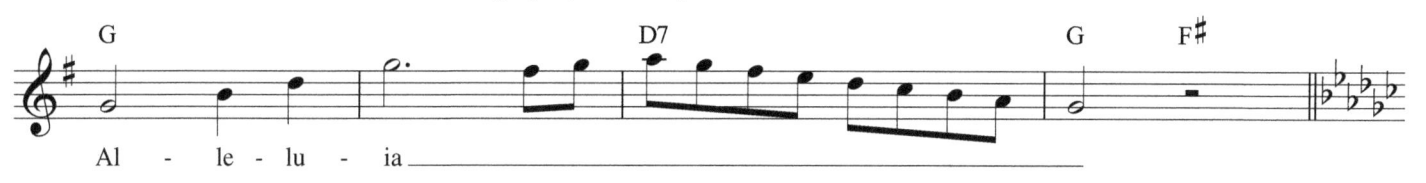

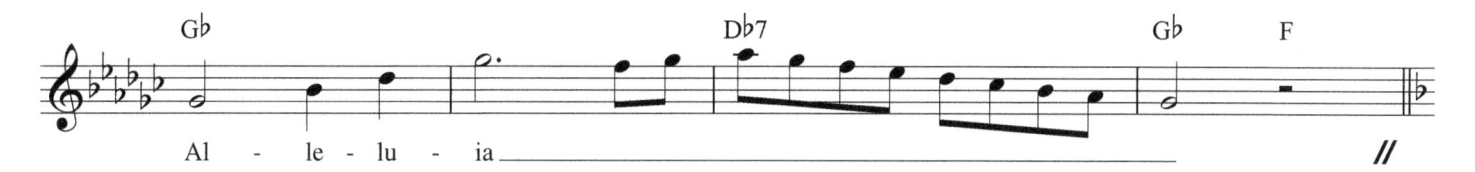

Continue to travel down by half steps, concluding nice and low in your range.

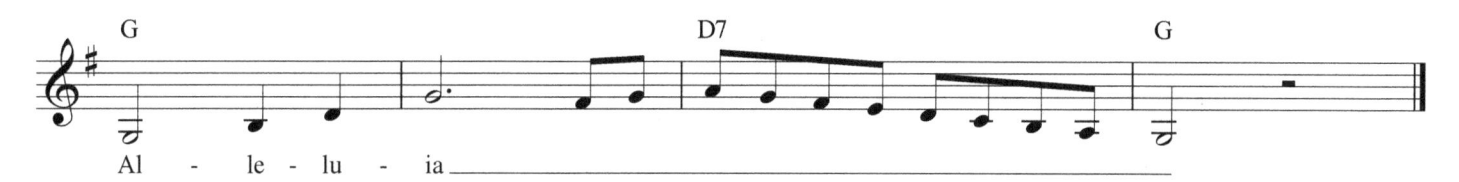

EXERCISE 11. ELASTIC BAND, ALTERNATING MAJOR/MINOR

A wide elastic band that is used at the gym makes a terrific device to aid flexibility by helping you to visualize engaging more of your body when you sing. Hold the band in front of you, arms outstretched, about six inches apart. As you sing, stretch the band outward to about two feet as you ascend, then let it relax when you complete one phrase. This will help your *body* to feel the elasticity that your voice can generate, even while you go "up" in pitch. (Be careful not to over-tense your arms by using a very short length of band; rather, you are encouraging your body to stretch.)

In this exercise, allow yourself a small pause at the top octave note, as if you're at the top of a Ferris wheel with the best view, right before it goes forward again. Take as much time as you need to be clean, flexible, and accurate, all on one breath.

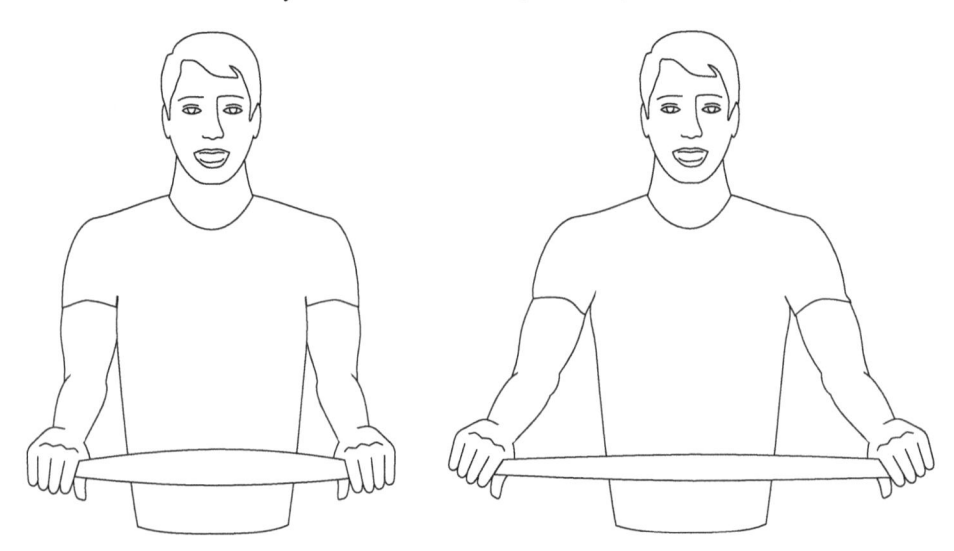

Fig. 6.13. Elastic Band

TRACK 14

Ranges: High: Low:

Zee

Zee

Continue up by whole steps, opening the "ee" vowel somewhat as you get higher to avoid tension or pressing. Lower voices stop at an E or where you're comfortable. If you feel like moving your body along with the recording on this exercise, that's perfectly okay.

Zee

Continue to travel down by whole steps.

AGILITY AND RHYTHM

> **TIP: YOU ARE NOT A PIANO**
>
> The piano is a percussion instrument, with felt hammers that hit strings to produce sound. Because we learn to speak or sing largely by imitation, often when we work with a piano, we tend to imitate its action. However, the way your voice produces tone is actually similar to the function of a trombone or a violin. So, when you work together with a piano accompaniment, be careful not to unconsciously imitate it. (Unless, of course, you want that sound, artistically, but that's another story.)

EXERCISE 12. CREATING MELODIC SPACES WITHOUT ADDING BREATHS

In this exercise, you are stopping the flow of sound within a rhythmic pattern that is traveling up a scale by thirds. Take your breath at the top of the octave, marked by the check mark. Conserve your air to last through the four bars; avoid taking a breath, out of habit, at the melodic rests in the exercise. We'll do it first in normal time, then double time, and in both major and minor keys.

🔊 **TRACK 15**

Fig. 6.4. Melodic Spaces Exercise 1

Continue to alternate major with minor, and normal time/double time, as you ascend by half steps.

FLEXIBILITY EXERCISES FOR BLUES AND R&B RUNS AND JAZZ IMPROVISATION

EXERCISE 13. MOVEMENT AND FLEXIBILITY

Now that you're warming up, we'll take the exercises faster and add complexity. If 150 beats per minute (bpm) is too fast and all your notes are not clean, slow it down a little. Remember, keep the melodic line foremost in your mind, picturing all the eighth notes as part of one larger melody, like beads on a necklace strand.

The major pentatonic scale is used in this exercise. When you learn to improvise over basic blues changes, sticking to this set of pitches is a great place to start: you can't sing a "wrong" note. It's interesting to note that many spirituals use the pentatonic scale, meaning their melodies consist only of these five pitches: consider "Amazing Grace" and "Swing Low, Sweet Chariot." The major and minor pentatonic scales likely originated in Africa.

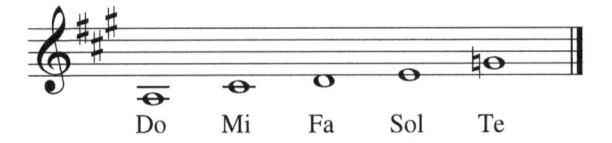

TRACK 16

Fig, 6.5. Major Pentatonic Scale

As with the previous exercises, travel up by half steps. If the starting note, above, is too low, start a little higher. We'll take this one pretty far into your upper register. Let the sound get thinner and lighter but not breathy, never pushed or forced. Let the vowels be open, not pinched, especially the "ee" vowel. Lower voices: go only as high as you are comfortable, perhaps to an F.

Now that we're moving along, travel down by whole steps, and complete as low as you are comfortable without pressing down your larynx.

FLEXIBILITY EXERCISES FOR BLUES AND R&B RUNS AND JAZZ IMPROVISATION

TIP: REMEMBER, AVOID "DOING THE MUPPET"

Muppets move their jaws up and down with every word. When your jaw does this on phrases while you are singing just one vowel, that means your jaw is tight. Massage the jaw muscles in the area of your back molars as you sing, to help them release. Use a mirror: have you been doing the muppet?

EXERCISE 14. MINOR PENTATONIC RUNS FOR AGILITY AND NOTE CHOICE

As before, ascend by half steps. Then, find out how low in your range you can descend, comfortably.

Seeing patterns within an exercise makes it easier to sing the intervals accurately. In this exercise, locate the tonic (Do, or A in this key), both at the root and one octave up. Then, locate the fifth (Sol, or E in this key). Once you hear these clearly, locate the seventh (Te, or G in this key). When you can reference these notes solidly in your mind, they become like harmonic markers, or sign posts, making the other pitches much easier to hear and sing consistently.

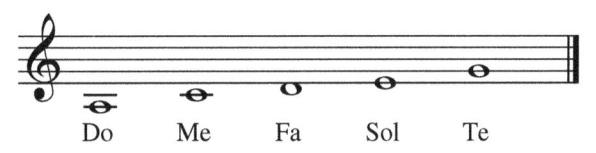

Fig. 6.6. Minor Pentatonic Scale

TRACK 17

Fig. 6.7. Minor Pentanonic Exercise 1

Variation 1

This exploration of minor-pentatonic runs is based on an exercise by my Berklee colleague, Kudisan Kai. Start with the exercise, as written. This will help you build flexibility and consistency. Then, make up your own patterns using the minor pentatonic pitches. Experiment with notes in different octaves, too. Any of these notes will sound good together!

By Kudisan Kai

Fig. 6.8. Minor Pentatonic Exercise 2

Variation 2

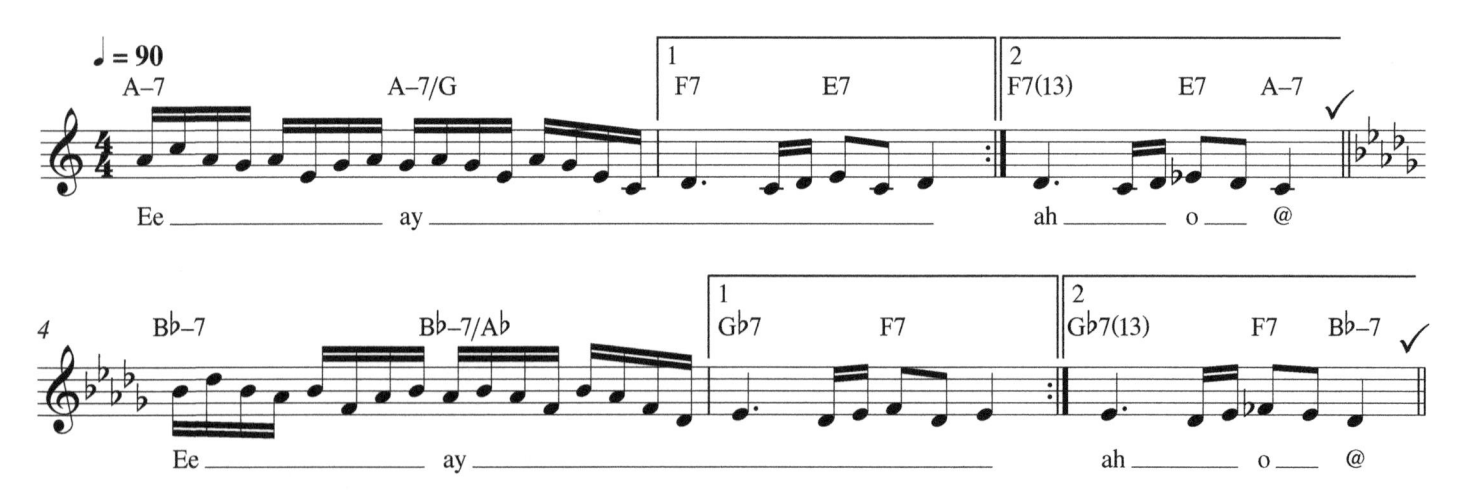

Fig. 6.9. Minor Pentatonic Exercise 3

FLEXIBILITY EXERCISES FOR BLUES AND R&B RUNS AND JAZZ IMPROVISATION

EXERCISE 15. MAJOR PENTATONIC MOVEMENT AND AGILITY

Work this exercise as comfortably high as you can, always focusing on stretch and flexibility.

🔊 **TRACK 18**

Lower Voices

You are singing the piano's "black keys" to start, as an arpeggio in the key of G♭.

Oo _____ Ee _____

Higher Voices

The pattern for higher voices is the same. We'll begin higher, though still low in your range.

Oo _____ Ee _____

EXERCISE 16. CAT ("C@T") VOWEL USING MINOR PENTATONIC MODE

This exercise will help you create a vowel tone used commonly in contemporary music, using the bright "aah" vowel as in "pak the cah in Havad yad." Don't be afraid of a strong, bright tone; nor is it about exaggerating to the point of sounding nasal by pressing tone into your sinuses. This vowel shape is created by broadening the roof of your mouth or palate, allowing the air to flow up against the roof of your mouth and forward. It is decidedly *not* bel canto. It's good to have fun with it, too.

We'll use the word "cat," with the vowel illustrated as "@." Don't be concerned if you think your voice sounds less appealing when you're trying out this exercise. The goal is to lift your soft palate, while creating a broader, flatter version of the domed space in the roof of your mouth. The sound is bright and high. It may never be a "pretty" sound. Is that really *always* important? A bright treble-heavy tone will help cut through a live band that is amplified, and also create flexibility throughout your range. We'll take this sound through a minor-pentatonic scale.

150   **CHAPTER 6** The Exercises

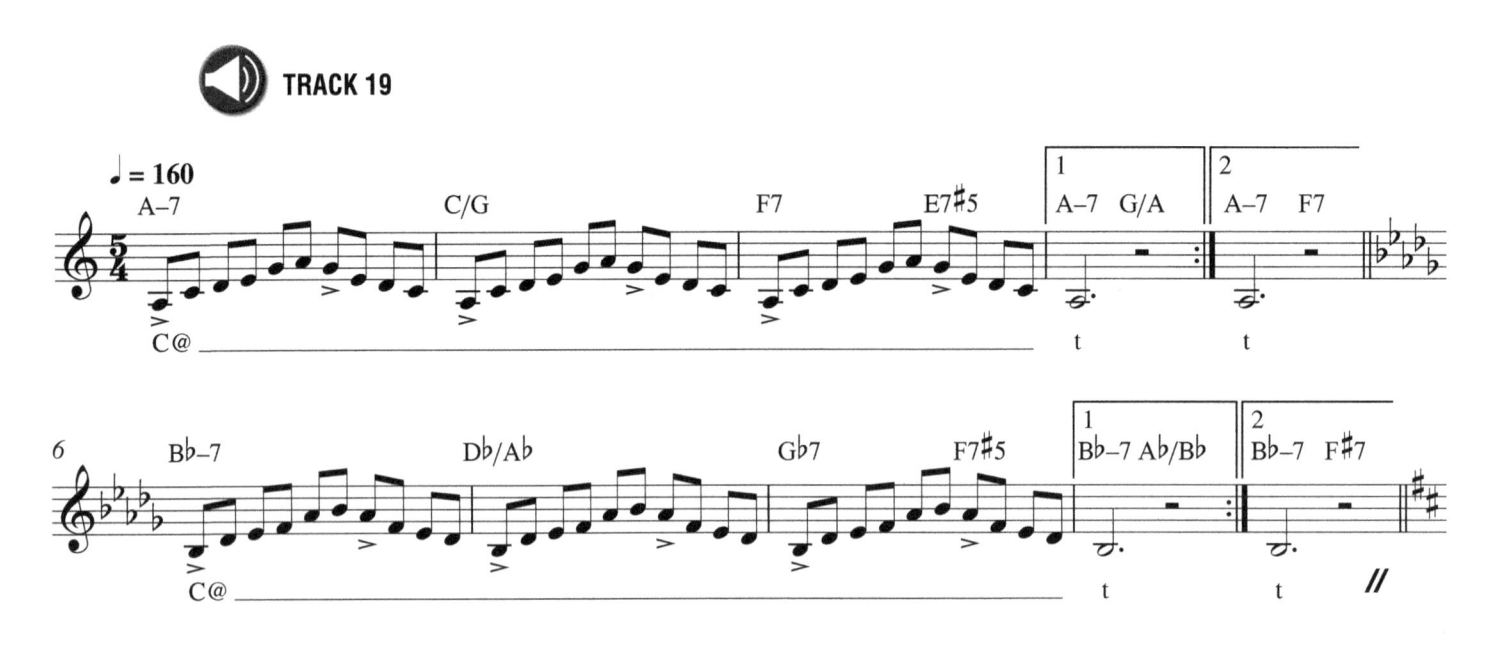

🔊 **TRACK 19**

Continue up by half steps (or whole steps, now that you are warmed up)....

Then, travel down by whole steps until you're low in your range.

EXERCISE 17. LYDIAN MODE

Take the Lydian mode slowly at first to hear the intervals affected by the sharp 4, then speed up when you are solid on the notes.

🔊 **TRACK 20**

Fig. 6.10. Lydian Mode

FLEXIBILITY EXERCISES FOR BLUES AND R&B RUNS AND JAZZ IMPROVISATION

TIP: SWING FEEL

A swing rhythm is based on a triplet feel. It is used in many styles besides jazz, such as country, hip-hop, and reggae. Furthermore, jazz styles don't always use a swing feel. In printed music, when you see:

♫ = ♩♪ (triplet)

...the publisher is indicating that the eighth notes—the subdivision pulse of the meter—swing. However, a swing is not as literal or precise as triplets. Swing is a relaxed feel that aims to be "in the pocket," or to groove. The best way to understand a good swing feel is to listen to master players.

EXERCISE 18. SCAT SYLLABLES USING MAJOR/MINOR, AND STRAIGHT EIGHTHS/SWING EIGHTHS

Try the exercise both ways with the recording, with an even-eighths rhythm ("straight eighths"), and then swung. The syllables in the exercise are suggestions; you can make up your own, too.

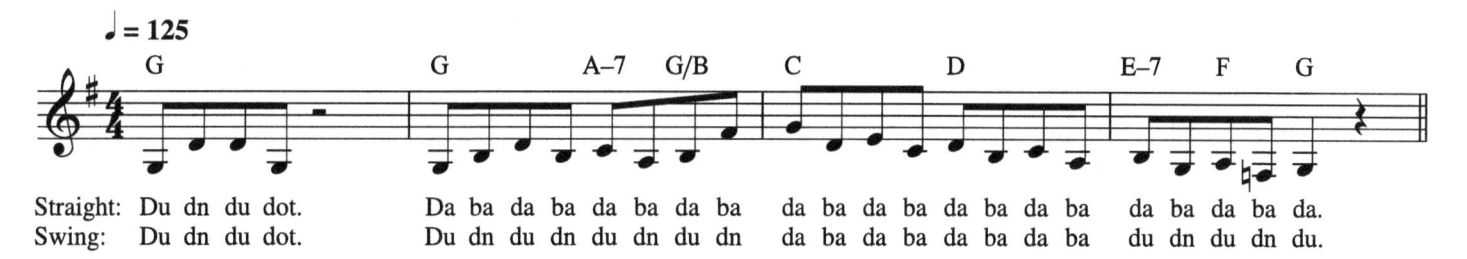

TRACKS 21–22

Straight: Du dn du dot.   Da ba da ba da ba da ba   da ba da ba da ba da ba   da ba da ba da.
Swing: Du dn du dot.   Du dn du dn du dn du dn   da ba da ba da ba da ba   du dn du dn du.

Fig. 6.11. Scat Syllables Exercise

EXERCISE 19. BOSSA (LATIN) RHYTHM EXERCISE

In this exercise, the rhythm is relaxed, yet "in the pocket," and seeks a balance of legato and staccato within one phrase. The exercise varies slightly every four bars in a twenty-four bar pattern, going between the I and ♭II chords. Keep your tongue relaxed as you articulate the various syllables. They are not "right" or "wrong" syllables; you can vary them if you like. Remember, though, singing the same two syllables such as "doo-bie doo-bie" repeatedly becomes uninteresting very quickly, so look for at least three syllables for variety.

TRACKS 23–24

Bossa feel, easy and in the pocket
♩ = 140

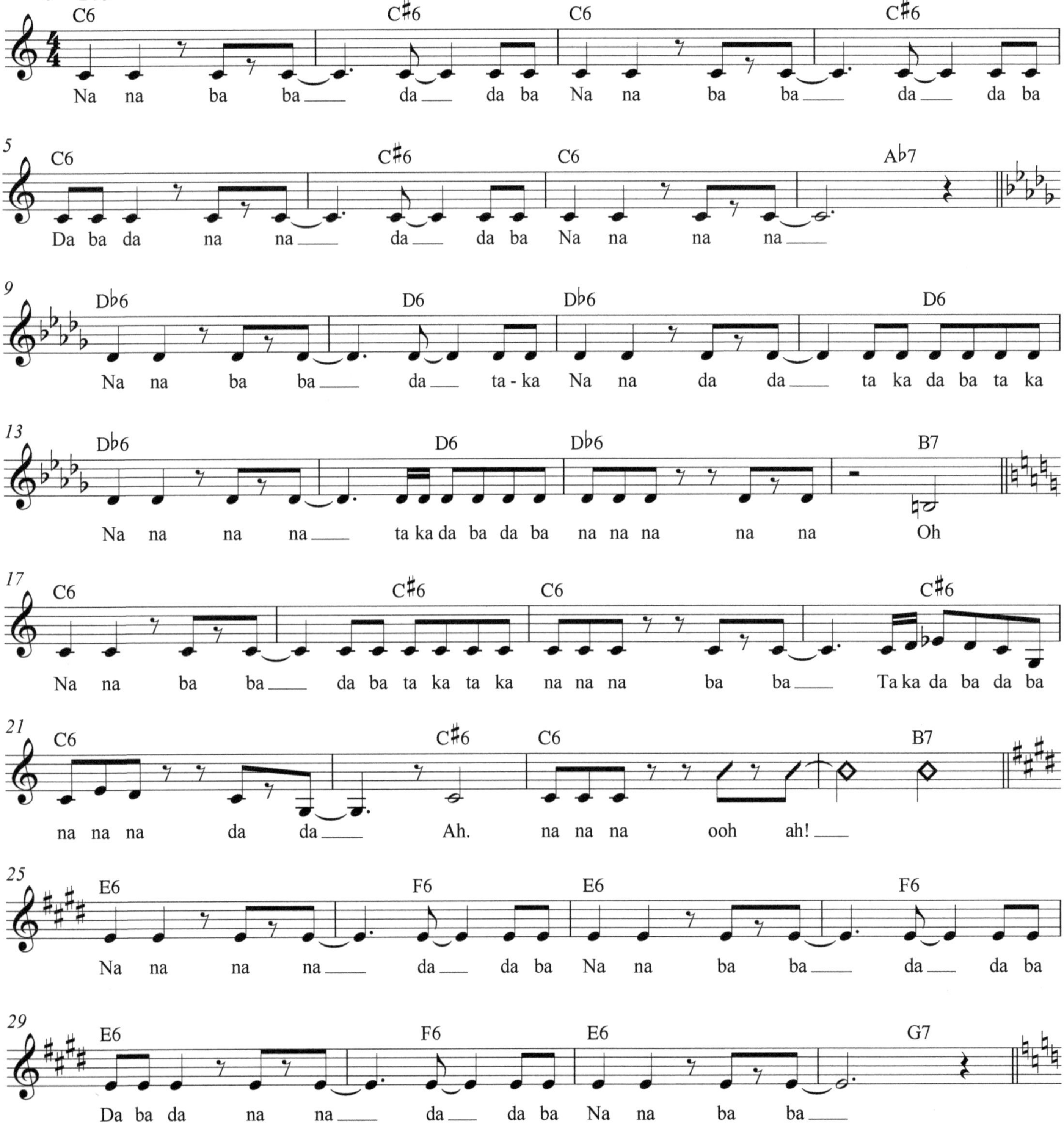

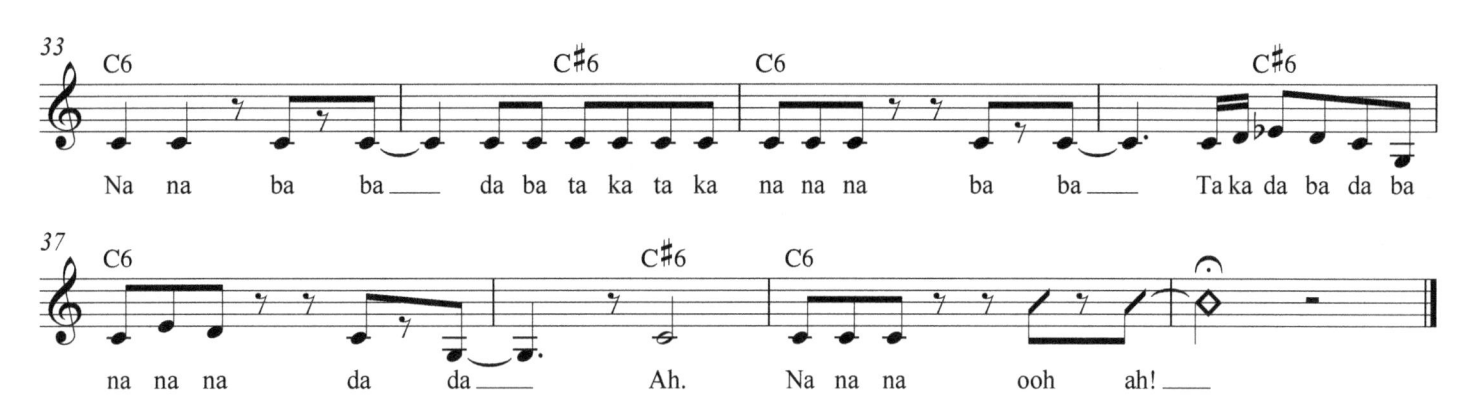

FLEXIBILITY EXERCISES FOR BLUES AND R&B RUNS AND JAZZ IMPROVISATION

Fig. 6.12. Bossa Rhythm Exercise

EXERCISE 20. SWINGING A CLASSIC

This is a traditional-style exercise modified by swinging the eighth-note rhythms.

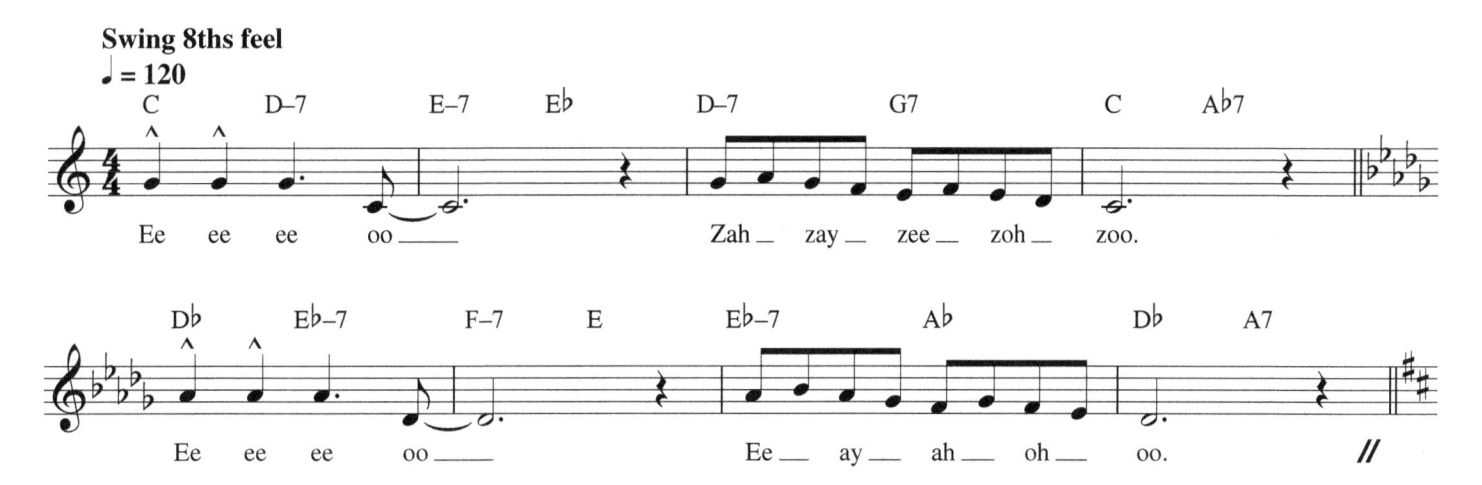

TRACK 25

Continue up by half steps...

Now, travel down by half steps.

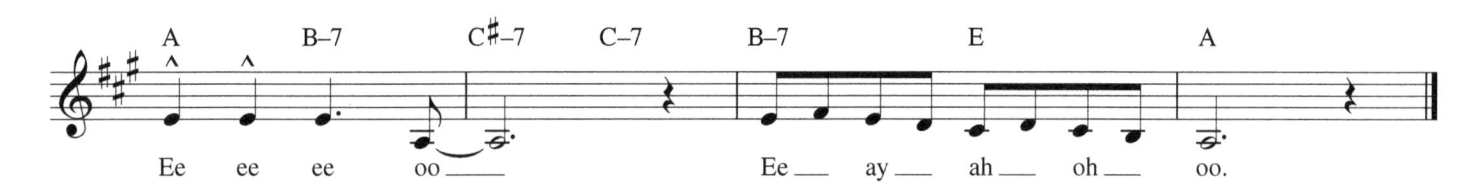

POWER

EXERCISE 21. POWER EXERCISE VOLUME SWELL: SOFT TO LOUD, THEN LOUD TO SOFT

This exercise takes you through shifts between registers as you change volume on one note. The slower you can tolerate going through the transition points without constricting, the better. It will teach your muscles to resist constricting through detailed register shifts and, with repetition, will give you superb flexibility. You may dislike the sound at first, especially if your voice does not change smoothly initially. That is normal. This isn't an exercise for vocal beauty. It's about building power with healthy technical control.

Begin on a very clean, soft tone, then gradually crescendo as if you were adjusting a volume knob on your stereo, one number louder at a time. With 1 being super soft and 10 being as loud as you can sing or yell, begin at about level 2. Gradually increase your volume to about an 8 while holding one vowel. Allow your vocal mechanism to shift registers as it gets louder. It will likely shift into "belt" or loudest tone. Be sure that you are not constricting your neck muscles or lifting and tightening your upper ribs; this is very important so that you *do not strain*. Don't fight the shift, and keep your breath supportive. *Embrace* the moment when you feel your voice changing; take your time through that area. When done correctly, this exercise gives you facility in the tough area around register shifts that occur between soft and loud tones on any given pitch, such as shifting into falsetto or belt voice.

Fig. 6.29. Volume Knob

When you decrescendo, repeat the exercise in reverse. Again, take your time through each number on the dial.

POWER

TRACK 26

[Musical notation: pp ee ——— Ah ff AH ——— ee ——— pp]

Or, try it out first up an octave (as demonstrated on the recording):

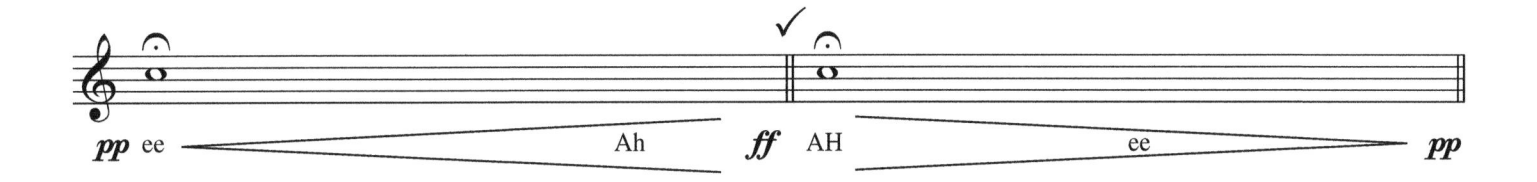

[Musical notation: pp ee ——— Ah ff AH ——— ee ——— pp]

TIP: BALANCE

To keep your body balanced, visualize opposites at work while you sing. When you sing notes that are moving "up," internally picture your body going down. When you sing notes that are moving "down," internally picture that you are going up.

EXERCISE 22: OPEN PHARYNX (THROAT)

In this exercise, stay within the lower to mid range of your voice. The arrows indicate continuing your support through the end of each three-note phrase, then lifting off at the end of each measure.

TRACK 27

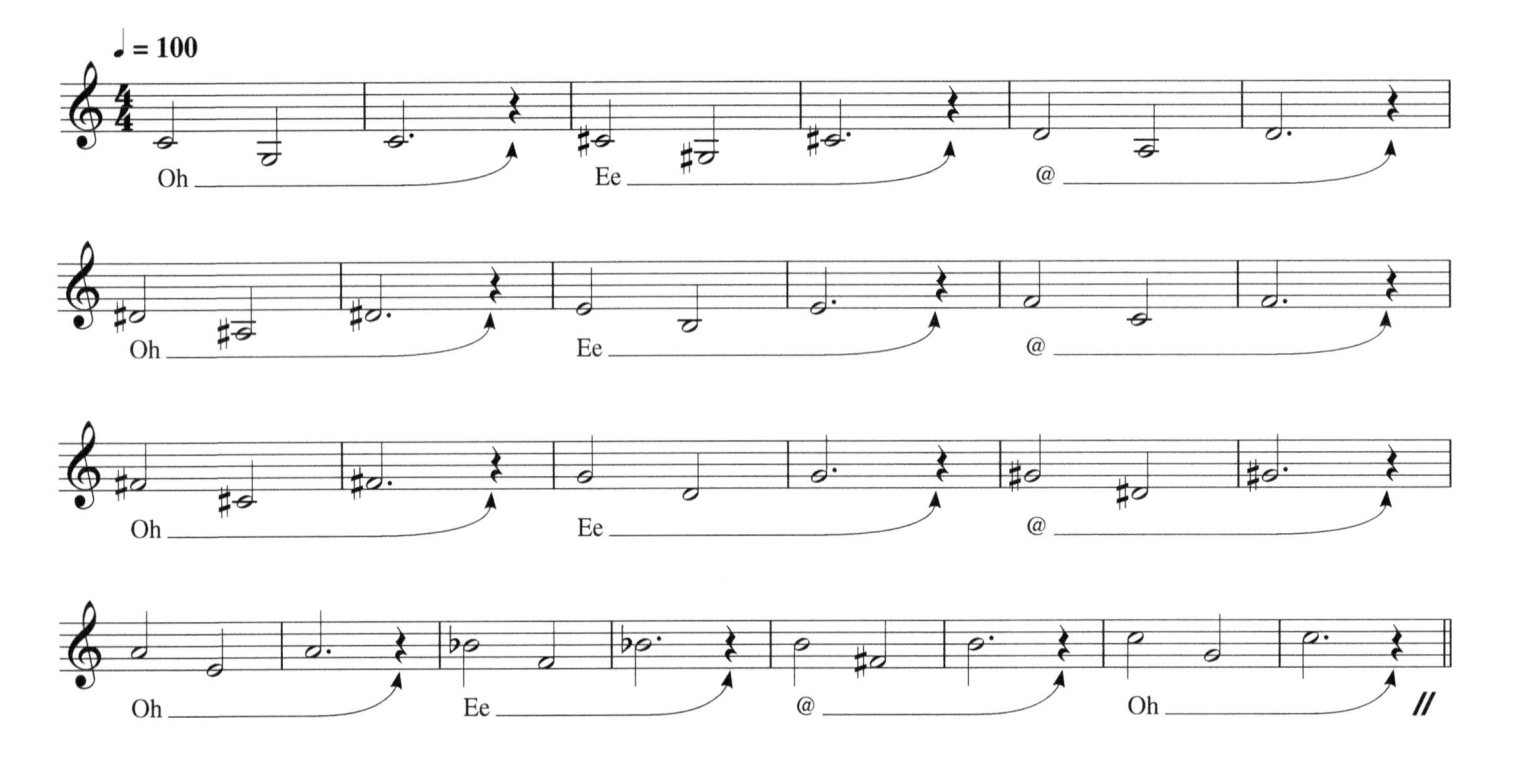

Continue up by half steps...then, travel down.

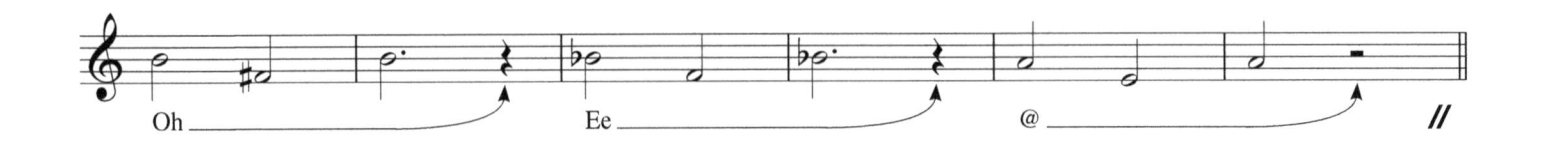

End about where you started.

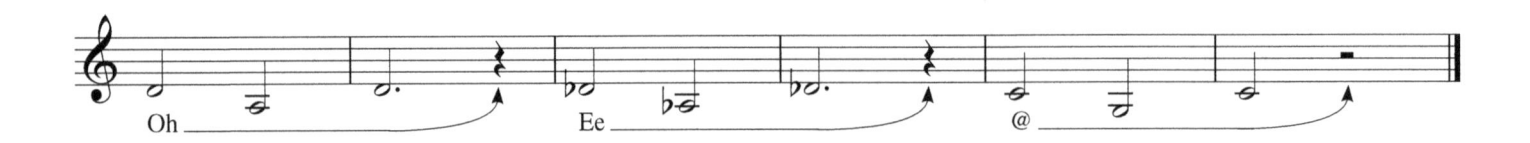

BELTING

Belting, or loud full-voice singing, is commonly used, and also abused, in contemporary styles. It can be done safely. The previous exercises have been working up to it. Belting—sometimes a form of controlled yelling—should not be done before you are fully warmed up and flexible. Exercise 21, "Volume Swell," is the first step to healthy belting: it trains the laryngeal muscles to sing through transitions in registers without strain.

Belting is used poorly when a loud "chest voice" is pushed up beyond its limit. How do you know you're at the limit? Muscles can only stretch so far. It may hurt, your voice gets tired quickly, your neck muscles bulge, you turn red, your chin rises. If your voice is hoarse after you've sung, you've been straining.

As we've seen, there are two primary muscles involved in controlling the vocal folds: the cricothyroid muscle and the vocalis muscle. One stretches for higher pitches, the other thickens and shortens the folds for louder, lower notes. Imagine a rubber band. As you stretch it, it gets thinner. If you don't allow your vocal folds to thin as the muscles stretch for higher notes, you will strain.

The secret sauce is to employ loud "mix" tones sooner. "Mix" means simply a little of this, a little of that. There is no perfect recipe for mix. You are in mix voice if you are not entirely in "chest voice" (the fullest lower tones you have that push out belt) or if you are not entirely in "head voice" (the thinner tones that travel high in your range). Exercise 16, "C@t," is designed specifically to develop mix voice. So, instead of pushing your chest voice as far as it will go—until you find yourself switching to a wispy, thin sound before your voice cracks—use this *third* option sooner, during that transitional place in between your ranges. (This is where passaggios are.) Tenor voices can usually belt full voice to higher pitches than baritones; altos can usually bring belt voice, especially when blended in mix, to fairly high pitches before needing to make shifts in register. When ascending in belt voice, sopranos who have a full lower voice may find the need to shift to a lighter tone earlier than altos.

Healthy belting is difficult to teach from a book. You really need to be coached by a teacher who understands the mechanics of it. It is like learning how to lift 150-pound weights from a book. You might be doing it correctly, or you might be lifting the weight and hurting yourself over time, with a blown shoulder showing up later on. Let's avoid injury! These exercises will help you find your range of healthy belting in your own instrument.

However: If in doubt, don't do it. Many known singers have wrecked their voices by belting badly, again and again. Or, they don't rest adequately in between strong periods of singing, and wear themselves out.

EXERCISE 23. LOUD OPEN LONG TONES

In this exercise, your pharynx is open and spacious, like a cathedral. Allow the sound to resonate throughout your mouth, being mindful not to pull it back down your throat as you ascend. **Tip:** Hold your tongue as you sing so that it cannot retract.

Even though I've indicated a swell in volume, you may not need to crescendo to get louder as you follow the melody up, as pitches tend to be naturally louder when a melody rises.

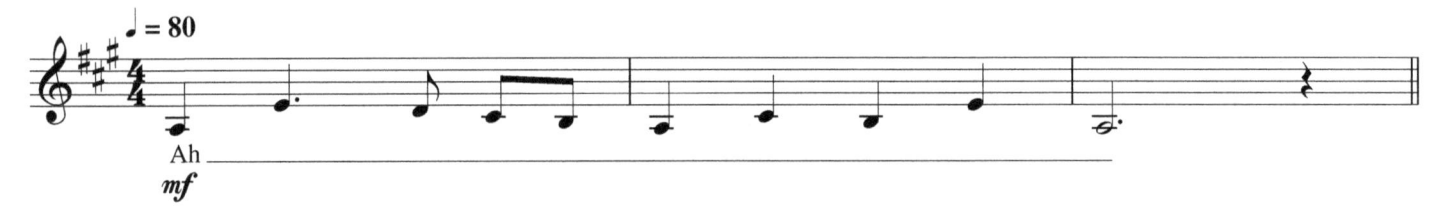

🔊 **TRACK 28**

Ah
mf

Fig. 6.13. Long Tones Exercise

EXERCISE 24. 12-BAR BLUES

Use the 12-bar blues as a starting point for singing blues. This exercise will help you develop strong singing technique with melody. The 12-bar blues form is simple. I think of it like a circle: the 12 measures keep looping around and around with each new verse and then under solos. Once you are comfortable with the patterns here, which are melody with embellishments, make up your own in a similar fashion. Remember, blues is about moaning, expression, emotion—perfect voices and perfect tone are not important at all.

BELTING

Higher Voices

🔊 **TRACKS 29–30**

High key
12 bar blues, rock feel, straight 8ths
♩ = 120

Hey — yeah — Hey — yeah — Hey
hey — yeah — Hey — uh uh uh mm
— Oh — *Inst.*
Ooh ooh — Ooh Mm —
Ooh Oh — Yeah, — mm — mm mm. — Oh —
— ho — Yeah — ah ah ah — mm. — Oh — oh.
Oh — Yeah — Ah — hah — oh — Yeah.

Fig. 6.14. 12-Bar Blues Exercise 1, Higher Key

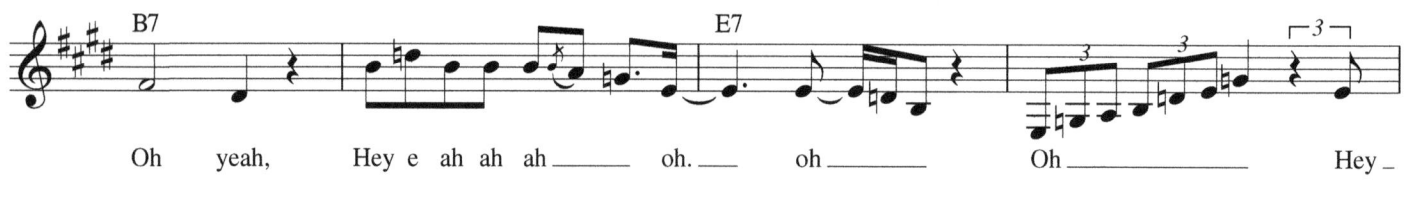

Fig. 6.15. 12-Bar Blues Exercise 2, Lower Key

INTERVALS, CHROMATIC MOVEMENT, AND SCAT

EXERCISE 25. INTERVALS

This exercise will help you build interval accuracy. Recognizing each interval is necessary for sight-reading and very helpful when you are improvising. Become familiar with the relationships between the pitches. The original exercise uses the names of the intervals, but if you prefer solfege syllables, use them instead. This is a useful choral exercise, too.

TRACK 33

Fig. 6.16. Intervals Exercise

EXERCISE 26. CHROMATIC AND RHYTHMIC DETAIL

Using both chromatic movement and two rhythm patterns, this exercise is ear candy. Don't be frustrated if you don't nail it the first time. It may take practice.

TRACK 34

Zay _____ Zee _____ Zoh _____ Za _____ Zu _____

Tay _____ Tee _____ Toh _____ Ta _____ Tu _____

Fig. 6.17. Chromatic Exercise

TIP: SINGING LARGE INTERVALS

When you need to sing a large interval, such as an octave, think of springing off the bottom note and landing on the top note like a cat jumping up on a table. You want to avoid bringing the weight of a lower tone up as you ascend. Instead, lighten the tone by thinning it.

EXERCISE 27. TRITONES

These three phrases take you through a tritone relationship between C and F#, first as quarter notes, then eighth notes, then traveling through two octaves. If the highest notes are beyond your range, begin lower. You may sing these on any syllable(s) that are comfortable. Pitch accuracy is very important here, so take the time you need at first to be dead-on. **Tip:** Record yourself and listen back.

TRACK 35

Fig. 6.18. Tritone Exercise

INTERVALS, CHROMATIC MOVEMENT, AND SCAT

163

EXERCISE 28. SCAT SYLLABLES WITH INTERVALS

This exercise has two tracks, one with a bossa feel, using straight eighths (track 36), and one with a swing feel, using swing eighths (track 37). Experiment singing the patterns with these different styles, one at a time. The repeat in measure 12 takes you back to measure 1, to sing the exercise twice through.

🔊 **TRACKS 36–37**

Fig. 6.19. Scat Syllables with Intervals Exercise

EXERCISE 29. SOUL AND INTERVALS

This exercise is drawn from a tune by my friend and colleague Sarah Dan Jones.[1] I've adapted it as an exercise over the past several years to highlight using a soulful feel, combined with interval work. Repeat the chant in measures 1 to 4 until you are grounded and centered. Then, sing the melody. Be mindful of keeping the "ee" vowel in "peace" from constricting or straining; reaching up to that note may cause your voice to tighten.

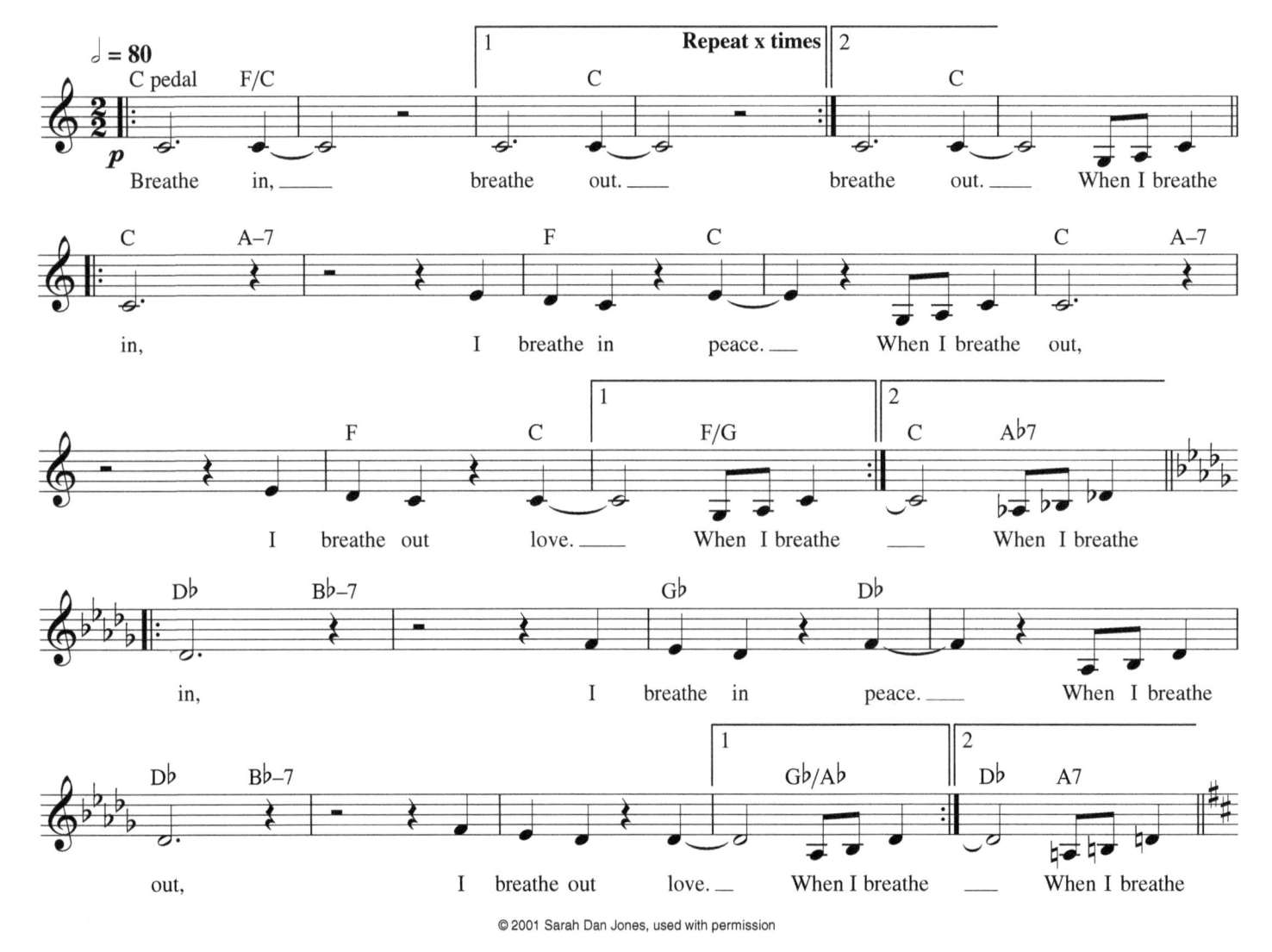

TRACK 38

© 2001 Sarah Dan Jones, used with permission

Fig. 6.20. Soul Exercise: "Meditation on Breathing"

---

[1] The complete tune is available at www.sarahdanjones.com. It is also published in a book of contemporary hymns: *Singing the Journey.* Boston, MA: Unitarian Universalist Association, 2005.

INTERVALS, CHROMATIC MOVEMENT, AND SCAT

165

EXERCISE 30. SWING SIXTEENTHS HIP-HOP GROOVE

This exercise takes you through quick runs with the swing sixteenth rhythm that is common in hip-hop styles. It utilizes the "C@t" vowel as a quality in the "ah" syllable. Once you get the hang of it, experiment with inventing your own patterns.

Lower Voices:

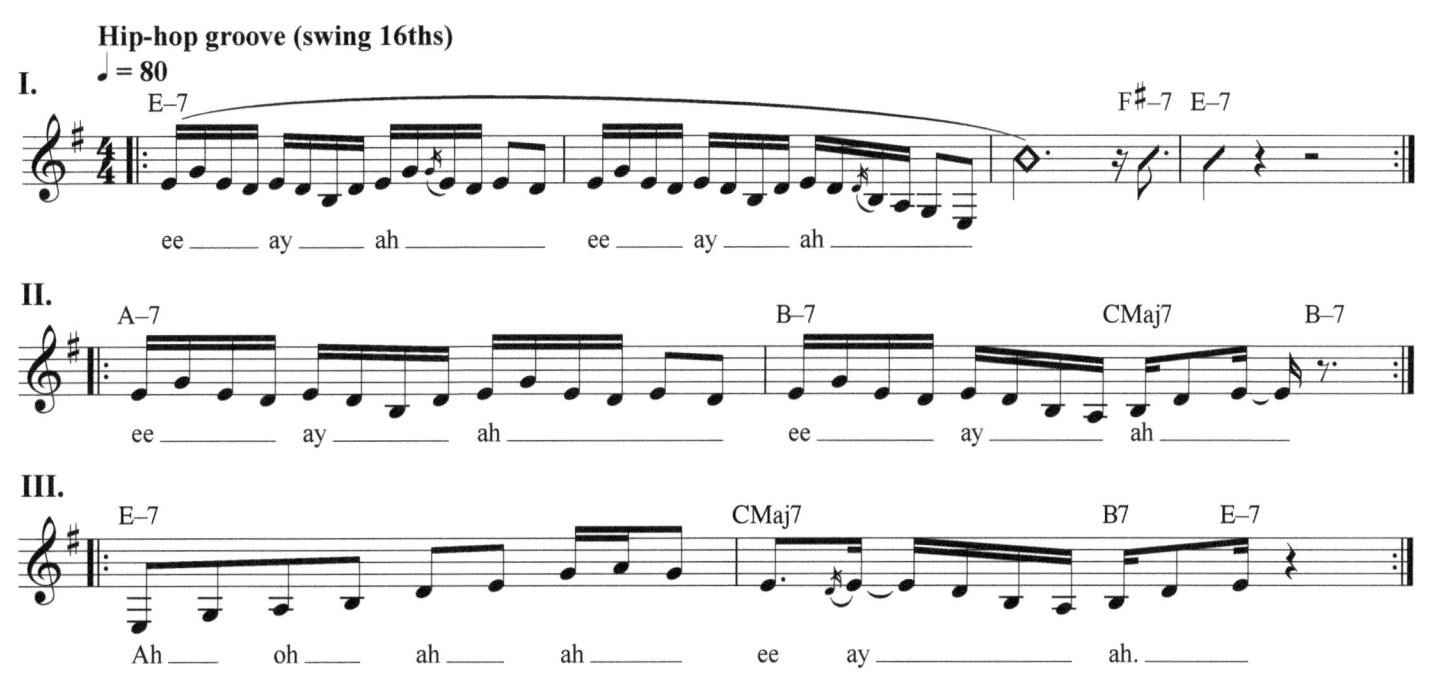

🔊 **TRACK 39**

Fig. 6.21. Swing Sixteenths Exercise 1

Higher Voices:

🔊 **TRACK 40**

Hip-hop groove (swing 16ths)
♩ = 80

Fig. 6.22. Swing Sixteenths Exercise 2

EAR CANDY

Below are exercises to challenge your ear. Singing these while concentrating on detailed intonation will help your pitch to become very accurate.

EXERCISE 31. ARPEGGIO WITH #5

🔊 **TRACK 41**

♩. = 70
Arpeggio with #5

Fig. 6.23. Arpeggio with #5 Exercise

EAR CANDY   167

EXERCISE 32. FULL DIMINISHED ARPEGGIO

🔊 TRACK 42

♩ = 80
Diminished scale

Fig, 6.24. Diminished Arpeggio Exercise

EXERCISE 33. MAJOR/MINOR THIRDS

🔊 TRACK 43

♩ = 90
Minor/Major thirds

Oo ee oo ee oo ee oo ee oo ee oo ee oo ee oo.

Da ba da ba da ba da ba da ba da ba da ba da ba da ba da.

Fig. 6.25. Major/Minor Thirds Exercise

EXERCISE 34. CHROMATIC SCALE DO TO DO

🔊 TRACK 44

Chromatic Scale Do to Do

Oo ee oo ee oo ee oo ee oo ee oo ee oo.

Ay ah ay ah ay ah ay ah ay ah ay ah ay.

Fig. 6.26. Chromatic Scale Exercise

CHAPTER 7

Tunes from My House to Yours

Here are four tunes for you to have fun with. Each one is recorded first with a vocal, then a second time with the instrumentation only so you can sing with the tracks. The final tune in the set, "Every Little Thing You Do," has a recording of the lower key available on the website that supports this book, www.jeanniegagne.com/YourSingingVoice.

CHAPTER 7 Tunes from My House to Yours

TUNE 1. BACKYARD BOP

🔊 **TRACKS 45–46**

Jeannie Gagné

Slow, Bluesy, percussive
♩ = 74 Swing 16ths

Bass line simile until Bridge

CHORUS
Splat! chick-a oom chick-a oom ta-ka bing boom hey-up! hey-up!

VERSE
1. Moss grows slow-ly, stead-i-ly creep-ing, inch-ing 'round my lawn.
It makes mu-sic as it tra-vels. Can you hear its tra-vel-ing song?

VERSE 2–3
2. I like moss, it feels so soft and pli-a-ble un-der my cold bare feet.
Bend the notes 3. Frog is sing-ing to his la-dy, rub-ber-band voice rings through the night.

Dan-dy-li-ons are an-oth-er stor-y, Pull them out for goats to eat!
La-dy croaks back, she bends the notes, and tells us ev-'ry-thing's all right.

CHORUS *Opening bass riff*
Splat! chick-a oom chick-a oom ta-ka bing boom hey-up! hey-up!

Splat! chick-a oom chick-a oom ta-ka bing boom hey-up! hey-up!

Words and Music © 2000 Jeannie Gagné

TUNE 1. BACKYARD BOP

Fig. 7.1. Tune 1: Backyard Bop

TUNE 2. DREAMIN'

TRACKS 47–48

Easy Jazz Swing
♩ = 110

(Lyrics:)

In the morn-ing when ev-'ry-thing is quiet, Just the sound of your heart-beat next to mine.
Dream-ing could nev-er com-pare to the real thing we're feel-ing right here.
float-ing on a love-ly cloud, yet when you hold me I feel the sol-id ground.

Ten-der in the still-ness, your love fills me com-plete-ly.
Sim-ple to pic-ture, al-ways and for-ev-er af-ter I must be dream-in'

lov-ing you feels so right. Eas-y I must

be dream-ing. be

dreaming.

Fig. 7.2. Tune 2: Dreamin'

Words and Music © 2008 Jeannie Gagné

Fig. 7.3. Tune 3: Look Inside for Love

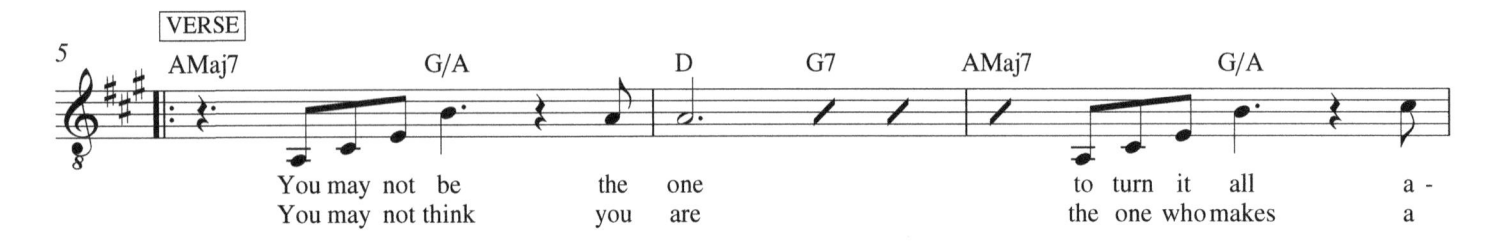

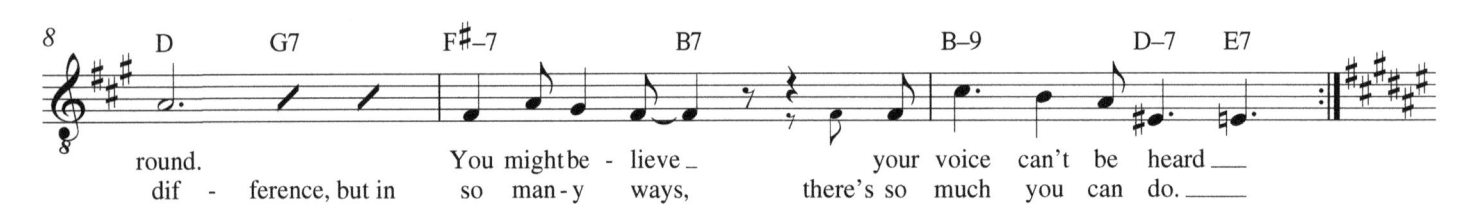

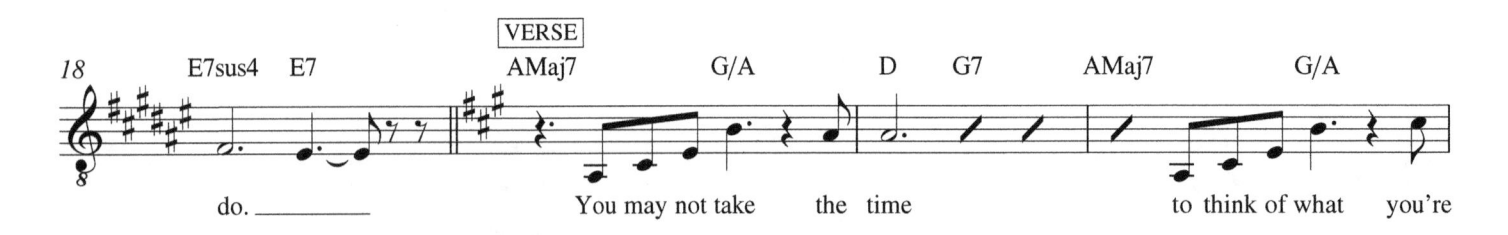

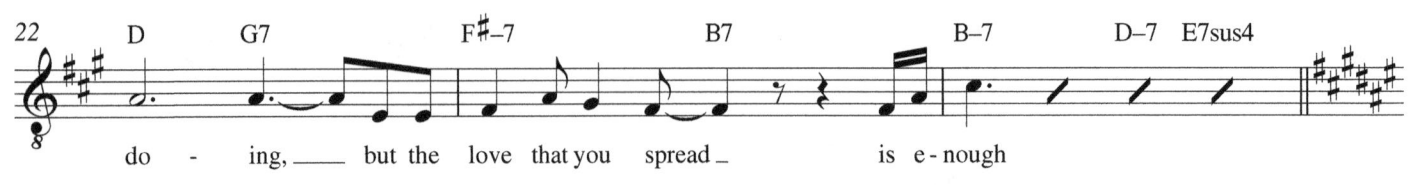

TUNE 4. EVERY LITTLE THING YOU DO

TRACKS 51–52 **HIGH KEY**

Easy Jazz/R&B Feel
♩. = 77

(Verse)
You may not be the one to turn it all a-round.
You may not think you are the one who makes a dif-ference, but in

You might be-lieve your voice can't be heard
so man-y ways, there's so much you can do.

(Chorus)
It's in the face that you show to the world. It's in the words that are true
You make a choice, wheth-er wrong or right, in ev-'ry lit-tle thing that you do.

(Verse)
You may not take the time to think of what you're do-ing, but the love that you spread is e-nough

Words and Music © 2007 Jeannie Gagné, Thaddeus Hogarth

TUNE 4. EVERY LITTLE THING YOU DO

175

CHORUS

It's in the way that you show that you care. It's in the touch that is true.

Ev-'ry-thing mat-ters and ev-'ry-thing comes from ev-'ry lit-tle thing that you do.

IMPROVISATION

CHORUS

It's the way that you com-fort a child.

It's in the love that is true. Ev-'ry-thing mat-ters and ev-'ry-thing comes from

OUTRO

ev-'ry lit-tle thing that you do.

Fig. 7.4. Tune 4: Every Little Thing You Do, High Key

LOW KEY

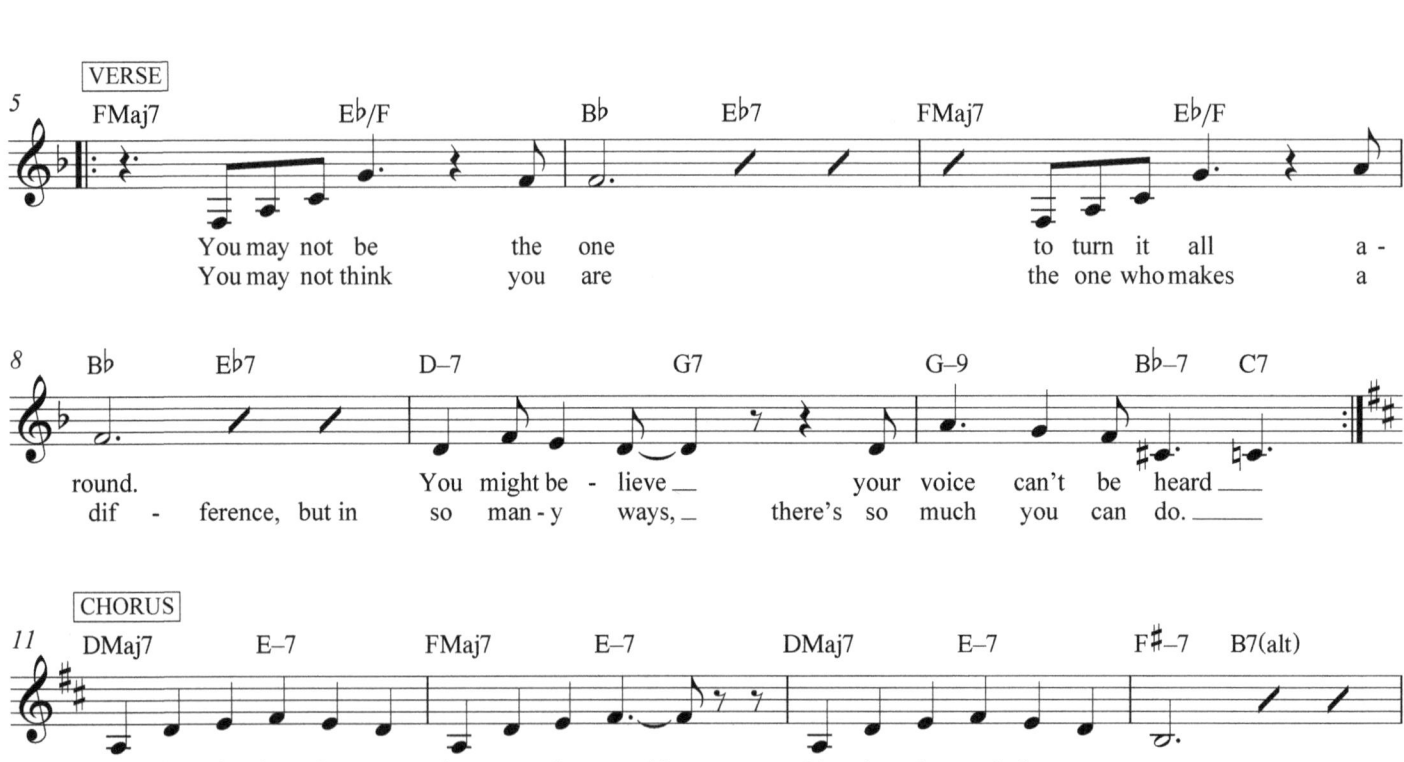

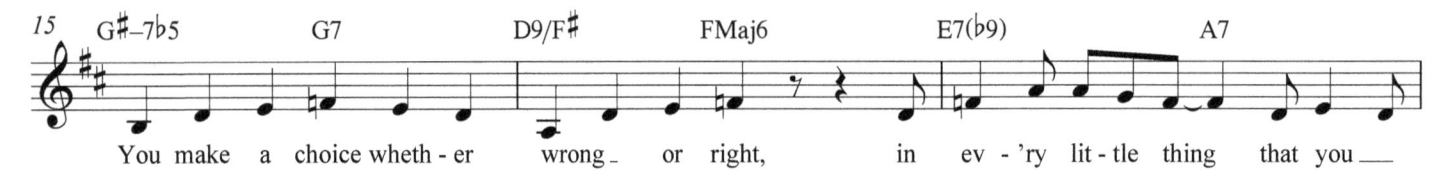

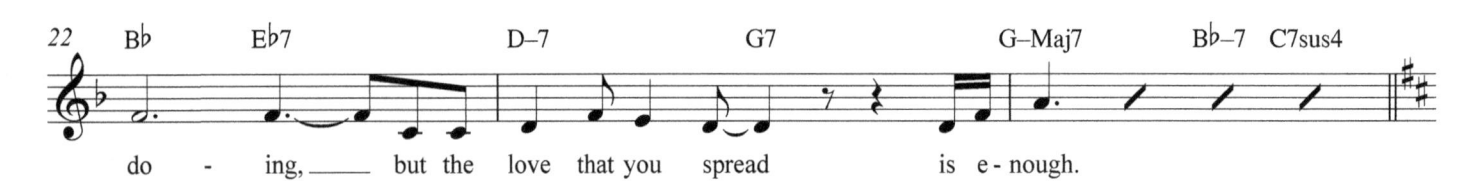

Easy Jazz/R&B Feel
♩. = 77

Verse:
You may not be the one to turn it all a-round.
You may not think you are the one who makes a dif-ference, but in so man-y ways, there's so much you can do.

Chorus:
It's in the face that you show to the world. It's in the words that are true. You make a choice wheth-er wrong or right, in ev-'ry lit-tle thing that you do.

Verse:
You may not take the time to think of what you're do-ing, but the love that you spread is e-nough.

Words and Music © 2007 Jeannie Gagné, Thaddeus Hogarth

TUNE 4. EVERY LITTLE THING YOU DO   **177**

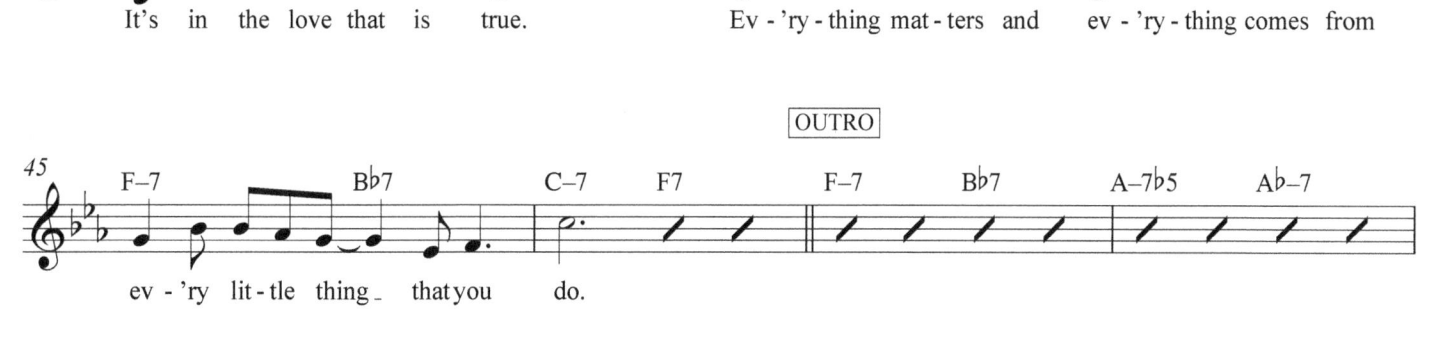

Fig. 7.5. Tune 4: Every Little Thing You Do, Low Key

PART III

Wisdom from Experience: Conversations with Extraordinary Artists, Musicians, and Teachers

INTRODUCTION

There is a process of musical maturity that comes to professionals over years of experience. Many artists create inspiring concerts, but when do you ever get the chance to ask them *how*? I decided to ask these seven highly gifted and seasoned artists what they think about in performance and as artists. What is it like on the other side of the mic? As motivational speaker Tony Robbins is fond of saying, if you want to get really good at something, ask people who already do it well *how* they do it. Find out everything you can. Ask a lot of questions. That's where the conversation section of this book comes in. There is a lot of wisdom on these pages. Enjoy.

CHAPTER 8

Patti Austin

Patti Austin is a Grammy winning recording artist who can sing in virtually any style—jazz, r&b, pop, even opera. She is also a producer, songwriter, and humanitarian. She began her professional career at the tender age of four, singing at the Apollo Theater New York City, then earning her first contract with RCA Records at age five. Growing up in Bay Shore, Long Island, Patti Austin was a child star who appeared on Sammy Davis Jr.'s television show. At age sixteen, she toured with pop vocalist Harry Belafonte at the peak of his fame. Patti Austin's father, Gordon Austin, was a successful trombone player who introduced Patti to major musical artists of the day. During the 1970s and 1980s, she was one of the top commercial jingle singers in New York City. At one time, she could be heard on seventy-five commercial spots simultaneously on television and radio. She grew up immersed in music. Producer Quincy Jones is Patti Austin's godfather. Diana Washington was her godmother.

Patti Austin may best be known for her pop hit "Baby Come to Me," a duet with James Ingram, and for "How Do You Keep the Music Playing." She had twenty songs on the r&b charts between 1969 and 1991, as well as success on the dance/club charts. In 2011, she co-produced "We Are the World 25 for Haiti." Her newest CD, *Sound Advice*, is a musically eclectic journey through songs that offer great advice. Patti Austin's humanitarian work includes co-founding the Over My Shoulder Foundation with CEO Dawn Carroll, "a non-profit mentoring organization established on the principle that the arts, entertainment, and media can positively impact millions of disenfranchised individuals." The foundation's mission is to teach that powerful mentoring can help those in poverty, improve school attendance and graduation, and decrease drug use and violence (www.overmyshoulderfoundation.org).

Patti Austin and I sat down to talk about her fifty-five year career, staying vocally healthy, and how she prepares for performing. We laughed a lot; she has a wonderful sense of humor. She told me many stories about her days in the jingle business and described a few life-changing moments. A strong businesswoman, she welcomed the opportunity to have a chat about the creative side of being a singer and producer.

MARKETING AND THE INTERNET

Patti Austin was positively ecstatic about how powerful a tool the Internet has become for marketing. "Now, it's easy to find your demographic," she explained, "because you can reach out to new potential fans in any kind of musical niche; you can make just about any record you want to make." That appeals to Patti a great deal. Her music is very eclectic from all her years singing a wide variety of styles, from opera to rock to r&b and jazz. "If I'm making country music," she says as an example, "let me talk to someone who's got a website about country music. 'Who is buying your country music? 13-year-olds with purple hair? How many are on your website? Well, we're getting about 500 hits a day. Why don't you send your 13-year-olds with purple hair to my website, and I'll send them back to yours, and then we will *all* get the 13-year-olds with purple hair [who like country]'." When Patti hired two tech-savvy people to research her potential markets and rebuild her website, her team discovered she has a huge audience in Asia. Her website went from 300 hits a day to 180,000.

Patti Austin learned about marketing during her lucrative fifteen years as a top jingle singer. Although she was already the number one vocal contractor in New York City for albums, Patti got into the jingle business almost by chance, when another singer/producer she knew fell ill and hired Patti to take her place on a session. Patti was lucky: no one would *ever* leave once they were in that elite circle of singers, she explained. The money was too good, and the competition too steep. This small group sang background on *every* commercial in those days. Occasionally, Patti would sing lead vocal, too. (If any singer did the lead vocal too often, agencies would stop using that person to bring in a fresh sound.) The real work was in background singing. These singers would go years without taking a vacation, for fear of being replaced. (A colleague coined it the "velvet handcuffs.") So, why *did* she leave the business? Who could walk away from that kind of success?

CHANGING DIRECTIONS

It began after fourteen years in the business, when Patti realized the jingle world had "ceased to be emotionally fulfilling." She was growing restless, questioning what she was doing for a living. Even though studio singing was creative, in a way—she had to perform with expertise in a wide variety of styles—she had become frustrated with the lack of artistic expression that came with the job. Non-musical advertising executives, trying to direct the singers, would frequently make ridiculous comments like, "Can you sing this an octave SLOWER?" (That actual quote became an inside joke.) Patti said, "After you get asked that for the twenty-fifth time, you want to blow your brains out. I said, 'I need to go back to performing, I need to go back to working on stage.' But, I knew that when I did that, I was going to lose a lot of money and a lot of security. Because when you're out there making records, you might love it. You might think it's great. But you're making the sign of the cross. You don't know if it's going to sell."

Even her big hit with "Baby Come to Me" was a stroke of luck. Only receiving marginal success at first, the song was discovered by a music director for the soap opera *General Hospital*, who had heard it on the radio in Florida. He started playing the song on the show, and "Baby Come to Me" became the love theme for the soap's two main characters. One Saturday, a radio program in Miami played the song while they recapped soap opera plot lines. That day, the station received 1,000 calls from fans who loved the song. Over the weekend, it sold 50,000 copies. But Patti's record label wouldn't work the song again, thinking the weekend's popularity was a fluke. So, Patti invested her own money to re-release the song, and *Baby Come to Me* became the number one pop record in the country.

Getting back to jingles, Patti Austin said there were three main reasons why she finally decided to leave the business. The first was following a casual conversation with her good friend, singer Valerie Simpson. She explains. "There was a new girl who had come in to sing on some sessions. She was not one of the brightest pennies in the coffer." Patti laughs. "We were at a party one night, and David Bowie was there. David Bowie was huge. This girl goes up to him and says," [Patti imitates a thick Long Island accent…] "'You're David Bowie. You're *good*. But you should really do commercials, you'd make a lot of money, like that!'" [Patti snaps her fingers.] A few weeks later, in the studio, the same girl and Patti were working together on a session, and she paid Patti a compliment. "Oh my Gawd," the girl said, "I love your music, you're so fabulous. I don't understand why you're not a household name!" Valerie Simpson sat across from Patti reading a newspaper, lowered it, and said, "'Because she's making all this money doing *this*,'" and went back to reading the paper. Patti

> "I said, 'Okay. That's what you do this for. *That's* what you do this for.'"

said to me, "For some reason, that comment bothered me. It hit me in a weird place. It ate at my craw." Patti said she started to feel like she was selling herself. But she didn't make a move, not yet.

The second reason was an experience she'd had at a children's hospital, where each Christmas the jingle singers would perform for the kids on the terminal ward. "It was just a great thing in life to do," Patti recalled. "Most of the kids we sang for were not going to be there the next year. It was really kind of deep." This particular year, as they were packing up to leave, Patti was approached by a woman who said, "Could you do me a really big favor? My little boy was in treatment when you were singing. Could you sing to my son, just a little bit? He would love it so much." Patti agreed to stay a little longer for the boy. "The kid had just been in oxygen treatment," she continued. "He was on a gurney, bandaged head to toe, burned over 80 percent of his body. The only thing that was exposed was his hand. I took a deep breath and went over. I held his hand. Just his little eyes were sticking out. I don't even remember what I sang to him, but he went right to sleep. So I said to her facetiously, 'Oh great. I give up my best song, and he goes to sleep.' The boy's mother was getting weepy eyed and chuckling at the same time. She said, 'No, you don't understand. He never sleeps.'" Sitting at the table with me, Patti's own eyes were welling up as she recalled that day. She apologized, saying, "Every time I tell this story, it messes me up." She explained. That moment was a profound turning point for Patti. Yes, she knew how fortunate she was to be working as a singer at the highest level in the jingle business, earning gobs of money. She would not even have been in that hospital ward on that day had it not been for her success. But, in that moment, Patti was touched so profoundly by the effect of her singing, she was stopped in her tracks. She asked herself honestly, was she happy? *Why* did she really sing? "After she said that," she continued, "I turned around and went into an alcove. I slid down the wall to the floor and I sobbed. I just sobbed, and I said, 'Okay. That's what you do this for. *That's* what you do this for.'"

The third reason Patti Austin left the jingle business was because of an event that has stayed with her throughout her life. When Patti was thirteen, Quincy Jones brought her family to the Newport Jazz Festival. Ray Charles was there, and Judy Garland was playing that night. Quincy insisted that Patti see Judy Garland live, but Patti wasn't interested. She knew that by that point in her life, Judy Garland was "a hot mess." Patti tells the story, "Judy Garland was drinking; she was trying to commit suicide every week. And her chops were gone. Her voice had gotten very warbly. There was no control because she wasn't taking care of her health. She was just a basket case. So, I didn't want to see her. I said, '*A Star Is Born, The Wizard of Oz, Meet Me in St. Louis*—brilliant. But not live, not now.' And Quincy said, 'You *must* see her.'"

Quincy talked Patti into it. She went to see the performance with her mother, while her father hung out with Quincy and the guys. What Patti had not anticipated was Judy Garland's amazing showmanship and her raucous sense of humor. Even though offstage she was a wreck, onstage Judy Garland was "funny, *funny*!" Patti said, "I found out from someone in the audience that she had been doing that same show for years, with not an inch of change in it. But it all felt like it just came off the top of her head: and that's hard to do. That's how brilliant she was as an actress and performer. She'd been doing it night after night, and it sounded like it just happened in that moment. It was one of the most brilliant performances I've ever seen in my life. It brought me to tears. It brought me to my knees—me and everyone else in the audience. By the time she was into the second song, people were standing up cheering. It was just insane. And she was frail, and messed up. It just didn't matter." The final moment of the experience was when Quincy took Patti backstage to meet Judy Garland. She came off stage, grabbed Patti's young face in her hands, kissed her forehead, and said, "Oh, you little cutie!"

LEARNING HOW TO *SING*

Seeing Judy Garland taught young Patti Austin how to *sing*. Years later, Quincy Jones explained to Patti, "That was like *Mohammed*, man. I knew if you saw her at an impressionable age, you'd meld into who you wanted to become as a singer, into who you are now." Patti said, "It was a seminal moment in my life. I'll never forget it. I made about twenty different determinations at that point: When I sing a song, I'm going to sing the lyrics. I'm going to tell the story. That's how you reach people. You can have the most beautiful melody in the world, but if you are singing a song with lyrics, you've got to tell that story. When Judy sang "Surry with the Fringe on Top," you could see people in the audience bouncing along like they were on the carriage with her. You could *see* the fringe because of where she put the words—how she created the conversation with the lyrics in the body of the melody. That totally changed the way I performed from that day on."

Patti had years of practice learning how to sing lyrics by delivering jingle commercials as if she were in love with the product. "I brought my Judy Garland with me into the jingle business. Part of that was looking at that copy, looking at those words." She explained that to sell the product, you had to make it sound like you had sipped that morning cup of Maxwell House coffee. "Yet, the truth was, I had a client over here who was looking at me like a ham sandwich, and he hadn't eaten in three weeks. And I had a producer over there giving me the same look. And I've got this copy in front of me that I have to sing, and make it sound like I *believe* it."

One time, the background group was in the studio recording their *seventh* jingle that day, which happened to be a Budweiser commercial. After they sang a take, the producer in the control room said, "Can you sing it again? It sounds kind of tired." The singers looked mischievously at each other, knowing their singing was fine. They also knew they would sing the next take exactly the same way. When they went back over to the microphones, they became very animated. They sang the spot again, but this time they put big, exaggerated smiles on their faces. Then, the client said, "That's IT!" After the client left, they listened back to both takes. They were identical. The singers thought that was hilarious. All they had done differently was move a little and smile broadly. Bringing a stage-like performance into the studio had sold the client.

Patti finally left the jingle business after one last incident. "The powers that be were changing," she said. "Madison Avenue was changing. The people producing the jingles were getting younger. One day in the studio, the [advertising] client said to the [music] producer, 'Maybe this spot needs somebody who can do an Ella Fitzgerald thing.' And the producer said, 'Who is Ella Fitzgerald?'" That was it, the last straw. How could she continue in an industry where one of the greatest singers of all time was never heard of? She was all done. Patti said to herself, "It's *TIME*! Thank you, Lord! Thank you for permission to leave the room now!"

LEGENDS

During the years when Patti grew up, popular singers were known for both phenomenal technical skill and outstanding voices. Up at the Apollo Theater in Harlem, "there was a tradition in the Black music scene," Patti said. "It was all about you being a kick-ass singer. And people used to say, 'She's a flat-footed singer' because everyone I am talking about only had to stand there and sing. When Ella Fitzgerald sang three songs in a row, you'd just want to shoot yourself. She didn't have to do another thing."

Lena Horne was another phenomenal singer and actress, like Judy Garland. She was equally powerful in her one-woman show on Broadway, Patti recalled. Yet Lena Horne "was not like the kick-ass black girl singer. She was an all-around entertainer. She had done film, so she came from that musical film tradition. She had that chop. Judy loved Lena, and she watched her to get a lot of what Judy had on stage. Lena had an energy that I've never seen a black female vocalist express before." I had to agree with Patti, having been fortunate to catch Lena Horne's one-woman show on Broadway, too, when I was young. It was truly extraordinary. "Lena was the only person who I would say was entertaining on the level of Judy Garland or Sammy Davis Jr.," said Patti.

THE BIZ

Patti Austin says the record business has also changed a great deal since she started out. Back in the day, record company executives were musically astute and creatively involved with the artists on their labels. Many well-known recording artists benefited from label support in the early years of their careers. Nat King Cole, Frank Sinatra, and Count Basie—to name just a few—would never receive that kind of artist development now. Giving another example, Patti explained, "The days of Motown—when they signed you, taught you how to walk and talk and interview and be fabulous—are gone. It's all on you, now. You have to brand yourself. You have to market yourself."

Patti Austin believes the recording business struggles today for survival because it killed itself with its own practices, shifting away from artist development to focus strictly on the bottom line. Record company executives who once had understood the artistic side of music were replaced by lawyers. "It stopped being about somebody who had a sense of music listen to your demo tape and say, 'This is an artist we invest in because there's something creative going on here.'" Patti said today, a label decides to make a record based strictly on focus-group studies, to determine sales in a potential market. There is "tremendous bitterness in the music business by anybody who's been in it awhile." She was advised recently by a business associate, "Sometimes, experience can get in your way. Ignorance can be bliss when you're trying to get financing. You have to come at this not only as a creative person; you have to come at this as a business person, too."

> "You've got to make a personal connection. There is nothing like a live performance, nothing."

Staying true to your artistic vision is very challenging in this new environment. It is also essential for an artist. What is one piece of advice Patti would stress? You *must* perform live. All the Internet traffic you might generate—even using methods such as asking your Internet fans to choose your next single—cannot replace showing up in Des Moines or Ft. Lauderdale for a live show.

"You've *got* to make a personal connection," Patti said. "There is nothing like a live performance, nothing. I don't think anything will ever replace it. It's human contact. Look at indigenous people, people who are living the tribal existence (for lack of a better description). They all have one thing in common: at the end of the day, they get into a circle around a fire, and they talk to one another. Everyone in the tribe has to contribute either a story, a song, or a dance. It's their CNN. There is something in the hard wiring of humans that we have to have that sense of community, that connection. That sharing of music, that sharing of the rhythm, of the beat. The news."

Echoing my conversation with Ysaye Barnwell (see chapter 9), we discussed how, in many places around the world, the audience is part of the music. There is no separation between audience, musicians, and dancers. In the United States, popular music used to be about appreciating a singer who was much more skilled than you could ever be. "Now, it's about seeing someone do something you think you can do," laughed Patti, "and you are usually right. 'Oh my God, I can sound like that in the shower.' And if they just got out of rehab, even better!"

Artistic standards have shifted, too. To make the point, Patti told a long story about producing a remake of "We Are the World." (The original song brought many superstars into the studio together for the first time. It was written in 1985 by Michael Jackson and Lionel Richie for *USA for Africa*.) In the production meeting—where, incidentally, Patti was the only woman in a room with managers, agents, production staff, and camera guys—the team watched the original video of the song. "It sounded like crickets in the room when the song finished," Patti said. "It was Stevie Wonder, Bob Dylan, Bruce Springsteen, Billy Joel, Cyndi Lauper, the Pointer Sisters… Everyone was worried about being able to recreate this. It was a frightening revelation. Autotune—and a prayer. A whole lot of fixing in the studio after everyone has gone."

The good news is there were indeed some amazing singers on the new version—Tony Bennett, BeBe Winans, Pink, Barbra Streisand. When Patti rearranged the tune with Mervyn Warren, they added funky syncopation to the melody to modernize it. Patti describes showing the new syncopation to her good friend Barbra Streisand. "Barbra said, 'Patti, you know I don't do that.'" Patti replied, "'You do today, Barbra.' I sang it for her a bunch of times. I stood behind her and tapped her on the back while she was singing to show her the rhythm. That was just to help her get it in her bones." Patti was able to work with Barbra in this unusual way because of their friendship and their "mutual admiration society." Barbra Streisand's voice is brilliant, and in the end, she nailed it.

VOCAL HEALTH, FIFTY YEARS LATER

I asked Patti, more than fifty years into her career, how does she still sing with as much power and technique as ever? How does she take care of herself?

Her first answer: rest. Back in Bay Shore, Patti had studied voice with a former opera singer who learned the hard way how to take care of the voice. She passed that knowledge along to her students. Her teacher's mantra was, "You've got to get your vocal rest." Patti Austin always makes sure she does. It requires great discipline. Her teacher also taught breathing skills and stressed taking care of the whole body. Patti still follows this advice, too. At the end of a show, for instance, the band will want to go out and party. Patti won't go but instead retires to her hotel room to read or watch television, to settle back down after the energy of a performance. She saves going out for the last night in a run. "It never fails though," she smiled and said. "The next morning, the whole band will have an early flight home, and they won't go out!"

Patti Austin also avoids over-singing. She doesn't like the sound of a pushed tone. "It sounds strident to me," she said. "If you're singing right, it shouldn't ever sound like you're straining. Even if you go up there with volume, you need to have support." Patti wants singing to seem effortless, not like she's walking on a tight rope. "Plus," she continued, "I'm from the generation where everybody was cool. Even if you were singing some wild stuff, you were looking cool. Nat King Cole, Frank Sinatra. Finger snapping. I'm not about vocal histrionics. There are better ways to say something that's profound. If it's a great piece of material, it's all there. It's in the melody. If it ain't broke, don't fix it. I think a lot of that kind of singing goes on now because the music itself is not that strong. You have to do vocal calisthenics to make it interesting." I called that kind of over-singing "vocal break-dancing." She laughed.

BUILDING THE FLOW OF A SHOW

Patti Austin described how she puts together a set list for her shows. "I'm always going for drama." She admits, "I'm a drama queen. I'm always trying to milk it. I'm always going for Judy. I'm very old-school when I put the set together. I like to come out with something hopping and jumping, and then I want to start taking you on this ride. Usually, by the third or fourth song, I want to take your butt all the way back down, way down. I want to break your heart. Then, I'll gradually start bringing you back up. Usually that third or fourth song is something really touching, a beautiful ballad with some kind of lyric that's on the sad side."

Patti includes dialogue in between her songs and a lot of banter. "I constantly digress, and I'm all over the place," she continues, "and I cannot tell a joke to save my life. But I can tell you a story about my life, which is always a joke anyway [laughs], and that usually ties in to the music in some way. Or, I might go off into a political rant. But I want to take the audience somewhere. I'll have them laughing hysterically, then I'll take them into *Porgy and Bess*, 'My Man Left Me.' I beat them up, smack them around. Then, start climbing again. I try to make the climb based more on the music than on the lyric, which may not be profound. It's not necessarily a cerebral thing: it's the music. I usually do something very poignant before I do a closing number. Then, I make my closing number a barn-burner. I love doing up crazy, wild fun."

FIFTY-THREE YEARS AND STILL GOING

Patti Austin doesn't have a favorite kind of music. She says, "There is good and bad in every genre," and avoids dividing music up into categories. For a long time, her eclectic musicianship created challenges for her career. But she insisted on keeping her spectrum wide and would not be pegged into one genre. At one point, she even abandoned pop music altogether, and for the past eight years, she has been singing straight jazz, working with big bands and "crazy, exotic arrangements."

Patti Austin's album *Avant Gershwin* won her the 2008 Grammy Award for "Best Jazz Vocal." She'd waited fifty-three years before she won a Grammy. What advice would Patti Austin give a new artist? "Make the music you want to make. Find an audience, and send it out to them. You don't have to wait for a record company to make a decision. It's the most freeing time we've had in the record business. If you're an artist and you have half a brain about how to market yourself, these are the pioneer days."

Patti Austin will keep on forging a way for her career to grow and evolve. She is a survivor and a pioneer with an old-school ethic. She is creative, superbly gifted, and smart. Patti Austin is in music for life.

CHAPTER 9

Ysaye M. Barnwell

© Dwight Carter Photography 212-932-1661

Dr. Ysaye M. Barnwell came to mind immediately when I decided to include conversations with artists in *Your Singing Voice*. Her superb work as a performer, educator, and writer spans many decades, setting a high standard for those who wish to create profound experiences through singing, performing, and teaching. She is perhaps best known as a member of the vocal group Sweet Honey in the Rock, the Grammy Award–winning *a cappella* ensemble. Fondly referred to as simply "Sweet Honey," the group epitomizes the type of concert experience that exhilarates me, as well of millions of others. People of all ages attend Sweet Honey concerts, including many generations within one family. Audiences leave their concerts feeling inspired, uplifted, moved, singing, and knowing that they've been to an *event*—not just to a concert.

Founded in 1973 by Dr. Bernice Johnson Reagon, Sweet Honey (www.sweethoney.com) is a six-woman *a cappella* group with deep roots in the sacred music of the African American church—spirituals, hymns, and gospel—as well as jazz and blues styles. Playing only percussion instruments, including shakers and hand drums, whoever's not singing the lead vocal creates a vocal accompaniment. Voices blend together in rich harmony and with engaging counter-rhythms. Their collaborative style is distinct from a group in which a lead singer is supported by backup singers. Members take turns singing the lead melody in performance; sometimes the singers take turns singing the lead within one song. On some songs, in the tradition of congregational singing, the lead singer improvises and calls out the verses, which are then sung together in harmony by the group. The sixth member of the ensemble is not a singer but uses American Sign Language to interpret each song for the deaf and hearing impaired. She accompanies every song with gestures and beautifully animated facial expressions.

Dr. Ysaye Barnwell has been with the group since 1979. A choral composer in her own right, she wrote many of the internationally published Sweet Honey in the Rock works. "We Are," "Wanting Memories," and "No Mirrors in My Nana's House" are among her most popular pieces. "Wanting Memories," her best-selling recording, was a top forty hit in Hawaii. "We Are" and "No Mirrors in My Nana's House" have both been illustrated into beautiful children's books. Her book, with four illustrative CDs, *Singing in the African-American Tradition: Choral and Congregational Vocal Music* (1989), is a superb resource for learning how to sing in traditional spiritual styles.

I first met Ysaye Barnwell back in 2004 at the Unitarian Universalist Musicians Network conference where she held master classes on topics such as song leading, empowering people through singing, and how to sing spirituals and gospel accurately in a way that honors these traditions. It was a powerful week. Ysaye Barnwell has inspired thousands of people around the country with workshops that get people singing. These workshops, together with the compelling music she creates with Sweet Honey, are why I chose to speak with her for this book.

PLANNING A CONCERT

I began by asking Ysaye to list the top things she thinks about when planning a concert. Her first consideration is, what shape are the singer's voices in? "Because Sweet Honey rotates leads, everybody sings everything," she said. "So, it might be that I want somebody to sing something in particular, and they're saying, 'I've been on a plane for fifteen hours and I can't go there.' Okay, fine, so scratch it, let's bring in something else. I want each person's voice reflected in the program. I might ask them if there are some options for what they feel like doing." Ysaye said the songs are planned on the day of the show, sometimes even onstage. This practice arises from their emphasis on music from oral traditions, which is often spontaneous. (Joey Blake discusses a similar approach in our conversation in chapter 11.)

Bearing in mind what members feel they can sing that night, Ysaye next considers, "What's going on in the world that we might want to address? Everybody knows we're at war. Does Sweet Honey have to comment on the war in every performance? Sweet Honey is odd because we have an audience that comes for many reasons. Part of the reason that they come is because they want to hear themselves reflected on the stage, position-wise." She said her audiences want to feel affirmed, sometimes politically. "It's not possible to affirm everything at every concert. So, it has to do with what's going on in the world, but it also has to do with what community are we in. Are there particular things going on in the community that we might want to either comment on or reflect on in the music?" Ysaye said the program may shift in the moment if it looks like something's happening in the audience or "something catches fire." I've even seen her switch to a different song, once it had already begun, when the first song just didn't feel right.

How does Sweet Honey learn about what is going on in the community where they're headed? "It's a conversation on the way there from the airport. What things seem to be important to people, what's in the newspaper? What have we heard in the news about that particular location within the past few weeks, if anything?"

Sweet Honey performs a range of musical styles. They want to represent as many of those styles as possible within a program. The exception is when the program has been tailored specifically for their host sponsor. "We just did a concert for the 150th anniversary of the African Episcopal church. So, we wanted to be sure that African-American sacred music was represented well in this program. But in general, we want to do a wide variety in terms of our musical palate, because that's part of who we are. We are not a gospel group, we are not a rock group, we are not a jazz group, we're not any of that. We're all of it! And so we want people to *hear* all of it."

ECLECTIC FROM THE START

In a music business that is genre-driven, Sweet Honey stands out as a diverse group that has always been eclectic. They have stayed eclectic for the nearly forty years since Bernice Johnson Reagon founded them. They embrace new musical influences from time to time, especially when they get a new member. Ysaye said, "I think because of how it was formed, Sweet Honey always had a number of different styles. It was formed out of the D.C. Black Repertory Theater Company where Bernice Reagon was the vocal coach. She used all kinds of music to help actors develop their voices. In the course of that, people said, 'Wow, the music is really good. Why don't we take the music to the stage.' And they started doing that, and they took everything. It's always been an 'everything' group."

Ysaye Barnwell knows that people return to see Sweet Honey again and again because their experiences are so powerful. She recognizes that not all artists strive to forge a deep connection between audience and performer. "I think it's really important for me to try to make a distinction here. There are performers, there are musicians—musicians who perform in what I will call a 'popular' mode as opposed to a 'traditional' mode. Sweet Honey comes out of a traditional mode. So, we are not doing what's commercial, we are not trying to be in the top 40. It would be great if we were; it would be great to sell millions of CDs. But that's not why we exist. We exist out of a real frame of mind that says what we do, in many ways, is a service to the people that we represent. It is in service to our culture and everything that came before.

"So, if you look at it that way, then you understand. You develop an attitude that says that music is a tool of the community. It's a *tool*, it's not entertainment like that. If you understand that you're working with a tool, you understand something about the power of the tool—the potential of the tool to do some kind of work. You don't take it lightly, and you don't take it for granted."

This distinction is crucial. An artist may be motivated by her goals of personal success. She may want to be in the top 40, to be commercial, to make millions of dollars. When she wants to be on stage, singing for herself, her audience probably accepts it. To Ysaye Barnwell, that's fine, but that is not what Sweet Honey is about.

TOUCH AND HEALING

The members of Sweet Honey need to be touched and healed by the music that they are performing. Although the women do sing for themselves, in a way, Ysaye stresses that their goal in singing is much broader than their own enjoyment. She said that if they were not looking to be touched and healed themselves by the music they make, "then there would be no by-product that's going to touch or heal anyone else. So, if five people show up, it's okay. We're still going to sing like we would sing if there were ten thousand people there. The five—the number—will not impact what we do on that stage. We are clear that we have to create something in that moment that touches us. If it touches us, it will either touch five people or ten thousand people. But if we're not touched ourselves, *nothing* will happen. There will be no magic that night."

How does Sweet Honey know what their audiences are looking for? What kind of feedback does Sweet Honey receive? "Sometimes, they don't know what they're there for, but they tell us how they've been touched by the music," explains Ysaye. "It's been as extreme as, 'I didn't even feel like coming here. I was really thinking about doing away with myself, but my friend made me come. Y'all have changed my life.' Or, people tell us all the time that they use our music at funerals, and at christenings, and at weddings. There are people who tell us,

'I've been listening to Sweet Honey for fifteen years. It got me through college, it got me through x, y, z.' People tell us that all the time." Fans of Sweet Honey bring their loved ones to concerts to share in the experience. "They bring their mothers because something reminds them that there's something they know their mother will tune into. And they bring their children because they want their children to be inspired. There have been concerts where there are *three and four generations* of people.

"It's *very* deep," she continues. "Grown people say, 'My mother used to drag me to Sweet Honey concerts all the time. Now I'm dragging my children because we really, really love y'all.' We were just in Gettysburg, Pennsylvania, and there was an interracial couple. The woman was the one who organized the whole concert. We were talking to them about how they met and how people respond to them and all that stuff. The guy said, "I took her to a Sweet Honey concert, and that kind of sealed it.' He was white. People tell us all the time what the music does for them."

I said, "I think that a performer or group of any musical style can reach audiences in a way that goes far beyond just being entertaining. The musical genre isn't important for this effect to happen. It comes from the artist." Ysaye added that going to a live concert is an energetic experience and a human experience. "Something different is going to happen than when you just sit at home and listen to that music." She pointed out that even when music is designed to be very entertaining, with "get up!" energy to make the audience feel good, that doesn't lessen the impact that a connected performer can have. "I think that if people don't touch the audience, they don't get there. They don't get to be on that stage night after night, if they're not touching somebody. That's the 'It' factor. They have 'It.' And if you don't have 'It,' then you just don't go nowhere."

"IT"

I asked Ysaye: "What exactly is this thing we call 'It'? You and Sweet Honey definitely have it, as your audiences will testify."

She replied, "You know … it's really hard to say. I have another life in public health, and I've gotten into discussions with people often, in the health field, around public health education. How do you get anybody—adults, in particular—to change bad habits, or what we consider unhealthy habits? That could be anything from smoking cigarettes to having sex without condoms. We're talking about intelligent people, like ourselves, who might get into a situation and just get caught up by the moment and know that we should do x, y and z, and then we don't do it. Then, we get into trouble. And/or we have a habit, and we know that we should break that habit, but we can't do it. Then, somebody says something, and that something registers inside of you so profoundly that you never have to do that habit again. Not only do you never have to do it again, you don't even have to do anything to *compensate* for the fact that you're not doing it anymore. Like smoking.

"I call that the 'magic word theory.' Somebody says something that's a magical word for you. It doesn't touch anybody else. But somehow, it registers inside of you. That's the same as the 'It' factor. It's very difficult to know what 'It' is, because 'It' touches different people in different ways, but 'It' touches.

"So, I might say, 'Wow, there is something about the quality of this singer's voice that just makes me want to cry.' And there's somebody else whose voice I don't really like, but damn, he's saying something different and just as powerful as it can be. We could just have two different opinions, but there's something going on that's touching both of us."

Ysaye Barnwell thought there might be something universal about experiencing music, even though the touch of magic is likely a little different for everyone. The music, the magic, reaches out and grabs each of us in whatever place we happen to be. Dr. Barnwell doesn't know what words to use to describe that magic. She can't describe exactly what "It" is. But there's no question about it, when "It's" there, you know it.

We agreed that singers need to develop their own authenticity—need to be comfortable putting that out there in their music. Ysaye recalled, "There's a lesson that I learned some years ago. I wrote a song called 'No Mirrors in My Nana's House.' When we would sing that song, I would see people in the front row, some of them would be white, and they would be crying. I would say to myself, 'Well, what on earth are *they* crying about?' My song is talking about my nose is too flat, and my skin is too black, and blah, blah, blah. Why are they crying? And then a gay choir wrote to me and said, 'We want to sing 'No Mirrors in My Nana's House,' and I said, 'Well you can't change the words!' [laughs] And they said, 'Oh no. We don't want to change the words. We really love the song!'

> When an artist is specific, "the kernel of truth rings forward."

"I realized from that one song that when artists are as *specific* as they can be, that is when they are as *universal* as they can be. So, if you take your most specific core and share that, I think everybody will understand it. I think that's the same reason why everybody all over the world knows about the spiritual [song form]. I think that it is so specific that it is universal. Somewhere, everybody has had this feeling of being downtrodden and oppressed. You could be the only blue-eyed person in a brown-eyed family, or a rail thin person in a heavy family. In some way or another, you get it."

When an artist is specific, "the kernel of truth rings forward." People see that and understand that you are sharing your truth. When the music is honest and true, people find ways to relate it to themselves. They put themselves willingly in the artist's shoes. "Very often, you don't know your audience, so you just have to be true to yourself," Ysaye said. "I think your audience will reveal itself to you."

WORLDVIEW

We talked about Mark Baxter's idea (in chapter 10) that whatever colored flag you put out, you will draw people to you who like that color. The point is to be consistent, to be yourself. Agreeing with this idea, Ysaye discussed the world view in western cultures, which is radically different from the world view in traditional cultures. This impacts how western musicians approach their sense of personal authenticity.

"When I do my workshops, I have to start with the worldview. I have to explain to people, there need not be any fear of singing here, because you showed up. If you showed up, we're going to sing! And I don't want to hear, 'I can't sing. I can't carry a tune.' I don't even allow people to talk about it. Because we could spend the whole weekend or the whole week hearing people talk about how they *can't do*, etc., etc."

The tradition in western music that is taught, she continued, is paper-based. The western musician is expected to reproduce music from a piece of paper perfectly, and in the same manner every time. "Now how do you go from that to playing the thing until it's playing itself, or singing the song until it's singing itself? How do you get there, unless you change the student's worldview, or expose them to a radically different worldview. Then they realize they are dealing with two different languages." The western worldview is one language; the traditional worldview is a different language. It requires distinctive skills to make music from either place. "'Cause if they don't understand that they are dealing with two different languages, how do they make the translation?"

Ysaye Barnwell recalled the PBS series about jazz created by filmmaker Ken Burns. (You can still access the footage and transcripts on the PBS website, www.pbs.org/jazz/about/.) "There's a point that was made; I don't even know if he knew he made it or if he intended to make it. The point is this (and I hope you understand the context in which I'm saying it): as jazz began to evolve, there were musicians who began to play what they heard, what they transcribed. They were very good at playing it, but they did not take it to the next level. The people who *created* it kept taking it to the next level. Other musicians kept learning it. That's how they would move to the next level. But the creation and the evolution of the form of jazz basically came from the people who were creating it."

To emphasize her point, Ysaye talked about the music of jazz trumpet player Miles Davis. "There were people who would transcribe all of Miles' solos, and they could play them. They could play Miles as good as *Miles* could play Miles, or anybody else. But, Miles was always *evolving*. So, Miles would be really different tomorrow than what he was today." In other words, people who were transcribing Miles' music, or reading it, could only be where he had *already been*.

"We're talking about a distinction that is sharp. You have a culture that reads and has an expectation that the proficiency and the excellence in performance have to do with how you deliver what's written on the page. That's western culture. In traditional culture, or in African-American culture, the tradition says there's *no rule* that you have to do this the way you did it last night. In fact, there ought to be *something else* happening, don't you think?"

To let the spirit of a piece of music play itself through you, she said, don't try to duplicate your playing each time. This attitude—this language—is totally different from a paper-based western approach.

Ysaye Barnwell is also trained in western music. She studied violin for seventeen years. She understands playing violin, playing in orchestras, learning concertos. So, she understands the distinction between the two worlds very well. Even still, "I don't really know how to talk to really well-trained musicians in the western sense about improvisation. I think my whole approach to improvisation is radically different from theirs."

Emphasizing the point, she recalled a recent conversation with a very prominent classical musician about how he plays a *cadenza*, an improvised passage of a piece. He said he writes it out and memorizes it. She laughs. "I was blown away! Didn't the composer intend for you to have a creative moment, and not the same creative moment every night?"

Even for very skilled classical musicians, the word "improvise" can be frightening. "They cannot, they don't know where to begin. That so amazes me. I figure, if you know scales—this is coming from a classical position—if you know the form, you ought to be able to create something."

Improvising has not been taught in classical training. It is not the expectation. "As long as it's not the expectation, you're not going to do it."

We went on to talk about how jazz is often upheld as a classical music art form that is unique to the United States. Some educators believe that you need to understand and be true to how the music was originally done, and will be critical of you if you modify away from that tradition too much. "To me, that is a problem with who's teaching the form," she said. "That's like saying to an actor, 'Deliver these lines in the same way that Kate Hepburn would, and do not venture to find yourself in those lines.' That's the way composition is taught. Write something in the style of Bach. Okay, but when do I get to the point where I write something in the style of Ysaye Barnwell? How am I expected to make the *transition* if I'm always copying what Bach and Beethoven did? *How* do I make that transition?"

WRITING

"It's a challenge. It's like when I teach songwriting, I find myself teaching very differently from how other people teach. I don't go to the same places. Where I start is very different. Yes we'll talk about melody, but we'll talk about it really differently."

She compares her writing process to "priming the pump." She may begin with only a few notes, or a brief recording of an idea. She might come up with short phrases that are rhythmic or melodic. Even if she doesn't incorporate those phrases in the work, the process of jotting down small ideas gets her creative process underway.

Because her schedule is so demanding, Dr. Barnwell no longer has the time to sit down daily to write. She misses that. Instead, she composes primarily when she is commissioned to write a piece.

"If it's a totally blank slate—they don't give me a theme or anything like that—then it's a little harder. I have to figure out a phrase here and a theme there." The piece she is commissioned to write will usually fit into a larger setting or work, along with other elements that she needs to consider. "For instance, I have a piece to write for two different children's choirs, so I'm trying to get the sounds of the choirs in my head. I'm trying to figure out what I can write that might change the tone and texture of what they normally do.

"I always want to give people things to sing that will make some sense to them. I keep thinking that people who are learning this music are going to sing this song over and over and over. What should happen to them *after* they've sung it over and over and over? They shouldn't just be bored with it. Something should click in their heads, like, 'Oh wow. I never understood this before,' or, 'I never thought about this before.' That's always a goal to me, my own personal goal. At some point, I hit on something that just starts pouring stuff forward. And after that, it's pretty much done."

CHAPTER 10

Mark Baxter

Photo by Janet Caliri

Mark Baxter is a vocal teacher with a unique pedagogy. He is also a working vocalist. His website profile (www.voicelesson.com) begins simply: "Some people are born to sing. Mark Baxter was not one of them. Undaunted, he studied, probed, inquired, explored, practiced, and applied his findings until he achieved the voice he had always wanted." Three thousand gigs and many hundreds of voice lessons later, Mark Baxter—a recognized authority in his field—regularly attends medical seminars to keep his knowledge fresh. He is passionate about learning about the voice. He has studied neuromuscular massage, nutrition, the Alexander Technique, acupressure, reflexology, and various relaxation techniques. With locations in L.A., New York, and Boston, as well as Skype and iChat options, Mark Baxter makes himself available to anyone who wants to study singing. His long and impressive list of students includes many who are touted to be among the best singers in commercial contemporary music. Many of Mark Baxter's students are also themselves vocal teachers. I studied with him for a time and learned a great deal from him. He is a wonderful teacher.

I knew Mark Baxter would be the perfect person to speak with about building a vocal instrument and learning how to perform from one's true "authenticity." We met in his small yet immaculate voice studio in the Boston area. Adorning his walls are hundreds of CDs from students. The rest of the wall space is covered in mirrors. Everywhere you turn you either see someone's hard work in a CD or a mirror that makes it impossible to hide from your own grimaces, gestures, breathing, or posture.

FOCUSING ON TECHNIQUE, NOT SONG STYLING

Many contemporary singers take voice lessons to gain power and agility for styles like rock or r&b. But unlike most teachers, Mark Baxter does not work with students on songs or styles of singing. He focuses instead on gaining knowledge and control of the unadorned instrument. His lessons teach how to strengthen the voice by singing without tricks or devices that singers commonly "hide" behind in order to cover weaker areas of the voice.

Even though Mark does not work on style, per se, the topic of performing comes up constantly in his teaching. His lessons frequently provide a kind of "performance therapy," the missing foundation. "This is why I focus on the technical stuff. I find that singers are very split, distracted by their own mechanics. Right at the moment when they should be dialing into the nut of their performance—the real beauty of it—they notice they've got this audience in front of them. So they become very self-aware and begin to police or micromanage their mechanics.

> **"When the technique is there, the singer is free to focus on the real power of music: to create a moving experience, for both the musicians and the audience."**

"What a shame," he continued. "The trust of their reflexes, the *trust of their technique*, is the limb that allows them to delve deeper into themselves."

"What I say over and over in my lessons is I think the audience does go to be moved," he said. "*What moves a human being is another human being, being moved*. So you sing for yourself. Basically, you sing to move yourself. In doing that, you give the audience permission to join you."

But when a singer is distracted by worry about singing well, he or she loses the ability to move audiences emotionally. The performance becomes an emotionless process of only "moving pitches." The performance never goes anywhere for the audience because "we're all waiting for the singer to settle into the driver's seat."

Over-rehearsing a song also comes out of fear-based thinking, Mark says: the fear of messing up. But when technique has been strengthened first, a deep well of ability allows us to take a song and perform it the same way every time, if that's our choice. Preparing in this way also frees us to interpret a song in different ways. When we have practiced the technique and environment of a song, rather than a precise way of singing it, we are not locked into one interpretation.

Mark said preparing in this way takes a little leap of faith. It takes trust both in the audience and in your own skills. "I feel that's why people want to rehearse a set of songs over and over. They're nervous about mechanics being exposed. They're afraid of forgetting lyrics. In my teaching studio, I also find that it's difficult to separate the emotion from a particular song. When people are practicing a song, they're practicing the *emotion*. Then, when they get up on stage, *that's* when they worry about their mechanics. People practice backwards!"

Mark believes that people who really want to sing are already working on songs and style on their own anyway. It's up to the student to learn the lyrics, know the melody and arrangement, and figure out the reason why he or she chose that song. It's personal. Instead, he'll help them with *how* to sing. "There is an expectation that if you rehearse a song and all the steps of it," he says, "that you will be able to replicate it. But to me, the truth is, it's never quite the same as the actual performance. It's like driving over to a friend's house rehearsing what you're going to talk about. Let's say you go over to someone's house because they're distraught they've just lost a parent, or something. And you're rehearsing what you're going to say on your ride over. To me, that is so contrived. Just go over to this person's house knowing they're a dear friend of yours, that you care about their situation, that you have a deep vocabulary to draw from, and that you have *the courage of silence* just to be there for somebody. All of those elements are going to end up being used.

"It's only in driving home from that person's house when you will know what was necessary. You may go over there and laugh! You may find they're in a better mood than you expected, and they're cracking jokes about their mother, and it was all very light, and that's what that person needed at that time. But to go there with a big speech about death already rehearsed would not allow you to be sensitive in the moment. You'd miss an opportunity."

I asked Mark how he addresses the frustration students sometimes express when they work exclusively on technique, worrying they won't know how to apply what they're learning to an actual song. He will tell the student, "If you gotta ask me when you can sing a song, then you are not in love with singing songs. I'm doing this with you because I think this is stuff you don't do at home. I'm assuming that you sing all the time, and people are telling you to shut up, because you're always singing. I'm assuming that, because you're calling yourself a singer." If a student is bored with the exercises and wants to sing a song, they're probably "a little tight, emotionally." Mark uses their tension, pointing it out to them when it shows up in technique. To help reduce tension, he teaches relaxation techniques, which he believes are important to include in the lesson.

Where Mark feels he can be helpful is on technique—on the naked voice. "I'm very consistent with my clients in that I'm just always going for the physical—always going for the foundational. We talk a great deal about performing and singing and stuff, I don't deny them that, but I always start the same way in that I'm going to reinforce these [vocal] reflexes in them. I feel that's the vitamin they don't take on their own."

In the beginning of his career, Mark noticed that he was singing better on the way home than at the gig. He wasn't warming up enough. He would either blow out his voice on stage, wrestling to make it exciting, or he would finally loosen up by the time the show was over. It was extremely frustrating when he wasn't ready to *really* sing until the last song in the show. This frustration led him to start taking voice lessons.

"For me, personally, it takes a long vocal warm-up. It's an all-day event to get ready for that gig, because I've got a lot of blocks. I want to use that stage for what it's good for. I want to ride that wave. I don't want to just run through some songs."

A GOOD SINGER SHOWS VULNERABILITY

> "We're lucky," he said. "We're singers."

Mark believes that to be a good singer, you must permit yourself to be vulnerable. "It's not everybody that's cut out to be so vulnerable and so exposed and so intimate. It's not a good fit for everyone's personality." We also get disappointed in ourselves. "When we sing," he continued, "there is an intended result that we have as a singer, and often we don't meet that intended result. But the listener is assuming that everything that came out of our mouths was intentional. All the audience knows is that we are on stage presenting ourselves. They think we must be thrilled with our voices! We're lucky," he said. "We're singers."

Singers can do things that other people dream about. Being on a stage creates an illusion for the audience. He said it's "smoke and mirrors. Woody Allen's line is, '99 percent of it is showing up.' So if you've got the guts to stand on stage, it's not talent—it's *courage* that allows you to get through the song. The audience is going to give you so much more license—so much more leash—than you'll give yourself. Only you are privy to all the little mistakes that you're making along the way." Mark believes audiences go to a show wanting and expecting to be moved, not to critique the singer, hoping he or she is bad.

"We've got a roomful of people rooting for you already. Of course, we never see it that way, as singers. We see it as a jury. And the jury has our face: every single person has our face. We're just assuming they are privy to all of our thoughts. Of course, they can't be. Actors are trained to stay in character when they miss a line, and that training is very important to keep the façade going. For singers, it's the same thing, in that if you advertise your displeasure with something, then you call attention to it, and everyone else is now privy to it.

EVOKING A MOOD IS THE MOST IMPORTANT FACTOR

Mark believes that when we perform well, we evoke a mood. It's not about singing perfect notes. Often people get up on stage for the wrong reason; they love the spotlight, but they don't love *singing*. Mark said, "Many students are in fame mode. Yet, an audience will be very *unmoved* if they're not buying into this person's fabulousness. I find it gets very awkward when a person discovers this on stage, in a room with people who don't agree with them. That's the talent show stuff and the beginning stages of people finding where they belong."

Sometimes, a singer chooses "the wrong song" or "the wrong genre." It is especially awkward if you find yourself on the wrong bill with a bunch of bands that don't sound like yours. Audiences don't mix, so this is difficult. In a show like that, it's very tempting to try to emulate the kind of music that's going on around you. As a performer, Mark has been in this situation, too, and knows first hand that trying to fit into a musical environment that doesn't align with your own music will never work. He holds a deep respect for musicians who hold onto their individuality. "I've never seen it fail. When someone in the audience starts yelling out 'You suck!' is when people are floundering on stage. All that means is they're trying to split the middle, they're trying to please everybody, and in so doing, they don't try to make a statement about themselves.

"When I'm playing with a punk band, if I go ahead and do my retro-soul thing, I get all these guys in Mohawks coming up and going, 'Hey, that was cool.' They're not going to like it, or I didn't convert them, but at least they're coming up and saying, 'That's cool.' And when I try to be a little more aggressive or punky, that's when they throw stuff! They smell a rat!

"It's the same for a classical audience. You'll get a more mature person saying, 'Well, it really wasn't my thing.' They don't throw stuff, but it's the same response. They may respect a punk thing, saying, 'Well, that was certainly aggressive.' They don't know what to say, but they know they just saw the real deal. I find that authenticity is something that non-musicians *are* sensitive to."

AUTHENTICITY

Authenticity, Mark says, is the courage to be yourself. Finding this authenticity is essential. "We've got so many layers of imitation in us that it requires a little shaking of the tree to get that bad fruit to come off, and what sticks is who we are," he said. This is why repeating drills and mechanics allows the singer to work on the true instrument. Practicing impressive, fancy tricks does not. "When that kind of stuff gets shaken off, you're left with a naked truth—which is very attractive to others, and not so attractive to you." This takes courage. There are, of course, artists who are very skilled at vocal gymnastics, who love themselves and pull it off authentically, and their audiences love them, too. There are also artists with unattractive voices who can still express a song very effectively. It would be pretty funny, Mark pointed out, to hear these artists singing one another's material. "And so, to each his own. That's what's so hard to develop.

"I always see it in those superstar line-ups, the 'We Are the World' kind of shows," he said. "You see all these incredible, different people up on stage, and the audience is cheering every one of them on for that little thing that they do." Combining artists on a program who seem opposite from one another can be very inspiring.

Mark said that all singers are influenced by artists who inspired them. But *admiring* artists who came before you, who have impacted your development, is very different from *imitating* them. "When you get the B-level act or artist, you hear kids who are coming up but who haven't really found themselves yet." A singer who only imitates another artist, such as recreating a beloved r&b artist's riffs, hasn't put enough work into finding his or her own blend of musical influences.

Mark Baxter believes you can signal to the audience that you are telling the truth by how you release your voice. "I'm a big fan of releasing the area of the throat just above the larynx. There is a lot of study now being done about that effect at about 2800 Hz. It calms animals down, and it calms kids down, and it lets everybody know that there's no danger. The opposite occurs at about 8 kHz. Real nasally, shrill singing gets everybody bouncing off the wall. It might be intentional if you're in a metal band or punk band or something." There are many different signals that get expressed along with your message. "I find it infinitely interesting that people have such a radar for authenticity. It's a human thing, not just a cultural thing."

When a singer is authentic, and consistent, audiences will respond. Mark believes the premise that you should be able to sing for everybody is false. Popular television shows that ask the contestant to be strong singers in several styles are unrealistic. People enjoy big CD collections because we're eclectic, and we like different moods. But no single CD has everything we like on it. It can't, not authentically.

Yet, as artists, so often we want to please everybody, to reach everyone. We want to put all of our own different moods and different sides into our music. But, for consistency sake, artists have to make the difficult decision about what *not* to include. It's like raising a single-color flag, trusting that the people who also like that color flag will come to hear you. "You don't know who they are yet. You've got to raise your orange flag first, the same color every night. Then, the blue people will leave the room, and just the orange people will stay. That's who you want to sing to, anyway."

EMOTIONS ARE UNIVERSAL

As a seasoned performer, Mark Baxter is aware of encouraging an emotional response from his audience. "To me, love is love, hate is hate, joy is joy. What I've learned is you don't have to be specific. If you're singing a song about a girl, and you want people to feel that feeling of first love, you don't have to think about Jane and evoke those feelings. You can call it up by thinking about your dog or your mother or your daughter. You can evoke that love—that kind of moving sensation.

"I call it a wave. *I want to stir the waters within myself, and then I want to surf that wave.* Singers who don't know what the song is about are singing in placid waters. The artist in me, the singer, wants to create just the right-sized wave that the audience can handle. That will take you through three minutes of 'shooting the curl' and 'running up against the edge of the board.' You're taking that wave any which way you want, once it's created. It's about going for an internal feeling. The real job is to create it." Once that wave gets going, a cracked note or a missed word couldn't matter less.

"It is by someone willing to go into themselves in front of you that you extend your protection. If somebody starts to cry in a crowded train station, that person is going to get a lot of aid. I think that's a very human truth. Somebody starts crying, people reach out. And if somebody starts laughing, you're gonna ask, 'What? What?!' People want to share the joke. Those are just two very real emotions. When somebody's angry, people are going to say 'Why?' And when a couple's kissing, *everybody* understands what's going on. In any culture—there's no difference."

The singer presents acoustic demonstrations of emotions. "It's the singer's job to dial in that good stuff." When Mark Baxter is riding the wave, he tries not to pander to the audience. He has learned through experience not to over-read the audience to see what more they may need. "It's like that line from the movie: 'You had me at '*hello.*' When a singer is trying too hard, he sends out distress signals," he said. On the other hand, the artist who is playing the music from within themselves lures everybody in. "Through my years, I've learned it's about being exposed. You're aware because you're on a stage. I'm aware there are people in the room, so I'm including them, but I'm trying to make it not about them. It's *for* them that I make it for myself."

A PERFORMANCE IS AN INVITATION

That being said, Mark continued, an artist does create a musical set with expectations of what the audience came to see. It's like hosting a party. "I want people to have a good time. When I'm doing a show, I expect to take them to several different places. I know I want to go into a ballad at some point, but I'm not going to start with that. My favorite thing is to hit them pretty hard at the beginning, to get their attention. It's an unconscious room at first, and so I like to make some noise. I love to start out with rhythm because rhythm is so primitive. Banging drums, or clapping. Or, I'll start out just singing *a cappella* because it makes me so vulnerable on stage. It's that crier in the train station. I know I'm going to get a lot of attention up front. I'll get people's focus. And once I have it, I honor it." It's not about forcing a group of people to come along. It's not coercion. He used to yell, "Come on!" trying to get the audience involved too early. "I found out that looked needy—when I reviewed the tapes!" [Laughs]

It is always an invitation, never a demand. Mark describes building a set of songs as a kind of baiting, to bring the audience along with him. Then, there is a place somewhere in the show where the music gets very intimate, bringing the energy down, such as singing a ballad. Or he may do a dance number, so the audience *has* to get moving. By the end of the concert, he loves to come back up on a positive, high note. "It's kind of like a roller coaster where we go up a little bit, and we go down and end on the highest hill there."

And what is the result for the audience? When people tell him he took them along on a ride, up and down on that roller coaster, then he knows he has succeeded as intended. When someone says, "Oh, that sixth song just killed me!" it lets him know the audience went on the ride with him. But if they say, instead, "Great show, what a good voice you have!" or stand back with folded arms, that means they didn't come all the way with him. "And at the end, I know very quickly whether I got tangled up in myself or whether I went there or not." He will be extremely disappointed with himself if he did not immerse himself in the music to create that ride. "It's so rare to get an opportunity with people in a room like that, giving you permission. It's one of those things where you want to hit it out of the park, and sometimes we strike out. That's a human element there.

"I hold myself wholly responsible. I never want to blame an audience or a circumstance or the sound equipment or anything like that. It's all up to me. I'm not going to damn myself about it, but I'm definitely going to review so that next time I can be smarter and more prepared. So it's a learning experience either way for me."

LEARNING TO UNDERSTAND YOUR AUDIENCE

As a performer, Mark changes his interaction with the audience depending on how many people are there, as well as on the venue itself. When he plays for a small audience, his approach is very personal. He enjoys this kind of performance very much. "I've played for intimate coffee shops and songwriter workshops with twelve people in the room, and they're all writers. Obviously, in the coffee shop, I don't say, 'Hey, thanks for coming down tonight! What's up in the back! Hey you!' That obviously won't work." A better way is to bring it down a little bit. Treat it like a rehearsal in front of them. "I'd rather talk with the guys on stage and not make the audience feel so exposed."

When Mark is planning for a concert, he has a short list of factors he considers. The first factor is the venue, including the size of the room. The second factor is whether it's a band show or a solo appearance. The third factor is the length of the set. Is it three songs, or a forty-minute set? "I don't feel you can really evoke a mood in three songs, so I will do something a little safer," he said. "If I have forty minutes, I will go a little deeper, be a little riskier, because hopefully I'll gain some trust by then."

The fourth factor is the expected size of the audience. "The larger the audience, the quicker they homogenize, so there are easier things to do with a large audience." A small audience, made of a few strangers in the room together, is not going to homogenize easily. "It would take a seminar to get them to meet or an AA meeting." [Laughs] If it's an intimate setting with a small audience, he will gear the set list a little differently to make them feel comfortable. He doesn't want them to feel overwhelmed by the music or feel uncomfortably intimate where they think they are supposed to "hold hands."

However, within the content of the songs themselves, a small audience can handle a wider range of emotions, and more details in the song, than a larger audience can. A larger audience wants big gestures, instead. "You'll get everybody too restless if you go into detail too soon with a big audience," Mark said. He also makes sure that he acknowledges a big audience, though he does not rehearse what he's going to say. He feels that is like planning what you are going to say to that friend when you drive over to his house. "If you're just present, you don't need to rehearse anything. Rehearsing job interviews—same fear. And, of course, you want the standard answers at your disposal, but you gotta go to a few job interviews to get good at it, so you're not rehearsing it on the way there. You've just got to relax and answer the questions given to you. And that's very hard. You want the job, you want them to like you, so you're nervous. Boy, if that isn't like standing on stage, I don't know what is." Eventually, you become familiar with how your audience is responding.

WHEN IT'S ROCK OR WHEN IT'S JAZZ

I asked Mark if he finds that the culture or style of the music affects his experience on stage. We compared rock with jazz. In rock shows, the musicians are putting on moves, whereas jazz musicians are focused more on their own experiences and on creating really interesting music. "I always view rock shows as throwing a New Year's Eve party every night," he said. "As the host of that party, even if you don't feel good, you're going to put on a smile and greet everyone at the door and be concerned about their welfare." A jazz concert feels more personal. "It's like you've just dropped by your friend Tom's house, who's a little eccentric. Sometimes Tom answers the door in his underwear, and he's like 'come on in!' and he really doesn't treat you like a guest, you're just there. That's like a jazz concert. This guy Tom is very embracing in a lot of ways. He's not doing anything different than he would have done if you weren't there. There's a real opening there—a real trust. He's just watching TV, and you come over, and he's going to continue watching TV."

Mark Baxter grew up with rock music and knows it very well. He pointed out that there are many sub-varieties of rock music, some more "heady" than others. Nonetheless, there is a definite entertainment component to it. "If you're hosting a party asking people to come over, and your girlfriend just broke up with you, you're going to put on a good face and have a party. That's definitely rock 'n' roll. It's one agenda."

Mark Baxter began as a drummer. He moved onto keyboards next, and then, eventually, became lead singer. Once lead singer, he felt responsible for feeling the vibe of the room and responding accordingly, even making shifts in the set list. But his band just couldn't make adjustments even when the audience was small. It was frustrating. "I used to hate that in rock 'n' roll. You prepare this big show, and six people show up, and you have this big, bombastic set prepared. It's like you show up at the costume party and it's not a costume party. You have this Halloween garb on and everyone else is dressed regularly, and you feel like a fool. I used to hate that because the bands are typically very simple, so they don't adjust well on their feet. You get these four guys that just rehearsed all these big, Marshall riffs, and they can't jam and do something subtle 'cause there are only six people on a Tuesday night in a club. They'd look at me like, 'What do you mean, are we doing the third song or not?' And that killed me because I felt for the six people in the audience that were getting slaughtered by this arena show.

"It's really hard to get an elephant of a rock band to dance on one foot. Whereas someone coming to a coffee shop knows that's the deal, and it's more of a jazz feel. I really enjoy when a venue works like it's supposed to. I've never been in the circumstance when I've been prepared for an intimate moment and it's a packed house. [Laughs] I suppose that would work better. You get people to hush up and really get into you."

When your audience is more like a *crowd*, it has a different kind of energy. You need to be careful in these situations so the tribal energy of a crowd doesn't take over and become disruptive, he said. "I've seen Springsteen do this plenty of times. It's an award show, it's very upbeat, schmaltzy, a schticky thing. He'll come in and sing 'Philadelphia' or something, and of course, that will really be a downer. But, in the same context, the room can handle it. Everybody respects that he went in and did what he came to do. It's as if he's communicating, 'I want to say this for a moment, and it's going to change the mood, and then I trust that you'll find the mood again.' He's spoken on that in plenty of interviews where he does these four-hour shows because he wants to take everybody through all these different physical and emotional things. It takes time to get everybody beaten down to the point where they can handle this and then bring them back up again. I've found him to be a very, very brave performer in that he's willing to go against the energy of the audience sometimes. That's what a *leader* does." Mark said this courage is impressive.

STAYING CONSISTENT

An artist who is consistent with his or her musical style will invariably experience lean times throughout a career, as well as high times of popularity. It's a natural cycle; it happens to many of our favorite artists. "Any artist who's true to their heart is going to go through that point where they don't have a big fan population with them," Mark says. In contrast, some performers choose to change their music as trends come and go, putting out music that they hope will be popular. "These are the pop artists who just chase down the numbers," Mark says. "They're just pandering to that. They're always throwing a New Year's Eve party, so the numbers mean a lot to them. There are two different kinds of artists there, and they're both in pop music."

Mark continued. "I have such high respect for artists and such high respect for the artistic process. I feel it's such a necessary element of society and that it's not frivolous and it's not ear candy. I feel that it's so important." Our culture has become very glossy in order to deny the reality of our mortality, Mark believes. "We're going to die. I think the only reason we *can* discover this is because we can talk about it. When we have this internal dialogue about it, now that we're so self-aware, I think that's the forbidden fruit! Animals are in this blissful ignorance, they're so primal."

MUSIC IS NECESSARY

"I'm really providing a necessary role for society, just as a cop or as a fireman does. I'm equal to them. I know very few would agree with me. I'm just saying that music, in general, is so necessary as a human element, like eating and sex and shelter. Music is right there. Because we are primal, music allows us to experience each other on that primal level."

"I think music soothes us," he said. "It allows us to go back to that primal existence and see that we're all connected in every which way. We are lucky to be here! This is an incredible opportunity. Most days it sure doesn't feel like that, so music plays such a vital role in survival. I feel like I am really helping the army of musicians out there, and all I'm doing is equipping them. I can't sing it for them. But I feel that music teachers play a very vital role in giving people that courage, the tools to get out there and touch others, and equip them. We're teaching farmers how to farm, which has such a residual domino effect. Food for the soul."

> "Music soothes us. It allows us to go back to that primal existence and see that we're all connected in every which way. We are lucky to be here!"

CHAPTER 11

Joey Blake and Christiane Karam

Joey Blake and Christiane Karam are both eclectic, gifted vocalists who are passionate about bringing people together through music. They are on the voice faculty at Berklee College of Music. Joey is a founding member of Voicestra, Bobby McFerrin's a capella vocal ensemble. He has worked with Mickey Hart, Kenny Loggins, Rebeca Mauleon, Holly Near, and Rhiannon. He is producer, recording engineer, arranger, songwriter, and vocalist with the groups SoVoSo and WeBe3. Christiane, who grew up in Beirut with both Western and Eastern musical traditions, works with a wide range of musical genres and specializes in traditional and fusion styles from the Balkans and the Middle East. She is a composer and songwriter and has worked with Bobby McFerrin, Yanka Rupkina, the Assad Brothers, the Boston Pops, and the New York Arabic Orchestra; she is the founder, leader, and vocalist of the world/Middle Eastern music band ZilZALA.

We sat down together in their softly lit apartment over a wonderful meal they had prepared, with soft music, laughter, and warm friendship. We spoke about making music, community building, teaching, and performing. We spoke about *why* we are drawn to be musicians.

Photos by Jan Watson and Heather Matthews

AT THE HEART OF IT ALL

It has to be real. A concert that digs into the real gem of a performance always is. "I need to be sure that I'm singing from a real place, do I believe me?" Joey asked. "It's not about, 'Look what I can do.'" Christiane added, "Sound is vibration, and the human voice in particular, when sung from a place of truth, has an incredibly intimate and healing ability to communicate emotion, tell a story, and transform lives."

So, if concerts can be transformative, how do you get there? Do you plan it, or is this kind of powerful experience somehow *organic*? What are the top few factors that Joey and Christiane feel are the *most* important to consider when putting concerts together?

For Joey, creating a good experience for the audience is always an important goal. He tries to choose music and groups that bring him joy to work with. How does he stay real? Joey avoids going for big, flashy singing. It's not about showing off chops. Instead, he reminds himself, "I don't have to blow up the stage tonight." By not worrying about whether or not each gig is "the show of all shows," he can focus his energy on the experience and on the truth in what he is singing. It allows for the true musical gem of a performance to shine through.

Christiane, who grew up in a war-torn country, understands the powerful potential of music to foster peace, and to bring people together. She chooses music that she hopes will do exactly this. She wants her concerts to raise awareness toward this goal, lasting well beyond when the last notes have finished ringing.

When she's preparing for a concert, Christiane focuses first on the musical aspects. The songs, the players, and the blend of styles have to be right. Christiane is a world musician, with many influences in her palette; her performances blend a variety of music and musical guests. She strives to create new sounds and possibilities by exploring common ground between different musical languages. She has a wide swath of cultures and music that have sculpted her throughout her life, and she is always learning new music and techniques that influence her choices. She enjoys introducing audiences and students to new sounds they may never have heard before, and to new musical scales and rhythms. It is a fun challenge. For instance, music that was once part of ancient cultures can now become more accessible to wider audiences. Christiane enjoys building bridges between the old ways and new music.

MAKING "MEDICINE" IN LIVE MUSIC

So, how do you make music that is truly meaningful? How do you build an experience for the audience? In improvisational singing, Joey said, the first thing you do is to start singing. Clear the palate. "You have to quiet your thoughts before you can find the music that's going to come through you in that moment." Clearing the palate allows us to go deeper than our usual thoughts. When we can transition out of the moment that *was* before we sang, we can be present in the moment that *is, now*. Then, we need to be wholly open to going with whatever singing wants to come forward. You cannot plan for this. When you get yourself out of the way, then *real* music can be revealed. It will come through you.

"Genuine artists are like channels," added Christiane. "They have this ability to ground themselves and open themselves up just enough to let energy through. The audience is yearning for that openness." Open channels allow for passage. They make space. Musicians create space for the audience to connect through. Channels. Openings. Passageways. "This space we create allows them to be part of the music and the experience, even if they're not musicians. That's what makes every Bobby McFerrin concert so joyous and unforgettable. When he sings, the audience becomes part of the music making and the circle comes to life. Everyone gets to be part of the magic. Everyone is *inside* the music. There's nothing like it."

For Joey, a performance vibe that is inclusive helps to draw the audience in. "As an artist, you have to figure out when and how to engage the audience. Energy onstage—having fun—translates to the audience. They get to be a part of the show." Does Joey design what experience he hopes the audience will leave with? No. There is so much that happens in live music that you don't need to plan as much as you think. The interaction in performance that can happen between the musicians and the audience is a beautiful thing. He added, "You can feel when they're with you, and that will change what I'm doing. If we go out there and have fun, everyone else will, too."

Christiane feels a responsibility to be invested in the music she performs.

> **"It's like medicine. We are like healers."**

When she sings about what is meaningful to her, feeling and believing it, she can share her connection to the music with the audience. The audience feeds the performer, and the performer feeds the audience. It is a reciprocal experience. There is a give-and-take of energy that happens at a very deep level. "It's like medicine. We are like healers," she said.

DETACHMENT, NOT EXPECTATIONS—FEELING IT

"Tori Amos once said that we all struggle not to get too attached to what happened the night before," Christiane continued. When a performance is great, naturally, we want that experience again. The challenge is to avoid building up an expectation of what we want this new night to be like or to sound like. "Tori said that every night before a performance, she peeks out from backstage and looks at the audience. She smells the air. She figures out what the recipe is going to be for that night. She puts herself into a place where she is working with what is, right now. That's different from working with her own thing that she set up. Great performers do this. They know how to let go. It's hard, and sometimes the energies are not aligned; either we're in our own way, or the sound system is problematic, or the audience is in a different place than we are. But these things are all necessary to help manifest the next magical moment. Ultimately, it's what we learn from each experience that moves us forward—and not holding onto any of it, allowing it to simply be what it is. That's why improvisation is so great. It's a crash course in surrender."

This got us talking about big performances, like a huge stadium show, where there is often a separation of hundreds of feet between the band and the fans. When the venue is that big, there is no way for the artists to really *feel* the people. All the band hears is the roar of the crowd; all they see is a big audience enjoying their show. And all the fans see are their favorite artists off in the distance and bright, flashing lights. It can be a compartmentalized experience.

Joey said, "These compartmentalized places—you're talking about 15,000 seats or more—are so big and so broad that what you experience way over here somewhere [he points to his right] is different from what happens way over there somewhere! [he points to his left]. There is no experience of a whole room. Each person in the audience is going to have their own experience. There might be someone sitting right here who just had a great time all night. Then there might be someone sitting way over there whose audience section was rowdy and obnoxious."

Christiane wondered if this kind of giant show somehow feeds a deep, primal part of us. Perhaps it reaches a hungry place inside, satisfying an unsettled discontentment. Joey suggested that when the music is aggressive or angry, "It can bring out things in us that are not the most inclusive or warm or fuzzy." Christiane said, "Depending on the kind of music, stadium shows could sometime have an aggressive energy, but they can also be extremely spiritual and uplifting."

"For example," she continued, "I saw Tina Turner a few years back at the Fleet Center. It was gorgeous, beautiful. There were 20,000 people there, but it was *Tina Turner*. She doesn't have that angry energy. She has a very deep thing. It's rock, it has an edge to it, but there's something about this woman that just transcends. It's a big stadium, a lot of people. But it didn't get out of hand. Because there's something that she projects that is about healing and connecting that came through."

CIRCLE SINGING

Half of the beauty of a concert is watching the musicians create, Joey said, experiencing making the music with them. This interaction produces a variety of improvised music that would not have been on the CD. That's definitely true with his group SoVoSo.

SoVoSo stands for "from the soul to the voice to the song." The group is experiential and rooted in the circle singing tradition. The group forms half of the circle, and the audience is the other half. Without the audience, there is no circle, no community.

> "Each live performance happens only once–and the next one can never be the same."

The singers give and receive this "medicine," that Christiane describes, with the audience. For Joey, this makes it worth doing. The songs are the vehicle for the experience, but are only the shell. Being in the moment is essential: the real experience comes from being present. Each live performance happens only once—and the next one can never be the same.

Joey also performs with the artists Rhiannon and David Worm in an improvisational trio, WeBe3. The three are founding members of Voicestra, the vocal ensemble created by Bobby McFerrin. "It's just improv," Joey explained. "We walk on stage, and whatever happens is what happens. It's an experiential thing, all based on the circle. Without the other half of the circle, the audience—without community—it's as if you are putting the music out into oblivion. It's that experience of both of us feeding each other that makes it worth doing. So, you think about ways of putting music out that will generate a response. That response will give you something else to feed off of—to build something new, in the moment. That's why the tunes can only be a shell, or just a guideline, just like a music chart. These are the directions. Where you go is based on your own musical experiences and what you bring to it." The directions could be an actual song with a beginning, middle, and end, or they could be the loose structure of an improvisation. "The improv itself usually gets built out of the songs that we've sung and the reactions we've gotten, and the audience experience, and the feel of the energy in the room at that moment. We all create an aesthetic that happens inside a room. That's why live performance is so great."

IMPROVISING

Joey described how he teaches improvising. "We talk about how it's done. I'm usually in the middle, giving out parts, and then we start going. After a while, I start bringing people in, maybe to complete something, like a musical line, that I haven't finished. I always tell my students, the first thing you want to do when you work in a circle is just start singing. The first thing that comes into your head, you should just go there. Because that's usually what the feel is in that room at that moment. If you sit there and try to think about it and try to be clever, it's not authentic anymore. You're not going with the mood of the music. The music is already out there. It's already in the air. All the notes that we sing are a vehicle to let that music come through. So when you open yourself up to that music, then you can get yourself out of the way. Then the real music can come through and be heard."

From his studio, powerful, rich sounds waft into the Berklee halls when Joey teaches. Improvising, circle singing, classical styles, breathing techniques, and tone production are a normal part of his lessons. When he sings, Joey focuses on the pure vowel, making sure he has adequate breath support. That's all he needs to do. The rest happens by itself. This is what he teaches his students, too. "It's by *listening* that you get the timbre of the vowel, and that gives you the style." Modify the tone: modify the style. While many approaches focus on talking about head voice or chest voice, Joey believes it can sometimes get students hung up on the terms and further away from their "true" voices.

"I'm all about music and how it works with community—how community helps us, how we help each other," said Joey. "It's a very precious thing to be an artist. People should be musicians because they *are* musicians, not because they want to learn how to be musicians. If you don't love what you do, you'll never be good enough at it to make any money. That's really what it's about. You have to do something because you love it—because that's just what you are. So it's important to discover for yourself what that thing is for you, whatever it is—something you have to do whether or not you get paid for it."

Christiane always seeks to bring out the best in each of her students. Her style is loving, inclusive, warm. She also expects hard work, and her students love her. Her world music ensembles and classes literally bring students from all around the world together in song. "I deeply believe in music's endless potential to connect us with one another and bring us to this peaceful place of oneness from where we all come," said Christiane. She believes that when musicians share their truth, "they can bring love and healing to the world."

CHAPTER 12

William Allaudin Mathieu

W.A. Mathieu, who prefers to be called Allaudin, is a pianist, choral conductor, composer, educator, and author. For over fifty years, his career has been a rich journey through many diverse areas of music, including theater, North Indian raga, and classical composition. In the 1960s, he served as arranger and composer for the Stan Kenton and Duke Ellington Orchestras; musical director for Chicago's Second City Theater (which he helped found), and San Francisco's Community Theater; in the 1970s he taught at the San Francisco Conservatory of Music and Mills College. He founded The Sufi Choir, which he directed from 1969 until 1982. He is the composer of a large variety of chamber pieces, choral works, and song cycles; and the author of four books on music. For twenty-five years, Allaudin was a disciple of North Indian vocalist Pandit Pran Nath. Allaudin's website (www.coldmountainmusic.com) offers numerous albums, ranging from big band to Sufi choral music to sound cycles to piano and chamber compositions.

His prose writing delves deeply into what makes music tick, examining topics like listening, harmonic experience, and the contemplative side of being a musician. John Coltrane once said of him, "Mathieu is consistently proving himself to be one of the best in musical theory."

In 2005, my friend Suzanne Hanser, Ed.D., MT-BC, Chair of Music Therapy at Berklee College of Music, introduced me to Allaudin's first book, *The Listening Book*,[1] which has since become required reading in my Berklee classes. Written

---

[1] Mathieu, William Allaudin. *The Listening Book: Discovering Your Own Music.* Boston, MA: Shambhala Publications, 1991

in short, meditational-like chapters about listening, practicing, and managing our thoughts, *The Listening Book* is both simple and profound. Drawn from decades of musical and life experience, Allaudin's work is inspiring and wise. As you read *The Listening Book*, you begin to hear sounds that are around you all the time, sounds you probably never noticed before. You become aware of how music gets under your skin. My students love this book.

The Listening Book has been very popular, since its publication in 1991, for musicians and non-musicians alike. I was eager to begin our conversation by asking Allaudin what inspired him to write it. He explained that, coming from a writing family, "I knew at a certain point that I had something to say, and I should probably write it down." He'd been writing journalistically his whole life, beginning in his twenties with music criticism for *DownBeat* magazine. He wanted to write a book that says what he knows about music. So, he began by writing "the big book," a ten-pound exploration of music theory called *Harmonic Experience: Total Harmony from Its Natural Origins to Its Modern Expression* (1997). But once he got deep into it, Allaudin realized that he needed to explore listening first. So, he wrote *The Listening Book*, followed by a second book, *The Musical Life: What It Is and How to Live It* (also published by Shambhala), which, because it discusses overtones intensively, got him closer to "the big book." Finally, he could approach his tome, but ultimately, counting years of teaching and music-making, *Harmonic Experience* took thirty years to write. Allaudin laughed as he said, "It made me crazy, no doubt about it." A fourth book, *Bridge of Waves: What Music Is and How Listening to It Changes the World*, was published in 2010.

BIG EARS

There is a chapter called "Big Ears" at the end of *The Listening Book*, which recounts in beautiful, poetic prose a moment of transformation in Allaudin's life. For many years, Allaudin taught all-day seminars, followed by an evening concert. Eventually, he noticed something perplexing: after his seminars people would typically say, "Thank you. I really needed that." But after his concerts people would say, instead, "That was very interesting." Why were people getting something out of his workshops but not so much out of his concerts? What was he doing wrong? The word "interesting" got under his skin. One day, in Boston, it hit him: he suddenly realized that his *intention* in the seminars was to be helpful to people; there was little ego in it. But his intention in the concerts was to show his skill, to blend different techniques and music in order to create something that was indeed objectively *interesting*. On that day of transformation, he asked himself bluntly, what *was* his life's purpose? To be giving or to be interesting? Was the music he played in concerts an expression of his life's purpose?

We talked about moving and being moved in performance. I asked Allaudin if he thinks most musicians are intentional about moving their listeners. "It's a tough topic," he said. He wondered, how can you say with certainty why people perform music? Human beings are complex.

"I came to realize through that episode, and through many like it over the years, that people make music for many reasons," Allaudin said. "I think experiences that happen to you when you're playing or singing in a concert have to do with how you're coming into the concert hall and how you're waking up that morning and why you're doing music in the first place. Your performing experience has to do with your development in your whole life, up to that point. People make music to amaze, to make money, to over-power, to magnify themselves, to sell shirts. There are so many reasons to make music. It's very revealing to listen to different [styles of] music with the question in your mind, 'What is the intention of this music?' Or you could more directly ask, 'What does this music want from me?'

"For instance," Allaudin continued, "listen to TV ads. Take seriously what the jingle writers are doing—the fact that the ad agencies are trying to sell you something. It's quite illuminating to see how music comes out when selling is the intention. Or, look at a horror flick. I was just watching (briefly) *Halloween* and listening to the music. It's the shadow side of what we do. It's the other side of our coin. You can almost understand your own impulses and your own clarity better by listening to music while inquiring into its intention."

STATE OF LOVE THROUGH MAKING MUSIC

Coming before people to commune through music is a luxury, he said, and also a responsibility. "The *communion* becomes the point, not the people." Allaudin said this communion is described by the Holy Trinity, as well as in the Arabic chant, "Ishkh Allah Mabud Lilla,"[2] "It's a typical mystical formulation," he said: "There's you, and then there's me, sometimes called the lover and the beloved. Then there's that state of being that allows us to be in love. So, in music, there's the musician and there's the listener, and then there's that state of being in which all of us exist at once: musician, listener, and connection.

"That's what we're looking for," he continued, "that special quality when the music is pure, and the musician is pure, and the listener is pure. By pure, I mean that the energy is going all around in all directions, like a circle, or globe. You can feel the energetic connection between the maker of the music and the listener of the music. They all become one thing. It's that one thing, between that three-ness, that we are looking for."

---

[2] pronounced a bit like "EESHKH Allah Ma BOOD Lee Lah," the phrase refers, roughly, to the attractive, cohesive force of nature.

Allaudin said that when you really *feel* the essence of someone, love is the medium. Love carries the experience; love *is* the experience. "I'm not referring to romantic love, but to the heightened sense of belonging to one human family. Music is magical," he continued, "in that it functions as a carrier wave of feeling that unifies the person doing it and the people receiving it. It's very mysterious, but after awhile, if you live enough years, you learn to devote yourself to that. It becomes the most important thing. It's not you anymore, it's not even them anymore. It's the *union* that happens. So, when you go into a concert hall looking for that union—and depending on the audience, they will be, too—then it happens. Of course, this presumes you know how to make music."

On his website, Allaudin writes of his album *This Marriage* (2002), "Rumi speaks of union with the divine—the Beloved—as a marriage. The title duet of this album offers images that remind us of such unions: honey dissolving in milk, women laughing together for days on end, the leaves and fruit of a date tree, a pale moon in a light blue sky. Musical duets can be like fine marriages in high art, replete with intimacy, ongoing trust, passionate joining, the cool trick of hearing the sound of another emanating from yourself, the being in another, but via the music."

Allaudin believes that performing musicians commonly seek this union, though there is a wide variety in what it looks like. "I think that punk-rock can be that union," he said, "and a mosh pit can be, too. It's just that it takes place at different levels of the psyche and at different levels of development. I also think that for some musicians, it's considered wimpy, or a sign of mushiness, to talk about it.

"I came up as a jazz musician, man, and let me tell you. You couldn't talk about these things or you were a 'fag,' an effeminate person, a weak person. I mean it. In truth, of course, jazz is love, created by musicians who are seeking union through their exploration of it. Jazz musicians are inevitably drawn to making music this way; but back in the socially unliberated days of the mid-twentieth century, it was something that was done but not discussed openly. Sixty, fifty, forty years ago, when jazz was still going through periods of explosive development, yet still borrowing heavily from European musics and principles, it had to keep its African and improvisational authenticity alive. So, it tended to become anti-scholastic and anti-European, which also meant anti-intellectual. That may still be true where macho blindly reigns, but the climate has changed these days. Today jazz is more and more heard as our American classical music—Louis is our Mozart, Bird is our Beethoven, Ornette is our Stravinsky—and intellectual, highly literate jazz musicians abound. We can talk about our hearts, find the good words.

WHY PLAY?

I commented that when everyone gets on stage, although we each have an intention, we may not, necessarily, be aware of it. Allaudin agreed. His students tell him: "I just want to play. I just want to do great music." He asks his students what their point is when they perform, asks if they have an objective, a goal. His students reply, "'I just want to say my piece, man, tell my story. I just want to bare my soul. I just want to make soul music, man.' That's it."

Sometimes, performing winds up being "ego mania." But when the music is much greater than the conscious intention of the players, then union can occur. "When you corner musicians who have some development," he said, "they'll probably get what's happening. But I don't know that musicians typically think very deeply about this.

"Imagine you play cello for the Boston Symphony Orchestra. It's probably very groovy to be in the cello section of the Boston Symphony Orchestra. Lots of great players, lots of great music. But why are you there? What are you actually doing right now? You're playing Beethoven and Shostakovich tonight, same as last night. Do you know clearly what you are doing with your life? There are a lot of possible answers." Is the point that being in the orchestra is an amazing experience and that is enough? Or is the point that it's easy to get lost in the routine of anything we do, even when that something is a rare and cherished experience like playing in the Boston Symphony Orchestra? It is the latter. We can become numb, or checked-out, even when we are doing what we set out to do and worked hard to accomplish. It is a paradox.

WHY LISTEN?

His comment got me thinking about the survey I'd conducted where one hundred percent of the people who responded said they go to a live concert in order to have an experience, to be moved. I told Allaudin that some people in the survey said they may really enjoy rock 'n' roll at home but it's too much of a volume assault to go hear it live. Or, they may like vacuuming to easy listening music but think it would be boring to see live. Sixty percent of the responders said they go to concerts for classical music or jazz or world music. I asked Allaudin if he thought the reason people choose to see live music might differ from the conscious intention of the musicians who are playing that music.

"Maybe, maybe not," he replied. "The reason this is difficult to talk about is that everyone is in a different place in their lives. You're really asking a question about how far along people are in their own awakening, in their own consciousness. I would think that a more developed human playing music is going to play it for more developed reasons than a less developed human playing music. The same holds for concertgoers who can—consciously or unconsciously—be affected by being in a communal space. When my wife and I go to the movies, we're sometimes the only people in the audience, watching it by ourselves. But if one more couple comes in, the entire experience changes."

"You have to ask yourself: if you went to a concert and there was a string quartet playing Beethoven but you were the only person listening to it, wouldn't that be different than at Alice Tully Hall with hundreds of people, where you could hear a pin drop and everybody's breath was modulated by the music? Where every single person was experiencing these *amazing* vibrational, harmonic energies in our bodies? We were all in it together—yes, having our unique experiences—but there is something we are all following that is elaborate and deep. That's important. I don't know if listeners generally recognize how important the rest of the audience is."

DISCOVERING ROCK

Allaudin went on to describe discovering rock music. Coming from the "uptight" University of Chicago mind-set, he had never been immersed in the kind of "people-music that was rising out of San Francisco in the middle 1960s," he said. "Suddenly, in '67, I go to the Fillmore and feel this tremendous openness in the atmosphere that was nowhere else in the country then. It was new. And I realized then why people made music together, whether or not I liked the music. But I found myself loving some of it. I became a Janis Joplin fan. I'd go listen to her and really, really get it. I'd be screaming along with her and everybody else! I have hearing loss in my left ear on account of Janis… yeah, I got a little too close to a ten-foot speaker at one concert. And I was personally acquainted with her, too, in those days; it was very nice to make that connection. She came to an ensemble improvisation concert of mine once, with a totally stoned, freaked-out friend who leapt on stage, and Janis and I had to talk her friend down. It all became part of the concert, of course."

Allaudin also went to hear the Grateful Dead in the late '60s. Those concerts were "fantastic because everybody was in this deep, ecstatic state," he said. "Sometimes, the music was pretty dark…but because everyone was going through it together, it was wonderful!" Rock 'n' roll can also create a disconnecting experience, he said. "There's a tremendous amount of negativity in it. There's a huge shadow in it. It's even worse with rap," he explained. And stadium-sized concerts have a legendary disconnect between the fans and the

> "I'd rather have… somebody pointing his guitar at me like it's a machine gun—than having somebody pointing his machine gun at me like it's a guitar."

musicians. "There's all this dark energy in the music. But I'd rather have this happening—somebody pointing his guitar at me like it's a machine gun—than having somebody pointing his machine gun at me like it's a guitar. So somehow, even though it's a crying out, which to us seems full of pain and alienation and negativity, somebody is getting healed. There's a lot of healing energy going on, even though it's in this very dungeon-like realm. You just have to honor it.

"What I'm trying to say," he continued, "is that when angst and a violent point of reference are shared through music, the sharing is just as important as it is for others of us to go out and listen to a Beethoven string quartet. It's the communality that's important. It's the sharing, not the angst, or even the ecstasy, that people ultimately go for. It's to be with others who are like you. Music is a unique magic for allowing that to happen."

TRANSFORMATION IN CONCERT

Does Allaudin think people listen to artists who seem to portray how they see themselves? He said that's difficult to say. For one thing, when 40,000 people gather in one place to hear a concert, it's more than just a concert—it's a phenomenon. Being at a major band event, like seeing a Rolling Stones stadium show, is historic. And sometimes, a live show will teach you to appreciate music that you thought you didn't like. Allaudin talked about how he learned to appreciate the specialness of hearing live jazz. He was mostly in the habit of listening to jazz only on records until he went to a Cecil Taylor concert in San Francisco. "I was just knocked out," he said. "So was everybody else. It was the best concert. I went to an Ornette Coleman concert last year, and it was the same as that Beethoven string quartet union. Everybody was transported. And there was no blue smoke curling in the air, no old guys on the make, and no chicks trying to get tips, nothing like that. It was because the music was absolutely fantastic, and everybody was getting it. And everybody was *getting* that everybody was getting it. It was enormously good...It was an ecstasy experience."

Allaudin said that after the Cecil Taylor concert, "People walked out with this wonderful glow. Cecil is a master musician, and you just hear him. I used to have this same experience with Pandid Pran Nath, my North Indian music teacher. The concerts were small—sixty, eighty, one hundred people, and it was like being in love with all these people at once. I would go to Pran Nath concerts and sometimes blank out. I wasn't asleep; I got into this somatic space where I knew I wasn't hearing the music anymore. It wasn't coming in through my ears, it was coming in through my pores, my cells! It was coming through a faculty that had just opened and could only open under these circumstances. And when this is communal—many people doing it together—that is high music."

Allaudin believes this type of experience is only too rare, not often consciously sought after. Once you have it you want more, but you may not know where to look for it. He wondered, what percentage of the six billion listening population has had that kind of experience?

Allaudin stressed, again, that being open to transformative experience in music has to do with where you are in your life. For instance, a troubled teenager who goes to a heavy metal concert can get a lot of good out of it. He said, "You can't be judgmental about this in any way. You're not a better person because you're more refined or more developed. There's no better or worse in this. The more awake you are, the less it's about being good or bad; you're just farther along. There's more of you there."

GETTING STUCK IN ONE'S HEAD

As we were speaking, I recalled working with Allaudin and his wife Devi Mathieu at a Unitarian Universalist Musicians Network conference in Denver, one summer, where they were keynote presenters. Their workshops were superb and eye opening. Allaudin recognized that this was a group of musicians who were very sincere people devoted to their work. The feeling among them was quite positive. He also felt that these musicians were generally "in their heads." He decided to sit still and feel the room before getting into his planned workshop. What he felt in the room was enormous intellectual curiosity. He said the group seems to think there's a series of puzzles they have to solve to get answers to their questions. This approach is mental. It's different from seeking truth energetically, kinesthetically.

Like everyone else, musicians can be susceptible to being stuck in their minds. Allaudin said, "In musical contexts that call themselves sacred, when there is some kind of communal intention, you can't think your way through these kinds of situations. You have to feel your way through them." At the Denver conference, he said, "I felt that my mission there was to draw people out of their heads and put them in their hearts. I wanted to sing for people, I wanted to have people sing, to have them deeply experience the music, to appreciate the simple beauty of being devoted to sound, to turn off their minds and realize what was connective (and thus sacred) about the actual experience of singing a single chord. I found that difficult at first, but it turned out to be successful. People got it. My problem is that I can only too easily get snookered by my intellect. In my workshops, when I start answering questions about overtones, it's all over." [He laughed.]

At the conference, Devi gave a presentation on the composer, writer, and philosopher Hildegard von Bingen. Hildegard was a groundbreaking church musician in the twelfth century, when few women wrote. Recognizing the intellectual tendency of the Unitarian Universalist group, Devi decided to limit the historical part of her presentation. Rather than give buckets of information, she wanted the group to *experience* Hildegard's music. Allaudin said Devi knew an experience of expansiveness would come simply from singing this sacred music together. The sound and feel of the music are at its core. "All you have to do is go to a gospel meeting," he said. "Just go to church with a good gospel choir on Sunday morning, and there it is, man."

When you are leading people through a prayerful state with music, Allaudin said, you need to be in a prayerful state, too. It doesn't matter what music you sing or play. "You're not going to be prayerful—by which I mean recognizing your inner being—just by using some kind of prayer or mantra." He said, "You're going to be prayerful by *being* prayerful. If you don't *do* the practice that you are teaching, what *are* you doing?"

MUSIC CAN TEACH LIFE LESSONS

After teaching music lessons for sixty years, Allaudin has recognized that music lessons are actually a cover for something even deeper than music. What is really being taught is helping students learn who they are and where they are in their lives. How do they handle their energy? How do they handle their realization, their level of maturity? Allaudin believes that, as a singer, you can't be truly singing if you're trying to please someone else. It's impossible. You have to go instead into that place "that is pleasure for you, that is your own deep rightness, your own deep autonomy. You can't be pleasing Daddy," he said. "Lillian Loran, Devi's vocal coach for many years, used to say, 'Nice girls can't sing,' to which I could add, 'naughty girls can't sing either.' The object is not to take on a nice-girl or a naughty-girl persona but to learn to sing through the person you authentically are without the mask."

When Allaudin performs, he enters into the music as fully as he can. He said, "I can't explain this, but I sense that music is a carrier of energy that is beyond the music. Music carries the deepest intention of the performer—ultimately there is no hiding, *even when you're hiding*. That's the beauty of music, and that's the responsibility you have for developing your own musicality—why you have to be the most integrated person you can be as well as the best musician you can be. The more masterful a musician you are—not only in terms of technique, but in terms of depth—the more your music can carry your intention. That's all you *can* do, really: allow your music to be so clear and so pure and so right, and in tune, and in time, allow it to be so lined up with what you are actually meaning and feeling in your life *right now* that people just *get* it. When that happens, that magic can occur." Allaudin believes that if the audience is made up of "like-minded souls who know the kind of communion they're looking for, then *whammo!*—it happens."

At the same time, you can't plan exactly what's going to happen. You might be distracted by the caterer or by your gear. "You might give a concert and have the impression you weren't connected. But what about those fifty years of practice you put in so assiduously? You brought that to the concert, too," he said, "so maybe you weren't as bad as you thought!"

It's like baseball. Allaudin explained. "The reason I love baseball so much is that the psychology of the team is gossamer, fragile as a spider web. All it takes is a little tweak to unravel it." He described baseball as a game where strong guys act macho, spit, flex their big biceps. Yet little things can tilt the feeling and momentum of the game. There is also the matter of balance, especially between teams that are well-matched. It's very telling, psychologically. "It's so beautiful to see," he said. "I think it's that way with music and audiences, too. The chemistry is complex, so sophisticated, so labyrinthine. All we can do, as musicians, is our best."

"The only thing you can say after it's over," Allaudin said, "is whatever the result, it would have been worse if you hadn't brought your best stuff."

Coda: Choices

I hope this book's eclectic mix of tools for contemporary vocal technique, for staying healthy, for accessing creativity, and for performing will give you what you need to become a strong contemporary singer. The recordings and exercises provide ample opportunity to practice and build your skills. The wise voices of the six phenomenal artists and teachers in this book have shared a snapshot of their musical journeys to inspire you to seek your own path. So, what's next?

KEEPING YOUR OPTIONS OPEN

One of the most exciting things about singing contemporary styles is the opportunity to be *you*. That's what contemporary singing is about. Your style will evolve constantly throughout your lifetime. There is no age limit, no voice limit. As the world gets smaller, styles and genres continue to cross-pollinate. The Internet makes it possible for you to collaborate and share your music with the whole world. It all comes down to what you put into it. The possibilities are endless.

Strong technique is essential. It gives you the tools you need to be expressive and creative. But making good music is way more than technique. It's about being willing to embrace your creativity, to look beyond what is popular at the moment to come up with something new, or to explore a style of music that you really love. It's about being willing to take chances. As a career coach once told me, you can sit in the bleachers and watch the game—that's safe. You won't get hurt. But to play the game, to be involved, you have to get on that field. That's where the fun and the action are.

Staying healthy in body, mind, and spirit is also essential. When you approach music from a holistic view, you can make decisions that embrace *all* of who you are. You can access and balance deep parts of yourself to express in your music. Your authenticity can shine. You can work with other musicians who align with your vision. You can learn to recognize what influences and teachers resonate with your inner music and being—or not.

Part of it is figuring it all out. What color do you want your flag to be? Why do you enjoy singing? What does it do for you?

There's nobody else with your voice. It's your music. It's your expression. It's your spirit. It's your voice.

The song is *you*. Enjoy singing it!

Keep the Conversation Going

Visit my website at www.jeanniegagne.com to keep up-to-date on my workshops, lessons, and performing. Drop me a line. I'd love to hear from you.

I hope you will give me feedback about this book. How was it helpful? Would you like to share it with a friend, school, or colleague? There's a blog section at www.jeanniegagne.com/YourSingingVoice where you can write in.

APPENDIX A

Bibliography and Recommended Reading

Adzenyah, Abraham K., Maraire, Dumasani, and Tucker, Judith C. *Let Your Voice Be Heard! Songs from Ghana and Zimbabwe*. Danbury, CT: World Music Press, 1997.

Barnwell, Ysaye. M. *Singing in the African American Tradition, Volume 2: Building a Vocal Community*. Hal Leonard, 2009.

Baxter, Mark. *The Rock-n-Roll Singer's Survival Manual*. Milwaukee, WI: Hal Leonard, 1990. Mark Baxter's excellent and easy-to-read vocal technique book. Mark Baxter appears in *Your Singing Voice, chapter 6*.

Beck, Robert J. et al. "Supporting the Health of College Solo Singers: The Relationship of Positive Emotions and Stress to Changes in Salivary IgA and Cortisol During Singing." *Journal for Learning Through the Arts*, 2(1) (2006). A review of studies that suggest singing is good for your health.

Berger, Harris M. and Del Negro, Giovanna P. "Bauman's Verbal Art and the Social Organization of Attention: The Role of Reflexivity in the Aesthetics of Performance." *Journal of American Forklore, 115(455)* (2002): 62–91. A fascinating look at the sociological phenomenon of "reflexivity," a kind of feedback loop that occurs in performance where the performer is self-aware, the audience responds, and that further affects the performer. Also looks at both jazz and rock groups in Cleveland, OH to see how musicians relate differently to audiences depending on the genre of music.

Bicknell, Jeanette. "Just a Song? Exploring the Aesthetics of Popular Song Performance." *Journal of Aesthetics and Art Criticism, 63*(3) (2005): 262–270. A philosopher's look at how the song form is expressed by a singer and received by an audience.

Bono and the Christian Right. 60 Minutes, CBS, Directed by Ed Bradley. Aired 11/20/2005. Ed Bradley's interview with U2's Bono, who does significant altruistic work internationally.

Brennan, Barbara A. *Hands of Light: A Guide to Healing Through the Human Energy Field.* New York, NY: Bantam New Age Books, 1987. This is the ultimate, scholarly work on the topic of energy healing, including inspiring drawings of "invisible" energy phenomena such as auras and the light used in Reiki healing.

Bruser, Madeline. *The Art of Practicing: A Guide to Making Music from the Heart.* New York, NY: Bell Tower, 1999. Bruser's book is a wonderful and useful resource for the musician. It discusses body mechanics for efficient playing on several instruments, body and mind states for practicing with ease, and developing performance confidence and warmth.

Cameron, Julia. *The Artist's Way: A Spiritual Path to Higher Creativity.* New York, NY: Penguin Group, 1992. Discussing "recovering" identity, power, integrity, abundance, connection, and other senses of self that are essential for the visionary work of artists, this comprehensive work combines aspects of religious faith with ways to tap into creativity.

Campbell, Don. *The Mozart Effect: Tapping the Power of Music to Heal the Body, Strengthen the Mind, and Unlock the Creative Spirit.* New York, NY: Avon Books, 1997. This groundbreaking book describes how music can be profoundly beneficial.

Carol, Shawna. *The Way of Song: A Guide to Freeing the Voice and Sounding the Spirit.* New York, NY: St. Martin's Griffin, 2003. This book encourages exploration of emotions and spiritual depth through free expression in unstructured singing.

Chopra, Deepak. *Reinventing the Body, Resurrecting the Soul.* New York, NY: Harmony Books, 2009.

Cooper, Morton. *Change Your Voice, Change Your Life: A Quick, Simple Plan for Finding & Using Your Natural, Dynamic Voice* (17th printing). New York, NY: Macmillan, 1984. This voice teacher to the stars writes like he speaks. Joan Rivers sums it up in her back-flap quote: "Before I met Mort Cooper, i spoke like this (sic). Now, thanks to his advice, I SPEAK LIKE THIS."

D'Angelo, James. *The Healing Power of the Human Voice: Mantras, Chants, and Seed Sounds for Health and Harmony.* Rochester, VT: Healing Arts Press, 2005. With a CD of mantras, chants, and seed sounds included, this book teaches vocal sound healing.

Davidson, Justin. "Measure for Measure." *The New Yorker* 82(25) (2006): 60–69.

Gaynor M.D., Mitchell L. *Sounds of Healing: A Physician Reveals the Therapeutic Power of Sound, Voice, and Music.* New York: Broadway Books, 1999. This book explores the healing power of sound and music with singing bowls, tone, rhythm, and song, written by a traditional physician whose understanding of healing was altered dramatically when he discovered these sound techniques.

Goleman, Daniel, Kaufman, Paul, and Ray, Michael. *The Creative Spirit: Companion to the PBS Television Series.* New York, NY: Penguin Group, 1992. This user-friendly book explores creativity.

Goodman, Gabrielle. *Vocal Improvisation: Techniques in Jazz, R&B and Gospel Improvisation.* Boston, MA: Goodness Music, 2010. A wonderful and useful book by one of Berklee's finest teachers.

Halpern, Steven. *Sound Health: The Music and Sounds that Make Us Whole.* San Francisco: Harper & Row, 1985.

Hunt, Valerie V. *Infinite Mind: The Science of Human Vibrations.* Malibu, CA: Malibu Publishing, 2005. A detailed look at human vibrations, with topics including the soul, emotion, biosphere, science and thought, mysticism, and healing.

Jourdain, Robert. *Music, the Brain, and Ecstasy: How Music Captures Our Imagination* (2nd printing). New York, NY: Avon Books, 2002.

Khan, Hazrat Inayat. *The Mysticism of Sound and Music: The Sufi Teachings of Hazrat Inayat Khan.* Boston: Shambhala Publications, 1991. Khan was a spiritual man who wrote profoundly about music.

Leeds, Joshua. *The Power of Sound.* Rochester, VT: Healing Arts Press, 2001.

Levitin, Daniel J. *This Is Your Brain on Music: The Science of a Human Obsession.* New York, NY: Plume, 2007. This fascinating work by rocker-turned-neuroscientist Levitin explores the connection between music and the brain, including topics such as how we are affected by music, why certain songs affect us more than others, and why a musician needs 10,000 hours of practice to become a virtuoso.

Love, Roger and Frazier, Donna. *Set Your Voice Free.* Boston, MA: Little Brown, 1999.

Mathieu, William Allaudin. *The Listening Book: Discovering Your Own Music.* Boston, MA: Shambhala Publications, 1991. This set of reflections encourages the reader to explore the essence of your music. Allaudin is interviewed in *Your Singing Voice,* chapter 6.

McCoy, Scott J. *Your Voice: An Inside View.* Princeton, NJ: Inside View Press, 2004. This vocal pedagogy text is anatomically and acoustically thorough.

Montello, L. *Essential Musical Intelligence: Using Music as Your Path to Healing, Creativity, and Radiant Wholeness.* Wheaton, IL: Theosophical Publishing House, 2002. Montello encourages the reader to uncover your innate musical "intelligence," with a focus on Eastern energy principles and with dozens of helpful, practical exercises. The book stresses using music and sound exploration as tools for well being.

Peckham, Anne. *The Contemporary Singer: Elements of Vocal Technique*, 2nd Ed. Boston, MA: Berklee Press, 2010. A highly respected and useful series by one of Berklee's finest teachers.

Peckham, Anne. *Vocal Workouts for the Contemporary Singer.* Boston, MA: Berklee Press, 2006.

Pert, Candace B. *Molecules of Emotion: Why You Feel the Way You Feel.* New York, NY: Scribner, 1997. This groundbreaking work by neuroscientist Pert goes deeply into how our emotions are connected between our minds and our bodies. A dense, deep, and amazing book.

Peterson, Lloyd. *Music and the Creative Spirit: Innovators in Jazz, Improvisation, and the Avant Garde.* Laynham, MD: Scarecrow Press, 2006. Peterson interviews forty-two major contemporary (mainly jazz) artists, including violinist Regina Carter, drummer Jack DeJohnette, and guitarist Pat Metheny, examining creativity, society, and musical tradition.

Ristad, Eloise. *A Soprano on Her Head.* Moab, UT: Real People Press, 1982. Full of stories from real-life inspiration and experience, Ristad's book encourages the reader to take new approaches to music-making to address problems that can so often be crippling.

Shank, Barry. *That Wild Mercury Sound: Bob Dylan and the Illusion of American Culture.* Duke University Press, boundary 2 29(1) (2002): 97–123.

Sloan, Carolyn. *Finding Your Voice: A Practical and Spiritual Approach to Singing and Living.* New York, NY: Hyperion, 1999. Dr. Sloan helps the reader look at several components of the complex art of singing, including self-image, vocal quality and sound production, self care, and societal influences.

Small, Mark. *Masters of Music: Conversations with Berklee Greats.* Boston: Berklee Press, 1999. Interviews with alumni superstars from Berklee College of Music are reprinted here from Berklee's alumni magazine. Many of the questions are about being successful in today's music business, sources of inspiration, and how the artist came to be a musician, writer, or producer.

Tomatis, Alfred A. *The Conscious Ear: My Life of Transformation Through Listening.* Barrytown, NY: Station Hill Press and Phoenix, AZ: Sound Listening and Learning Center, 1991. This is an autobiographical account of the development of Tomatis's groundbreaking work on sound acoustics, the ear, voice, and psyche.

Werner, Kenny. *Effortless Mastery: Liberating the Master Musician Within.* New Albany, IN: Jamey Aebersold Jazz, 1996. Werner's book is required reading in my classes. A jazz pianist, Werner writes about uncovering inspiration by removing barriers to creativity.

What the Bleep Do We Know!? DVD. Co-Directed by William Arntz, Betsy Chasse, and Mark Vincente. 2004; Los Angeles, CA: Lord of the Wind Films, 2004. This film, which includes interviews with notable physicists, as well as photos of Dr. Masaru Emoto's work with water molecules and projected thought, inspired me to link the power of intention with contemporary performance.

Wooten, Victor L. *The Music Lesson.* New York, NY: Berkley Books, 2006. Wooten's story-form tale of learning is full of rich nuggets for the music student.

The Zen of Screaming 2: Vocal Instruction for a New Breed. DVD. Directed by Denise Korycki, Written and Taught by Melissa Cross. Los Angeles, CA: Warner Brothers, 2007. Melissa Cross teaches healthy "growling" and "screaming" techniques, primarily for rock singers.

APPENDIX B

Glossary: Contemporary Rhythm Vocabulary

- **Backbeat:** Accented secondary beats, often beats 2 and 4 in 4/4 time. Usually played on the snare drum, sometimes on the toms, or occasionally on the kick drum in some reggae and pop/rock grooves:
    - In 4/4, beats 2 and 4
    - In 3/4, beat 3 or sometimes 2
    - In 6/8, beat 4
    - In 12/8, beats 4 and 10
    - In 4/4 with a half-time feel, beat 3
    - In 3/4 with a half-time feel, beat 1 of alternate measures beginning in measure 2.

- **Break:** Solo or *stop-time* indication

- **Broken time:** A groove with a steady tempo, but rhythm patterns are loosely improvised. Often used in the jazz idiom.

- **Busy:** Active or more syncopated

- **Chart:** Score, arranged lead sheet, or individual band part. May indicate the rhythm meter with *slashes* in place of melody. Often includes *stop-time* figures that tell the band to interrupt the groove and play specific rhythmic *hits*.

- **Comping:** Improvised chordal accompaniment, based on stylistic understanding of chord voicings and/or rhythms, to support the groove and harmonic structure of a song.

- **Concerted rhythmic figures:** See *stop-time* figures

- **Count off:** Speaking or conducting the meter, tempo, and beat subdivision of a song's groove to set it up one to two measures before the song begins. Ideally the count off is articulated in a manner that conveys both the genre and mood of the song, as well as qualities of the groove. In this manner, it is different from simply indicating tempo when starting a tune.

- **Downbeat:** In contemporary styles, the first beat of a measure, as well as any strong beat (i.e., beats 1, 2, 3 or 4, in 4/4 time). Must be equal to the value of the bottom number in the meter (time signature), where the bottom number always indicates what note value gets one beat of time. For example, in 6/8 time, downbeats are represented by eighth notes. Note: Traditional vocabulary often just calls this the "beat," saving "downbeat" for the first beat in a measure.

- **Drag:** Play too slowly; too relaxed; pull the tempo down; lag behind the beat

- **Feel:** Groove, style, or tempo. "Feel" may also specify a rhythmic subdivision, as in, "This tune has a triplet feel."

- **Figure:** Short rhythmic or melodic phrase

- **Freely:** Played with loose (flexible) time, or *rubato*

- **Groove:** The rhythmic style of a player or ensemble, characterized by tempo, musical style, use of syncopation, and so on.

- **Hits:** See Kick.

- **In the pocket:** A perfectly synchronized groove

- **Kick:** An accented *stop-time* figure or improvised rhythm, also called a "hit." Also, short for "kick drum," which is the bass drum in a drum kit.

- **Kicks (or hits) over time:** Rhythmic figures played in *addition* to the groove (rather than *instead* of it). Rhythm players integrate these figures with groove patterns without interrupting the time. Or, one instrument may be responsible for the kicks over time. Often indicated by writing rhythmic notation above the measure.

- **Laid-back:** Played with a very relaxed time feel, almost behind the beat.

- **Lock in:** Synchronize

- **Loose:** Poor synchronization; or, rhythms are less specific.

- **On top, or pushed:** Played with a slightly rushed time feel, almost ahead of the beat.

- **Open time:** Relaxed, loose, less locked-in; fewer notes played

GLOSSARY: CONTEMPORARY RHYTHM VOCABULARY

- **Pickup:** Note(s) or beat(s) that precede an important downbeat, such as a melodic line that leads into the chorus. For example, in "I left My Heart in San Francisco," the melody notes "I left my" are the pickup notes, and the word "heart" is the downbeat in the first measure of that chorus section. Pickup notes may also be used instrumentally to lead into sections of a song.

- **Play with an edge:** Play in time with a more excited feel, slightly ahead of the beat, or more aggressively. Time is pushed slightly ahead of the beat, e.g., snare hits in rock styles.

- **Push:** Play with an *edge*.

- **Rubato:** Free time, without a steady beat or pulse. Must be conducted. Most effective during an introduction but can be used anywhere in an arrangement. Often interchanged with *freely*.

- **Rush:** Play too fast; play with too much edge; play too far ahead of the beat.

- **Settle in:** Players synchronize well; the effort seems easier

- **Setup:** Improvise a very short rhythm that anticipates a written figure

- **Stop time:** Also called *concerted rhythmic figures,* stop time refers to rhythmic figures in an arrangement that are played collectively by all the players in the rhythm section. Replacing the established groove in the passage where they are written, stop-time figures are so called because the patterns of the groove are interrupted where these figures are played. Tempo and chord changes are not affected. When written *above* the measure, the groove patterns continue, and the stop-time figures are played in addition (see *kicks over time*).

- **Straight ahead:** Pure and simple groove, with less syncopation, i.e., basic, no-frills, rock groove

- **Tight:** A groove that is "locked in" or well-rehearsed, synchronized almost to perfection; established patterns are solidly maintained.

- **Time:** Groove, tempo, or rhythmic flow

- **Time slashes:** Written in the measure in place of the melody. Slanted across the middle staff line, time slashes represent the downbeats of the meter (time signature). For example, 4/4 time has four slashes, 3/4 time has three slashes, while 12/8 has four slashes (representing four groups of three beats). Chord symbols are written above time slashes to indicate where to change chords. Players *comp* their parts based on their understanding of that musical style, using this simple structural "map" of the song's form.

- **Upbeat:** A weaker beat in a meter; or, the next smallest, even subdivision. For example, in 4/4 time, there are four quarter notes per measure. The upbeat can be either quarter beats 2 or 4, or one of the subdivided eighth notes. When counting off a swing subdivision, articulate the upbeat with the syllable "a." (i.e., "a-one...a-two...a-one, two, three, four").

- **Walking:** A bass line style used mostly in jazz and country swing genres. The bassist plays embellished notes following the meter's bottom value, e.g., quarter notes in 4/4 time.

APPENDIX C

Online Resources

Voice Technique and Lessons

The Voice Workshop

www.thevoiceworkshop.com/somatic.html. This wonderful online resource is the method by voice teacher Jeannette LoVetri.

Vocal Anatomy

Vocal Focus

www.vocalfocus.com/vocal-anatomy.html. A website with animated views of the voice at work.

Voice Inside View

www.voiceinsideview.com. Scott McCoy, DMA's website that supports his vocal pedagogy text, *Your Voice, An Inside View*.

Health Resources

University of Iowa

Learn which medications are bad for your voice: www.uiowa.edu/~shcvoice/rx.html

The Singer's Resource

This website contains several pages of useful articles for singers about health, anatomy, and general care of the voice. www.thesingersresource.com/vocal_health.htm

Alexander Technique

To begin learning about the Alexander Technique: www.alexandertechnique.com

Body Mapping

To begin learning about body mapping: bodymap.org/main

Feldenkrais

To begin learning about Feldenkrais: www.feldenkrais.com

Reiki Training

There are many centers around the U.S. that teach Reiki, if you are interested in the training. As with many alternative approaches, do your research and be sure the practitioner is legitimate. Many people report beneficial results by receiving a Reiki treatment. Depending on what you receive Reiki for, it should not be used in place of receiving a doctor's care. You will definitely find a Reiki treatment stress reducing. It may very well offer you further insight into your energetic make-up and how that affects your physical make-up.

Center for Laryngeal Surgery and Voice Rehabilitation

At Massachusetts General Hospital, Boston:

www2.massgeneral.org/voicecenter

Voice and Speech Laboratory

Massachusetts Eye and Ear Infirmary, Boston:

www.masseyeandear.org/specialties/otolaryngology/voice-laboratory

Topic of Interest

We are composed of 65 percent water. Researcher Dr. Masaru Emoto exposed music, spoken words, pictures, and music to water, crystallized it, and found remarkable changes in water's molecular structure depending on the *emotion* it was exposed to. It seems incredible, but you can see for yourself.

http://www.youtube.com/watch?v=k1-0ulKgmio&feature=related

Musical Resources

Seventh String

Where is the lead sheet for that song you want to sing, in which real book? This website will find it for you. http://www.seventhstring.co.uk/fbindex.html

APPENDIX D

Excerpt from 5Realms for Artists: An Investigative Awareness Practice

Performance poet Caroline Harvey frames the yoga "five sheaths" as the *5Realms for Artists: An Investigative Awareness Practice.* The *5Realms* are: the physical realm, the emotional realm, the mental realm, the subtle energy realm, and the spiritual or inner wisdom realm. Harvey's work teaches the performer how to be more vulnerable and, thus, genuinely creative, as well as balanced in health and wholeness.

> This excerpt of Harvey's work describes a way to tune in to the five realms of our being. Her full work can be found at www.carolineharvey.com. (Used with permission.)

By Caroline Harvey

The 5Realms practice can be used as a meditative guide to building awareness of your whole body, helping to improve your clarity, focus, and overall health. You can track your 5Realms in any seated or standing position, while walking, before going to bed, during yoga, or during any other movement practice. What you find in your 5Realms will constantly change as your internal and external environments shift; tracking your evolving truth helps you stay connected to your natural creativity and flow. If you are using the 5Realms in this way, to build awareness, do your best to avoid judgment and analysis. This is a fact-finding mission. Simply note what you find without working to change or shift anything.

1. **The Physical Realm:** the state of the physical body, which includes all physical body parts, sensations, and movements. This realm includes the muscles and bones, the nervous system, the organs, blood, breath, digestive fluid, veins and arteries, and the membranous sacs around bones and joints. When working in this realm, consider questions like: Am I injured, tense, or in pain? Is there a body part that feels great? Do I

feel heavy/light? Tired/rested? Deep or shallow in my breath? Hungry or full? Quick or soft heartbeat? What is my shape, gesture, movement? Am I moving quickly, slowly, directly, indirectly? With strong or light effort?

2. **The Emotional Realm:** the state of the emotional body. When connecting with this realm, feel for a particular issue that is presenting itself: grief, joy, anger, frustration, love, worry, humor, sarcasm. You can also begin to connect the first and second realms by feeling for a particular body part or area that might pipe up in association with the emotional issue. As you practice deep awareness like this, your body will respond authentically to the internal message of a true emotion. Feeling the emotion is enough, you don't need to try to "show" it.

3. **The Mental Realm:** the state of mind. Is there a particular conversation, monologue, or event that is being held in your mind? Beyond that, what is the overall quality of your thinking? Chatty or quiet mind? Dull or bright thinking? Circular and repetitive? Or linear, one thought to the next? Is there a need to control your mind? Connect the first and third realms by asking, what kind of physical reactions does the quality of your thinking create?

4. **The Subtle Energy Realm:** the body's vital life energy/prana/chi/qi. You can also call this the "subconscious mind." There are many names for this realm, but all the systems agree that we are more than a physical body; we are also animated by an energetic, powerful force. To access this realm, ask questions like, do I have a sense that there is an energy flowing through me? What is the quality of this energy—smooth, light, heavy, quick, slow? Am I vibrating anywhere? Is there an area of my body that feels open and bright, or that another feels clogged, stuck, or stagnant? Am I energetically depleted, or hyper-stimulated and buzzed? What is the energy or mood of the piece I am creating, and can I invite that quality of energy into my body? How does my body want to move, gesture, or behave in response to this quality of energy?

5. **The Spiritual Realm/Inner Wisdom/Inner Physician:** the realm in which we sense our energy, or presence, as connected with the energy of the universe, the world, and/or the community or audience around us. You may experience this as an area, an ability, a spirit, a guide, a gut instinct, an image or message, a place, a sense, or a "knowing." This realm is connected to the universal source of vital life energy and it is the place in which we stop identifying as an individual and feel our deep interconnectedness with all beings.

About the Author

Photo by Mark Stallings

Whether it's jazz, rock, soul, folk/rock, singer/songwriter, blues, and, yes, opera too, Jeannie Gagné M.A. loves to sing. So, when people ask her, "What's your sound?" she describes a mixture of what calls her: a bit bluesy-soul, a bit jazz, a bit thoughtful/spiritual stuff, and a little edgy-rock for some sauce. "It used to be you had to define yourself in one genre, but these days it's just about good music!"

What matters is being authentic, real. What matters is building and nurturing our combined community. What matters is spreading a little love every day. We can do that through the music we make.

Jeannie Gagné ("Gon-YAY") is a vocalist, songwriter, pianist, guitarist, and professor of voice at Berklee College of Music. She teaches voice privately, and is co-founder and president of SoundationVox.com, which offers focused workshops for vocalists at all levels of contemporary performance. She wrote and teaches the Berklee Online course *Popular Singing Styles: Developing Your Sound* and teaches private lessons worldwide by Skype. Throughout her career of over thirty-five years, she has taught tens of thousands of singers to use their voices effectively to maximize their potential. A leading educator worldwide in vocal health, anatomy, and styles, and a classically trained soprano, she is also expert in several contemporary styles including pop/rock, jazz, R&B/soul, blues, and singer/songwriter. Her flexible method provides students with a solid foundation in vocal technique, styles, improvisation, and discovering their authenticity.

ABOUT THE AUTHOR

Jeannie Gagné encourages and nurtures what is precious within each individual. Part vocal technician and part life coach, she focuses on building healthy, career-lasting techniques for whatever style of music a singer is called to explore. She conceived and co-directed Berklee's Performance Wellness Institute for healthy and effective performance on all instruments. Among her course offerings is the groundbreaking class she created with jazz musician Stan Strickland: *The Body, Sound and Inspiration in Performance and Beyond.* Her company SoundationVox is designed to nurture and inspire singers at all levels.

Raised in New York City, Ms. Gagné received an M.A. in Wellness and Voice/Independent Study from Lesley University, Cambridge, and a B.A. in Music from Wesleyan University, Middletown, CT. She studied classical piano for a dozen years, later honing contemporary "comping" skills. At Wesleyan, she studied and performed West African drumming with master Abraham Adzenyah, instilling a deeply rhythmic approach to music. She is self-taught on acoustic guitar, which she has played since childhood. A singer, songwriter, and composer who received extensive classical vocal training, Ms. Gagné went on to a successful career in contemporary commercial music working with artists such as Philip Glass and Ravi Shankar, Frankie Paul, Penn & Teller, Stan Strickland, Terri Lyne Carrington, George Duke, Boston Big Band, and opening for Bare Naked Ladies. Her debut album *Wide Open Heart* (1999) boasts some of the industry's finest musicians, including Shawn Pelton (*Saturday Night Live*, Celine Dion, Buddy Guy), Kev Katz (Sting, Shawn Colvin, Aretha Franklin), and Mark Shulman (Suzanne Vega, Chris Botti). Jeannie Gagné's third album *Closer to Bliss* is soulful jazz originals and classics. Her second album *Must Be Love* (2005) features original and classic blues and rock songs, including "In My Quiet Sorrow," written for the best-selling book *Singing the Journey* (Beacon Press), which Ms. Gagné co-wrote. She has appeared on several recordings, television, and radio, and has sung on the soundtracks for *Anima Mundi*, *Feuille*, and *Forbidden Nights*. She is presently recording her fourth solo album. She is the author of several articles on music.

Now in her fourth decade as a professional musician, Jeannie Gagné travels nationally and globally both to share her expertise and to perform. *Downtown Magazine* wrote of her singing, "Few vocalists create images and stir emotions merely with the sound of their voice, independent of the subject matter of the song. All the great ones do, and Jeannie does, too." A Reiki master (the art of energy healing), Ms. Gagné leads workshops on vocal technique, empowerment, contemporary styles, demystifying improvisation, grooves and embodying rhythm, and uncovering one's authenticity as an artist. She and her family live in Massachusetts. For more information about Jeannie Gagné and her music, visit: www.jeanniegagne.com and www.SoundationVox.com.

INDEX

A

acid reflux, 21, 34
activities. *See* exercises
Adams, Brian, 106
aerobic exercise, 37
agility
    exercises for rhythm and, 138–45, *141, 144, 145*
    vocal exercise for, 143, 147–48, *147–48*, 149
airflow visualization, 29, *29*
    garden hose, 66
air pressure, 17, 26–27
Alexander Technique, 38
alleluia exercise, 143
Amos, Tori, 215
anatomy, vocal. *See* vocal anatomy
anxiety, 12
    deep breathing for managing, 27–28
    performance, 103–5
Apollo Theater, 181, 186
arms, movement of, 85–86
Armstrong, Louis, 78
arpeggio exercises, *166, 167*
articulation, 59
    rearticulation without glottal attack, 142
artists
    artistic and energetic presence, 96–97
    Austin's advice for new, 190
    commercial music and, 4
    consistency in, 211
    imitation of other, 61, 123, 206
    self-discovery of, 4
    specificity in, 196–97
artist statement, 100–101
arytenoid cartilages, *14*, 15
aspirin, 36
athletic movement, 86
audience, 96, 99
    adjusting set list to, 210
    Barnwell on, 196–97
    Baxter on, 207, 208–9
    Blake and Karam on, 215
    connecting with, 6, 114, 187, 216
    how much self to give, 119
    impact of performing on, 88–90
    learning about, 91, 208–9
    live music desired by, 110
    Mathieu on, 223–24
    size, 209
    song choices according to, 105
    survey, 110–11
aura
    chakras and, *115*
    touch, 119–20
Austin, Patti, 92, 181–90
    advice for new artists, 190
    children's hospital experience of, 184
    on concert planning, 189
    eclectic musicianship of, 189–90
    on Fitzgerald and Horne, 186
    Garland and, 184–85
    jingle singing career of, 182–84, 185–86
    on performing live, 187–88
    on record business, 186–88
    set list and performance flow, 189
    on vocal health, 188–89
authenticity, 44–46
    artificial, 95
    Baxter on, 205–6
    culture and, 95–96
    healthy ego and, 94–96
authentic movement, 86
Avant Gershwin, 190
awareness
    breathing, 22
    of energy, 116, 117, 118–19
    five sheaths investigative, 94, 244–45

B

"Baby, Come to Me," 181, 183
backbeat, 74, 80, 237
back-phrasing, 73
"Backyard Bop," 170–71
balance, cycles of, *41*
ballads, 173
band, working with, 112–13
Barnwell, Ysaye M., 191–99
    on audience, 196–97
    on concert planning, 192–93
    hit songs by, 192
    on "it" factor, 195–96
    jazz and western culture discussed by, 197–98
    songwriting and teaching of, 199
    on Sweet Honey, 193–95
bass, 79
bass drum, 80
Baxter, Mark, 43, 59, 201–11
    on audience, 207, 208–9
    on authenticity, 205–6
    on emotion, 206–7
    on mood, 204–5
    on music as necessity, 211
    on performance as invitation, 207–8
    technique focus of, 202–4
    on vulnerability, 204
beat
    back-, 74, 80, 237
    down-, 238
    finding, 81–84
    up-, 240
being seen exercise, 104–5
beliefs
    affirming, 50
    exercise, 48, *48*
    loops, 47–50
belting, 154, 157
    vocal exercises using, 158–60, *158–60*

INDEX

belt voice, 57
Bingen, Hildegard von, 226
biorhythm mapping, 52, *52*
Blake, Joey, Karam and, 213–18
    on concert planning, 214
    on teaching improvisation, 217–18
blues
    songs, 170–71
    vocal exercises for singing, *146–48*, 146–53, *150–52*, 158, *159*, *160*
body, moving while singing, 85–87
body mapping, 242
body warm ups, 129–32
    long steady breath release (SSS), 130
    single tone sounding, 130, *131–32*
    stretching, 129, *129*
book recommendations, 231–36
Bossa nova groove, 82
    Latin rhythm vocal exercise, 151–53, *153*
Bowie, David, 183
brain, 46–47
brain mapping, 47, 50
brain wave activity, 47
break (registers), 60–61, 237
breathing, 21–31
    action of, *24*
    air pressure and, 17, 26–27
    awareness, 22
    belly, 26
    deep, 27–28
    diaphragmatic, 24
    effortless, 22
    mechanics of singing and, 11–12
    planning, 66
    soul exercise and meditation on, 164, *164*
    vocal exercises with breath support, 140
breathing exercises
    airflow visualization, 29, *29*, 66
    on floor, 31
    SSS, 28–29, *29*, 130
    wings, 30, *30*
breathy tone, 106, 135
Brennan, Barbara Ann, 117
Bridge of Waves: What Music Is and How Listening to It Changes the World (Mathieu), 220
broken time, 237
Burns, Ken, 197
busy, 237

C

cadenza, 198
caffeine, 34
Cage, John, 6
call and response, 112
Cannabis, 34
Carey, Mariah, 58
Carr, Shona, 46
cartilages, larynx, *14*, 14–15
cat (C@T) vowel, 165, *165*
    using minor pentatonic scale, *147–48*, 149–50
CCM. *See* contemporary commercial music
Center for Laryngeal Surgery and Voice Rehabilitation, 242

centering exercise, 71
    single tone sounding, 130, *131–32*
chakras, 66, *67*
    aura and, *115*
    Reiki and, 120
Charles, Ray, 184
chart, 237
chest voice, 57, 58
chi, 44
chocolate, 34
choosing songs, 105–6
Chopra, Deepak, 232
choral singing, 9
chromatic movement, vocal exercise for, 162, *162*
chromatic scale exercise, *167*
Churchill, Winston, 71
circle singing, 217
classical music, improvisation in, 198
classical singing (traditional), 53
    contemporary contrasted with, 59, 128, *128*
    shifting to contemporary from, 124–25, 126
    swing eighths, 153
    vocal exercise for agility with accuracy, 143
classic songs, rhythmic subdivisions for, 77
Cobain, Kurt, 119
cold beverages, 33
Coleman, Ornette, 225
Coltrane, John, 219
commercial music, 4
comping, 79, 237
concentration, fusing two kinds of, 96
concerted rhythmic figures. *See* stop time
concert planning
    Austin's, 189
    Barnwell's, 192–93
    Baxter's, 208–9
    Karam and Blake on, 214
concerts
    rock contrasted with jazz, 209–10
    stadium, 216, 225
    transformative experience of, 225–26
    why people attend, 111
conditioning, 63
consistency, artistic, 211
consonants
    classical compared to contemporary singing of, 128, *128*
    English pronunciation key for, 127
contemporary commercial music (CCM), 247
contemporary rhythm vocabulary, 237–40
contemporary singing
    classical contrasted with, 59, 128, *128*
    excitement of, 229
    shifting from classical to, 124–25, 126
    styles of, 56
cool down, 68
count off, 238
    time feel variations with, *82*, *83*, *84*
country music, 73–74
creativity, student quotes on, 45–46
cricoarytenoid joint, *14*, 15
cricoarytenoid muscle, 16
Cross, Melissa, 32

C@T vowel, *147–48*, 149–50, 165, *165*
culture, 103
    authenticity and, 95–96
    Barnwell on jazz and Western, 197–98
cut time, 81
cycles of balance, *41*
cymbal, ride, 80

D

daily affirmations, 50–51
dairy, 34
Davis, Miles, 197–98
Davis, Sammy, Jr., 181, 186
deep breathing, 27–28
diaphragm, 23, *25*
    myth of breathing from, 24
    posture and, 25
    singing from, 26
diet, 34–35
digestion, 35
disco groove, *83*
distractions, 98
dos and don'ts, 38–39
double-time feel, 81
downbeat, 238
DownBeat, 220
drag, 238
"Dreamin'," 172
drumming, 73
    drum set, 80
    jazz, 74
    snare drum, 74, 80
    time feel variations and, 81

E

ear candy exercises, *166–67*
easy jazz/r&b songs, 174–77
EEG. *See* electroencephalogram
Effortless Mastery (Werner), 109–10
ego, 223
    authenticity with healthy, 94–96
Einstein, Albert, 3
elastic band, alternating major/minor, 144, *144*
electroencephalogram (EEG), 47
embodying rhythm, 85–87
emotion
    Baxter on technique and, 203
    song choices and range of, 105
    universality of, 206–7
emotional realm, in five sheaths, 245
energy, 114–20
    awareness of, 116, 117, 118–19
    realm of subtle, 245
    Reiki and, 115–16
energy awareness exercise, 118–19
energy grid, 52, *52*
English pronunciation keys, 126–27
Etheridge, Melissa, 106
"Every Little Thing You Do," 169, 174–77
excellence, 71
exercises. *See also* breathing exercises; practice; vocal exercises
    aerobic, 37
    agility and rhythm, 138–45, *141*, *144*, *145*

being seen, 104–5
    on beliefs, 48, *48*
    centering, 71, 130, *131–32*
    daily affirmations, 51
    energy awareness, 118–19
    glissando, 65, 137, *137*
    goals of, 124
    physical, 22, 23
expectations, 101–2, 120
    letting go of, 215–16

F

false folds, 15
falsetto, 58, 60
feedback, microphone, 108
feel, 238. *See also specific time feels*
figure, 238
Fitzgerald, Ella, 78, 186
5Realms for Artists: An Investigative Awareness Practice (Harvey), 94, 244–45
five sheaths, 93, *93*, 94, 244–45
flag analogy, 206
flexibility exercises
    for improvisation, *146–48*, 146–53, *150–52*
    movement and, *146*, 146–47
    with relaxation, 139
focus, 91
foods to avoid, 34–35
force, 19
forward-phrasing, 73
freely, 238
full voice, 57, 60
funk groove, *83*

G

Gandhi, Mohandas Karamchand, 7
garden hose visualization, 66
Garland, Judy, 92, 119, 184–85
General Hospital, 183
glissando, 65, 137, *137*
glottis, *13*, 15
goal setting, 68
Goodman, Gabrielle, 78
Graham, Martha, 86
grandfather clock analogy, 65
Grateful Dead, 224
groove, 238
    hip-hop, 165, *165*
    identifying, 81–84
    straight eighths, *82*
    straight sixteenths, *83*
    swing eighths, *83*
    swing sixteenths, *84*
    triplet, *82*
guitar, piano and, 79

H

habits
    conditioning and, 63
    styles affected by, 56
half-time, 81, *82*
Hands of Light (Brennan), 117
Hanser, Suzanne, 219
Harmonic Experience: Total Harmony from Its Natural Origins to Its Modern Expression (Mathieu), 220

Harvey, Caroline, 94, 244–45
headcolds, 35
head voice, 58
healing
   through toning, 8–9
   using music for, 7, 214–15, 218
health, 3–4, 92, 229
   Austin on vocal, 188–89
   authenticity with ego, 94–96
   belting and, 157
   benefits of singing to physical, 7–8
   holistic approaches to wellness and, 42–46
   web site resources for, 241–42
health practices, 31–39
   dos and don'ts, 38–39
   exercise and, 37
   foods and beverages list, 34–35
   hydration, 33, 129
   managing illness, 35–36
   mental thoughts and, 69–70
   speaking healthfully, 32
hearing, 46–47
heart, 94
   technique combined with, 92
hi-hat, 80, 81
hip-hop groove, 165, *165*
hits. *See* kicks
holistic approach, 42–46
Horne, Lena, 186
hydration, 33, 129
hyoid bone, 14

I

ibuprofen (Motrin), 36
icing cake, vocal concept of, 67
illness, singing during, 35–36
imitation, 61, 123
   admiration and, 206
immunoglobulin A, 7
improvisation
   Barnwell on jazz, culture and, 197–98
   Blake on teaching, 217–18
   in classical music, 198
   scat singing as, 78
   vocal exercises for, *146–48*, 146–53, *150–52*
   WeBe3 and, 217
Ingram, James, 181
inner physician, in five sheaths, 245
inner wisdom/inner physician, in five sheaths, 245
inspiration, 43
intention, 90–91, 220–21, 223, 227
intercostal muscles, 23, *25*
internal critic, 95
internal music, 43, 44
intervals
   large, 162
   scat syllables with, 163, *163*
   soul and, 164, *164*
   vocal exercise for accurate, 161, *161*
"in the pocket," 151
investigative awareness practice, 94, 244–45
"it" factor, 195–96

J

Jackson, Michael, 188
jazz
   Barnwell on, 197–98
   drummer, 74
   live, 225
   musicians, 222
   rock contrasted with, 209–10
   swing grooves, *83*
jazz singing, 78
   consonants in, 128
   easy jazz songs, 174–77
   vocal exercises for improvisation in r&b, blues and, *146–48*, 146–53, *150–52*
jazz swing songs, 172
jingle singer, Austin as, 182–84, 185–86
jingle songwriters, 221
Jones, Quincy, 181, 184–85
Jones, Ronnie, 112–13
Jones, Sarah Dan, 164
Joplin, Janis, 224
jump rope game, *64*, 64–65
Jung, Carl, 86

K

Kai, Kudisan, 148
Karam, Christiane, Blake and, 213–18
   on concert planning, 214
Kenton, Stan, 219
key
   English pronunciation, 126–27
   finding right, 106
   practicing in right, 113
   song choice and, 105–6
keyboard, 79
Khan, Hazrat Inayat, 28
kicks (or hits) over time, 238

L

laid-back playing, 238
laryngitis, 35
laryngologist, 20
larynx, 11, 102
   air pressure and, 17
   laryngoscopic view of interior of, *14*
   muscle movement in, 16, 18
   respiratory role of, 12
   vocal folds and, 13–15
Latin rhythm vocal exercise, 151–53, *153*
learning styles, 58
legato, 125
lip trills, 134–35
The Listening Book (Mathieu), 219–20
lock in, 238
long steady breath release (SSS), 130
"Look Inside for Love," 173
loop, 47–50
   changing, 49–50
   self-conscious, 97
Lopez, Adam, 58
Loran, Lillian, 227
loud open long tones, vocal exercise with, 158, *158*
lungs, steaming, 33
Lydian mode vocal exercise, 150, *150*

lyrics, 70–71, 113
    singing, 185

M

magic word theory, 195–96, Barnwell's
major/minor, exercises using
    elastic band, 144, *144*
    melodic spaces, 145, *145*
    straight and swing eighths, 151, *151*
    stretch, 141, *141*
    with thirds, *167*
major scale vocal exercise, *146*, 146–47, 149
marketing, Austin on, 182
mask, 60, *60*
Mathieu, W.A., xiv
    on audience, 223–24
    Coltrane on, 219
    on communing through music, 224–25, 227–28
    on intellect *vs.* sacredness, 226–27
    life's purpose and transforming moment of, 220–21
    on love and union through music, 221–22
    on music and intention, 220–21, 223, 227
    on music's life lessons, 227–28
    on teacher's concerts, 225
    on transformative experiences, 225–26
Mathieu, William Allaudin, 90, 219–28
    books by, 219–20
McFerrin, Bobby, 213, 215, 217
medications, 36
    web site on harmful, 241
meditation
    toning as, 8
    vocal exercise with breathing, 164, *164*
melisma, 137
melodic spaces exercise, 145, *145*
menstruation, 37
mental realm, in five sheaths, 245
microphone
    placement, *108*
    technique, 107–9
minor scale vocal exercises, *147–48*, 147–50
mistakes, 96
mix voice, 57, 58, 157
mood, Baxter on evoking of, 204–5
Morrison, Toni, 7
Motrin, 36
mouth
    open, 13
    roof of, 66
movement
    authentic, 86
    in depth, 86
    flexibility exercise for improvisation and, *146*, 146–47
    pedestrian, 86
    singing with, 85–87
    vocal exercise for agility and, 149
    vocal exercises for chromatic, 162, *162*
    voice warm up with increased, *136–37*
movement and fifths voice warm up, 135
muppet jaw, 65, 147
muscles. *See also* vocal anatomy
    conditioning, 36
    intercostal, 23, *25*
    isolation, 65
    memory, 50
    movement in larynx, 16, 18
    neck, 17
    shift in dominant, 60, 61
    tongue, 18–19, 37
music. *See also specific kinds of music*
    commercial, 4, 247
    communing through, 224–25, 227–28
    concentration on technique and, 96
    experiencing *vs.* intellectualizing, 226–27
    healing power of, 7, 214–15, 218
    intention behind, 220–21, 223, 227
    internal, 43, 44
    live, 110
    love and union through, 221–22
    necessity of, 211
    power of, 7
    prayerful state with, 227
    sheet, 243
    universality of, 196–97
    wellness and, 3–4
    Wooten on study of, 102
The Musical Life: What It Is and How to Live It (Mathieu), 220
musical theater styles, 125
The Music Lesson (Wooten), 47, 86, 96

N

Nath, Pandid Pran, 225
neck muscles, tense, 17
neti pot, 38
nodes, 20
"No Mirrors in My Nana's House" (Barnwell), 192
notation, rhythm, 75, *78*
notes
    changing volume on one, 154, *154*
    gradual reaching of higher, *137*
    high and low, 134

O

on floor breathing exercise, 31
on top, or pushed, 238
open pharynx (throat), vocal exercise for, 155–56
open time, 238
opera, 56
Over My Shoulder Foundation, 181
over-rehearsing, 202
over-singing, 188–89
overtalking, 39
overtones, 62

P

passagio, 60
PA system, 106
    sound of voice through, 109
pedestrian movement, 86
perfection, excellence instead of, 71
performance, 88–120
    audience impacted by, 88–90
    audience-inclusive, 215
    enjoying without, 10
    goal setting for, 68
    ideal environment for, 109–10
    intention behind, 90–91, 220–21, 223, 227
    as invitation, 207–8

letting go and, 92
magic of live, 187–88, 225
practicing daily before, 68
preparing for, 99
recordings compared to live, 61–62
steps to extraordinary, 91–92
subway, 88–89
technical aspects of, 107–10
technique and, 202
tips for, 113–14
unconscious, 97
visualizations for, 91, 98
vulnerability in, 204
performance anxiety, 103–5
performers
common qualities in strong, 93–94
intention of, 90–91, 220–21, 223, 227
personal energy, Reiki definition of, 116
pharyngeal constrictor muscles, 13
pharynx, 11, 12
expansion and contraction of, 16
vocal exercise for open, 155–56
phonation, vocal folds during, 16
phonosurgeon, 20
phrase, moving with, 87
phrasing, 73
consonants and, 128, 128
physical exercise, 22, 23
physical health. See also health
benefits to, 7–8
healthy habits, 31–39
physical realm, in five sheaths, 244–45
piano and guitar, 79
pickup, 239
Pink, 61
pitch
trouble matching, 62
vocal exercise for accurate, 162, 162
placement of voice, 58
play with an edge, 239
polyps, 20
pop artists, 211
pop/rock, 77, 237
pop/soul ballads, 173
positive practice, 70–71
posture, 23
diaphragm and, 25
SSS with, 28–29, 29
power singing, 19–20
vocal exercises for, 154, 154–56
practice. See also exercises; health practices; vocal exercises
Baxter on, 204
daily and performance preparation, 68
distractions and, 98
five sheaths awareness, 94, 244–45
in key, 113
mental, 54
positive, 70–71
schedule for, 68
successful outcome, 70–71
video recording of, 97
vocal concepts and visualizations for, 63–67
warm up and cool down for, 68
prana, 44

presence
artistic and energetic, 96–97
visualizing stage, 98
push, 239
push-phrasing, 73

R
r&b. See rhythm and blues
rearticulation without glottal attack, vocal exercise, 142
record business, 186–88
recordings
live performance compared to, 61–62
practicing with video, 97
registers, 57
changing, 19, 60–61, 154
commonly defined, 57–58
rehearsal
with band, 112–13
limitations and, 55
over-, 202
Reiki, 115–16
aura touch, 119–20
training resources, 242
resonance, 61–62
mechanics of, 12
open mouth for, 13
soft palate in, 12
vowels and, 59–60
respiratory system, role of larynx in, 12
Rhiannon, 217
rhythm, 73–87
Bossa Latin, 151–53, 153
embodying, 85–87
notation of, 75, 78
section, 79–80, 81
vocabulary for contemporary, 237–40
rhythm and blues (r&b)
easy jazz songs, 174–77
vocal exercises for, 146–48, 146–53, 150–52
rhythmic patterns, vocal exercises for chromatic movement and, 162, 162
rhythmic subdivisions, 75, 76
classic songs in each of five, 77
identifying, 81–84
rhythm section, 74, 75, 81, 107, 239
role of, 79–80
ride cymbal, 80
Robbins, Tony, 179
rock concerts, 209–10
rock groove, 82
rock music, 73–74
Mathieu on, 224–25
pop and, 77, 237
roll down/roll up, stretching exercise, 129, 129
rolling pin visualization, 137
Rolling Stones, 225
roof of mouth, 66
rubato, 239
Rumi, xi, 222
rush, 239

S
sailboat concept, 66
saliva study, 7

Scat (Stoloff), 78
scat singing, 78–79
　vocal exercises with scat syllables, 151, *151*, 163, *163*
Scott, Jim, 41
screaming, 39
scream singing, 32
Second City Theater, 219
self, 42–43, 96
　meeting true, 117
self-conscious loop, 97
set list, 71, 105, 189
　audience and, 210
settle in, 239
setup, 239
Shakespeare, William, 123
shape, of vowels, 59
sheet music, 243
Shelton, Jason, 72
shuffle, *83*
Simpson, Valerie, 183
singing. *See also* styles; *specific styles of; specific topics*
　benefits of, 6, 7–8
　circle, 217
　from diaphragm, 26
　high notes, 15
　during illness, 35–36
　impact and experience of, xiv–xv
　jingle, 182–84, 185–86
　just-for-fun, 69
　loudness of, 15
　low-to-high note and high-to-low note, 15
　lyrics and, 185
　mechanics of, 11–13
　moving while, 85–87
　over-, 188–89
　power, 19–20, *154*, 154–56
　power of thought in, 46–52, *48*
　right and wrong, 55–56
　speech-like, 124–25
　universal nature of, 4–6
"Singing in the Rain," 128
single tone sounding, 130, *131–32*
sit-ups, 36
6/8, 75
　time feel, *82*
smoking, 33–34
smooth glissando to 9th, 137, *137*
snare drum, 74, 80
soft palate, 13, *13*
　intentionally lifting, 12
　location of, 12
songs
　"Backyard Bop," 170–71
　Barnwell on writing, 199
　Barnwell's most popular, 192
　blues, 170–71
　choosing, 105–6
　"Dreamin'," 172
　"Every Little Thing You Do," 169, 174–77
　jazz swing, 172
　"Look Inside for Love," 173
　over-rehearsing, 202
　rhythmic subdivisions for classic, 77

soul
　ballads, 173
　intervals and, 164, *164*
sound engineering fixes, 61–62
sounding, centering with single tone, 130, *131–32*. *See also* toning
SoVoSo, 213, 217
speaking voice, 31–32
specificity, artistic, 196–97
speech-level singing, 125
speech-like singing, 124–25
spiritual realm/inner wisdom/inner physician, in five sheaths, 245
Springsteen, Bruce, 210
SSS
　long steady breath release with, 130
　posture for, 28–29, *29*
stadium shows, 216, 225
stage presence visualization, 98
steaming, lung, 33
Stoloff, Bob, 78
stop time, 239
straight ahead, 239
straight eighths, 75, *76*, 82
　vocal exercise for swing and, 151, *151*
straight sixteenths, 75, *76*
Streisand, Barbra, 188
stretching exercise, body warm up, 129, *129*
stretch major/minor exercise, 141, *141*
strobe light, for measuring vibration rate, 14
student quotes, 45–46
styles, 61–62
　choosing own, 124
　choosing songs according to, 105–6
　contemporary contrasted with traditional, 59
　evolution of personal, 229
　habits affecting, 56
　musical theater, 125
　rhythmic subdivisions for different, 75, *76*
　shifting from classical to contemporary, 124–25, 126
　Sweet Honey's eclectic, 193
　variations between, 8
subdivisions, rhythmic, 75, *76*
　classic songs in each of five, 77
　identifying, 81–84
subtle energy realm, in five sheaths, 245
subway performance, 88–89
surgery, 20
"Surry with the Fringe on Top," 185
survey, audience, 110–11
Sweet Honey in the Rock, 109, 191–95
swing, 77–78, *78*
　jazz, 172
swing eighths, 75, *76*, 78
　classical-style vocal exercise with, 153
　grooves, *83*
　scat singing with, 79
　vocal exercise for straight and, 151, *151*
swing feel, 151
　notation, *78*
swing sixteenths, 75
　vocal exercise with hip-hop, 165, *165*

syllables, vocal, 80
    Bossa rhythm exercise with, 151–53, *153*
    popping of, 108
    scat, 78–79, 151, *151*, 163, *163*
syncopation exercise, 138

T

Tagore, Rabindranath, 42, 133
Tai chi, 22, 39
Taylor, Cecil, 225
teachers, influence of, 53–54
teaching, 199
    Baxter on, 202–4
technique, 78
    Alexander, 38
    Baxter's focus on teaching, 202–4
    concentration on music and, 96
    emotion and, 203
    heart combined with, 92
    importance of, 69, 229
    legato, 125
    letting go as best, 18
    microphone, 107–9
    performance and, 202
    song choice based on, 105
    vibrato, 17, 125
temporomandibular disorder (TMJ), 37
This Marriage, 222
thought, 46–52, *48*
    belief loops and, 47–50
    changing patterns of, 102
    daily affirmations, 50–51
    healthy practices and, 69–70
throat. *See* pharynx
thyroarytenoid (TA) muscles, *14*, 15, 16
tight, 239
time, 239. *See also* swing feel
    broken, 237
    cut, 81
    feel, 81, *82*, *83*, *84*
    kicks over, 238
    signatures, 74
time slashes, 74–75, *74–75*, 239
TMJ. *See* temporomandibular disorder
toms, 80
tonal color, soft palate and, 12
tone, 61–62
    breathy, 106, 135
    lightening or fattening, 125
    practice for clean, 66
    single tone sounding, 130, *131–32*
    tritones vocal exercise, 162, *162*
    vocal exercises on, 66, 140, 158, *158*, 162, *162*
    volume of, 17
    whistle, 58
tongue muscle, 18–19, 37
toning, 8–9. *See also* sounding, centering with single tone
trachea, 11, *11*
traditional singing. *See* classical singing
traditional-style exercises, for agility with accuracy, 143
trap set, 80
triplet grooves, *82*
tritones vocal exercise, 162, *162*
true/false chart, *48*
"true" vocal folds, 13, 13*n*4
Turner, Tina, 216
12/8 feel, 75, *76*
    groove, *82*
12-bar blues, 158, *159*, 160
two-feel, 81
Tyler, Steven, 106

U

Unitarian Universalist Musicians Network, 192, 226
universality
    of emotion, 206–7
    in music, 196–97
    singing, 4–6
upbeat, 240

V

vibration rate, 14
vibrato
    mechanics of, 17
    modifying, 125
video recording, 97
visualizations
    airflow, 29, *29*, 66
    performance, 91, 98
    rolling pin, *137*
    vocal concepts and, 63–67
    vocabulary, 237–240
vocal anatomy. *See also* vocal folds
    arytenoid cartilages, *14*, 15
    cricoarytenoid joint, *14*, 15
    cricoarytenoid muscle, 16
    glottis, *13*, 15
    larynx, 11, 12, 13–18, *14*, 102
    larynx cartilages, *14*, 14–15
    pharyngeal constrictor muscles, *13*
    pharynx, *11*, 12, 16
    soft palate, 12, 13, *13*
    thyroarytenoid, *14*, 15, 16
    trachea, 11, *11*
    vocal cords, 11*n*3, 20
    vocalis muscle, 16, 157
    vocal mechanism, *13*
    vocal tract, 16
    web sites on, 241
vocal concepts, 63–67
vocal cords, 11*n*3
    polyps on, 20
vocal exercises, 133–67
    agility, 147–48, *147–48*, 149
    agility and rhythm, 138–45, *141*, *144*, *145*
    alleluia, 143
    arpeggio, *166*, *167*
    for belting, 158–60, *158–60*
    blues singing, *146–48*, 146–53, 158, *159*, 160
    Bossa Latin rhythm, 151–53, *153*
    calm clear tones with breath support, 140
    cat (C@T) vowel, *147–48*, 149–50
    chromatic movement, 162, *162*
    chromatic scale, *167*
    classical singing, 143, 153
    for clean tone, 66
    ear candy, *166–67*
    elastic band, 144, *144*
    for flexibility and improvisation, *146–48*, 146–53, *150–52*

intervals, 161, *161*
loud open long tones, 158, *158*
Lydian mode, 150, *150*
major/minor with thirds, *167*
major pentatonic scale, *146*, 146–47, 149
melodic spaces, 145, *145*
for mix voice, 157
movement and agility, 149
movement and flexibility, *146*, 146–47
open pharynx, 155–56
pitch accuracy, 162, *162*
for power singing, *154*, 154–56
rearticulation without glottal attack, 142
rhythmic detail, 162, *162*
scat syllables, 151, *151*, 163, *163*
soul and intervals, 164, *164*
stretch major/minor exercise, 141, *141*
syncopation, 138
traditional-style, 153
tritones, 162, *162*
voice warm ups, 134–37, *136–37*
volume change on one note, 154, *154*
vocal folds, 11–16, 11n3, *13*, 18, 39
avoiding straining, 157
dry, 33
false, 15
hydrating, 33
larynx and, 13–15
nodes on, 20
during phonation, *16*
swelling in, 21
thin or thick edges of, 15–16
"true," 13, 13n4
vocal fry, 57
vocal health, Austin on, 188–89
Vocal Improvisation: Techniques in Jazz, R&B, Gospel (Goodman), 78
vocal instrument
components of voice production, 10–11
daily variations in, 31
vocalis muscle, 16, 157
vocalizing, when unwell, 35
vocal mechanism, side view of, *13*
vocal range, song choices and, 105
vocal study, 52
learning styles, 58
teacher influence in, 53–54
traditional, 53
vocal syllables, rhythm section with, 80
vocal tract, 16
voice
belt, 57
chest, 57, 58
damage, 19, 20–21
full, 57, 60
head, 58
honoring limitations of, 54–55
medications harmful to, 241
mix, 57, 58, 157
naturally scratchy, 106
PA system sound of, 109
placement of, 58
quality of, 59
registers, 57
signs of healthy, 37
speaking, 31–32
strained or injured, 38
uniqueness of each, 57

voice production components, 10–11
Voicestra, 213, 217
voice warm ups, 134–37
increased movement, 136–37, *136–37*
lip trills, 134–35
movement and fifths, 135
movement variation with staccato, *136–37*
volume
one note with changing, 154, *154*
tone, 17
volume knob, *154*
vowels
Blake's focus on, 218
cat (C@T), *147–48*, 149–50, 165, *165*
English pronunciation key for, 126
resonance and, 59–60
shape of, 59
vulnerability, 204

W

walking, 79, 240
warm ups
body, *129*, 129–32, *131*, *132*
cool downs and, 68
voice, 134–37, *136–37*
water drinking, 33, 129
"We Are the World" (Jackson), 188
"We Are the World 25 for Haiti" (Austin), 181
WeBe3, 213, 217
web sites, 169
health-related, 241–42
sheet music, 243
vocal anatomy, 241
weight training, 36
wellness, 3–4
holistic approach to, 42–46
Werner, Kenny, 109–10
Western culture, Barnwell on jazz and, 197–98
whistle tone, 58
Whitehouse, Mary Starks, 86
wings breathing exercise, 30, *30*
Wooten, Victor, 47, 86, 96, 102
Worm, David, 217

X

XLR connection, 107, *107*

Y

yoga, 22, 38
five sheaths discussed in, 93, *93*, 94

Z

The Zen of Screaming, 32
ZilZALA, 213